COMPUTER PROGRAMMING
IN
PASCAL
THE
EASY
WAY

Douglas Downing
Seattle Pacific University

Mark Yoshimi
Computer Programmer, Allied Stores, Inc.

BARRON'S EDUCATIONAL SERIES, INC.

New York / London / Toronto / Sydney

All inquiries should be addressed to:
Barron's Educational Series, Inc.
250 Wireless Boulevard
Hauppauge, New York 11788

Library of Congress Catalog Card No. 84-2928

Library of Congress Cataloging in Publication Data

Downing, Douglas.
    Computer programming in Pascal the easy way.

    Includes index.
    1. PASCAL (Computer program language) I. Yoshimi,
Mark. II. Title.
QA76.73.P2D69 1984   001.64′24   84-2928
ISBN 0-8120-2799-X

PRINTED IN UNITED STATES OF AMERICA

9   100   9 8 7 6 5

Dedication

This book is for my family: Frank and Aiko Yoshimi, Diane Yoshimi, and my grandmother Teru Sasame.

Mark Yoshimi

Acknowledgments

We are deeply indebted to Linda Roberts and Marlys Downing for their assistance.

Contents

Introduction

Computers are designed to save work. A computer will be glad to do many boring tasks that you would rather not do. Also, because computers can work very fast, they can do many tasks that would be impossible without computers simply because they are too long.

However, a computer can only do exactly what it is told. It has no imagination. Therefore, you will need to give it very precise instructions explaining what you want it to do. Unfortunately, computers do not understand human languages like English (at least not yet). Therefore, you will need to learn a computer language in order to communicate with the computer. The computer itself can only understand a very complicated code consisting of 1s and 0s known as *machine language*. In the early days of computers, people needed to learn machine language in order to communicate with the computer. (When working with the very earliest computers, people needed to give instructions to the machines by plugging wires into circuit boards.) Machine language is very difficult for people to work with; so in the 1950s computer researchers began to develop *programming languages* (also known as high-level programming languages). Two of the earliest programming languages were FORTRAN, designed for scientific and engineering problems, and COBOL, designed for data processing applications. Learning a programming language is a bit like learning a foreign language, but it is much easier because there are not nearly as many words to learn.

When people learned more about computers, they began to understand more about what a good programming language should be like. Several new languages were developed and became popular. You may be familiar with BASIC, which is an easy-to-use language widely available on microcomputers. In this book we will learn the programming language called Pascal. Pascal was developed by computer scientist Nicklaus Wirth. Pascal was designed to encourage programmers to write orderly, logical programs whose meanings would be clear to people reading the program. The language is named in honor of Blaise Pascal, a French mathematician and philosopher who lived from 1623 to 1662. Among other accomplishments, Pascal studied probability, described an interesting arrangement of numbers now called Pascal's triangle, and built an adding machine that used toothed gears to represent numbers.

In this book we will start by pretending that we are creating the Pascal language ourselves. We will confront a series of problems. In order to solve the problem, we will imagine a new kind of command we would like our computer to be able to understand, and then we will describe how the problem is solved in Pascal. The purpose of this approach is to show the logic and motivation of each Pascal command. The main reason for introducing new commands is to save work (even if it looks as though new commands are introduced to torment you by making life more complicated).

The text includes examples of the usage of each command, and it also includes descriptions of the general form for each command. In the general form description, the parts written in capital letters need to be typed exactly as shown. The parts written in *italics* can be replaced by any appropriate item of your own choosing. For example, the general form of the IF command:

IF *condition*

THEN *statement1*

ELSE *statement2;*

means that IF, THEN, and ELSE must be typed exactly as shown, but you may choose whatever appropriate item you want for *condition, statement1,* and *statement2.*

Once we have learned the basic features of the Pascal language, we still need to consider the more general problem of how to write programs. A rigorously defined method of solving a problem is called an *algorithm.* Once we have created an algorithm, we need to translate it into a particular computer language, such as Pascal, so that a computer can understand it. In the last few chapters of the book we include examples of complicated Pascal programs taken from several different fields of application.

In this book we are assuming that you have a computer available that includes Pascal in an interactive environment. That means that you type your instructions into the computer at a keyboard and you see results on a CRT display screen. You may either have a Pascal compiler available for a microcomputer or you may be using Pascal in a time-sharing system where you work at a terminal that is connected to a big computer. Pascal can also be used in batch environments, but we will not discuss that possibility in this book.

The best way to learn programming is to practice writing programs. We have included suggested exercises for you to do to obtain practice writing programs in Pascal. We have included possible solutions to some of the exercises at the back of the book. However, note that there is often more than one right way to solve a computer science problem. Note also that you don't need to do all the exercises. More difficult exercises that require mathematical or other technical knowledge are marked with asterisks (*).

You don't need to know much mathematics to learn computer programming, although you do need to know some algebra and trigonometry to understand some of the applications discussed here. Skip over sections that seem too advanced mathematically. You should find plenty of applications that are not difficult to understand whatever your background.

You don't need to learn to program in order to use computers since you can buy programs that are already written by someone else. However, you need to learn to program if you are to appreciate the full power and versatility of computers and if you want to get your computer to do exactly what *you* want it to do. After reading this book, you'll be able to develop your own applications.

CHAPTER 1

Writing Programs in Pascal

Arithmetic Problems

People often need to do arithmetic calculations. Here are some examples of arithmetic calculations that you might face in everyday life or if you work at a financial institution or in a science or engineering job:

- Calculate the sales tax on an item if the tax rate is 6¾ percent, using the formula:

    Tax = 0.0675 × price

- Convert the amount of gasoline that you buy measured in liters into the equivalent amount measured in gallons:

    Number of gallons = 0.2642 × number of liters

- Calculate the amount of a foreign currency (such as pounds) you can obtain from a money exchange desk, if 1 dollar is worth 2/3 pound today:

    Number of pounds = $\frac{2}{3}$ × number of dollars

- Convert a temperature measured in degrees celsius into a temperature measured in degrees fahrenheit from the formula:

$$F = \frac{9}{5} \times C + 32$$

- Calculate the amount of money that you will have in your bank account if you start with $100, leave the money in the bank for n years, and collect compound interest at the rate of 5 percent per year:

Bank balance $= 100 \times 1.05^n$

- Calculate the height of a ball thrown straight up at an initial speed of 40 meters per second from an initial height of 10 meters:

$$\text{Height} = \frac{1}{2} \times 9.8 \times \text{time}^2 + 40 \times \text{time} + 10$$

(*Time* represents the time, measured in seconds, since the ball was thrown.)

Arithmetic problems can be very boring, and it is almost impossible to perform long and complicated calculations correctly the first time. It would help a lot if we could obtain a calculating servant that could do calculations quickly without making mistakes and without complaining. The best type of arithmetic servant, of course, is a machine. Let's start by considering how we could solve these problems with a pocket calculator. Suppose that the price of an item is $25. To solve the sales tax problem we need to type these keys:

and the result is:
    1.6875

Solving the problem with the calculator requires much less work than it would take to grind out the answer manually. However, if we have to perform this calculation many times, then even this much typing could become tedious.

We can also use the calculator to solve the other problems:

- 33.5 liters to gallons:

$0.2642 \times 33.5 = 8.85$ gallons

- 54 dollars to pounds:

$\frac{2}{3} \times 54 = 36$ pounds

- 21°C to °F:

$\frac{9}{5} \times 21° + 32 = 69.8°F$

- 100 dollars left in the bank at 5 percent interest for 6 years:

$100 \times 1.05^6 = 134.01$ dollars

- Time = 3.5 seconds:

    Height: $-0.5 \times 9.8 \times 3.5^2 + 40 \times 3.5 + 10 = 89.98$ meters

When the formulas become longer and more complicated, it is harder to perform the calculations correctly on the calculator. In more complex problems, we would have to perform calculations involving several formulas—not just one. Can we avoid all this work? Do we have any hope? Before the 1940s there was none; calculations like these had to be performed one step at a time.

The Need to Remember Instructions

We could save ourselves a lot of work if we had a machine that could *remember* its own instructions. That way we wouldn't have to type the instructions every single time we want the instructions used. For example, if the machine could remember the instruction, "Calculate the amount of the tax by multiplying the price by 0.0675," then it would be much easier for us to calculate the sales tax in any particular situation.

A machine that can store its own instructions is called a *computer.* Our next task is to figure out what instructions we want our computer to understand. A computer has no imagination. That means that we need to spell out exactly what we want it to do. If you tell a friend, "give me a hand," your friend will probably be able to figure out your real meaning. However, a computer will interpret everything you tell it literally. We'll develop a list of instructions that we want our computer to understand. Throughout this book we will add new instructions to our list when we think of a new task that we would like the computer to perform. When we are done, we will have created the computer language known as *Pascal.*

Computer Programs

A set of instructions for a computer is called a *program.* At the very beginning of the program we need a command that tells the computer that we are writing a program. The obvious command for that purpose is to type the word PROGRAM.

Therefore, the first word of our Pascal programs will always be the word PROGRAM:

```
PROGRAM
```

However, we will want to use the computer for more than one purpose, and so we will write more than one program. In fact, in this book we will write lots of different programs. Therefore, we will need a way to keep track of which program is which. When you need to keep track of different people, you give each one a name. Therefore, we will also give each program its own name. We can choose whatever name we want for a program, but the most helpful type of name is one that gives some indication of what the program does. In our case the program is calculating the amount of sales tax; so we may as well give the program the name *taxcalc.*

The first line of the program now looks like:

```
PROGRAM taxcalc
```

(Some computers require that all the words in a program be written in capital letters, but many computers also tell you to use lowercase letters. When lowercase letters are allowed, you can usually use either capital letters or lowercase letters, depending on your preference.)

There is one other useful bit of information we should add to the first line of the program. We don't want to take any chances that the computer won't understand what we mean. So we'll add the command (INPUT,OUTPUT) to the first line to make sure that the computer knows that we will want to feed some information *into* the computer (called *input*) and that we will also want to get some information *out* of the computer (called *output*). You may think that the computer should be smart enough to realize without our telling it that we will want to give it some input and get some output from it. However, remember that the computer that executes a Pascal program has no imagination, so it is best to give it very clearcut instructions.

Now the first line of the program looks like:

```
PROGRAM taxcalc (INPUT, OUTPUT) ;
```

Notice that we have put a semicolon at the end of the statement. The semicolon is there to tell the computer that we have reached the end of this statement and that we are ready to start a new statement. A Pascal program is made up of a series of statements, and we need some way to keep them separated. Therefore, we will add semicolons at the end of (almost) every statement. You may feel that it would be more natural to use a period as the end-of-statement marker, since periods are used to mark the end of sentences in English. However, we will want to use the period to represent a decimal point—it would be confusing to also use it to represent the end of a statement. Since we're not using the semicolon for anything else, it makes a good choice for the end-of-statement marker.

Now that we've identified the program, we need to describe exactly what we want it to do. The crucial instruction is based on the formula:

$$Tax = 0.0675 \times price$$

To make things simple, we would like our computer instruction to look as much as possible like this formula. We can, in fact, use the formula exactly as it is written, with only three minor modifications. First, we will, of course, add a semicolon at the end of the statement. Second, using the regular multiplication sign can create a lot of confusion since it looks too much like the letter x. Therefore, we will use an asterisk * to represent multiplication. Third, we will find that we have two quite distinct uses for the equal sign =, and we should keep these uses separate. In our situation the equal sign means, "We are commanding that the value 0.0675 * *price* be assigned to the name *tax*. We are giving you no choice in the matter." In an assignment command like this, we will add a colon : in front of the equal sign:

```
tax : = 0.0675 * price;
```

(We will use a plain equal sign when we want to ask a question, such as, "Does *price* = 25?" We will discuss that later.)

Now our program looks like:

```
PROGRAM taxcalc (INPUT, OUTPUT) ;
    tax : = 0.0675 * price;
```

Read and Write

Two important features are still missing. When the computer tries to calculate the value of the formula, it won't know what value of the price to use. We need some way to feed this input information into the computer. (Remember that the terms "input" and "output" are always used from the computer's point of view.) Therefore, we need a command to input the value of the price. Imagine that the computer is a person. Then there would be two ways it could get input: It could READ or it could LISTEN. Most computers can't listen to commands yet (although they likely will be able to in the near future); so we will use the command READ to indicate that the computer is supposed to read in some input information. The command READ(price) means that the computer will read in a value and assign it to the name *price*.

Now the program looks like:

```
PROGRAM taxcalc (INPUT, OUTPUT);
 READ(price);
 tax = 0.0675 * price;
```

We also need a command to remind the computer to tell *us* the answer. Suppose we told our arithmetic servant to calculate the answer, but then the servant kept the information to itself. That would be absolutely useless to us. We don't care whether or not the servant knows the answer; we want to know the answer ourselves. If the computer is a person, it could give output in one of two ways; it could TALK or it could WRITE. We will use the command WRITE to mean, "tell us the value of the output." The command WRITE(tax) means, "tell us the value of the tax."

```
PROGRAM tax (INPUT, OUTPUT);
 READ(price);
 tax := 0.0675 * price;
 WRITE(tax);
```

We've now completed the action part of the program. However, we need to make sure that the computer knows that the words *price* and *tax* are supposed to represent variable names. (In mathematics, a variable is just a symbol that stands for a value—often a number.)

Declaring Variables

You may think, "When I look at that program, it's perfectly obvious that *price* and *tax* are supposed to be variable names." But, since the computer can't figure anything out by itself, we will spell all this information out clearly. We will add a section at the beginning of the program called the DECLARE section. When you enter a new country, you need to stop at the customs office to declare your possessions. When you enter a new Pascal program, you need to stop at the declare section to declare your variables.

First, we'll write the word "variable" to indicate that we are declaring *tax* and *price* to be variables. To save us some writing, we can just write "VAR" as an abbreviation for variable:

```
VAR tax, price
```

Now we need to tell the computer what kind of variables these will be. Obviously they represent numbers, but we will later see that we use some variable names that are not numbers, and we will need to distinguish between two different types of numbers. When you count something, such as the number of lines in a Pascal program, the result is a number called an *integer*, such as 0, 1, 2, 3, ... When you measure something, such as the number of hours it takes to write a Pascal program, the result is called a *real number*. Examples of real numbers include 3, 2.45, 6½, 3.14159, and so on. Since the variables *price* and *tax* can take on values that are not integers, we will have to declare that they are real numbers. Therefore, the declare statement will look like this:

```
VAR tax, price: REAL;
```

Note that a colon : is included after the list of variables and before the word REAL. (If the value of a variable will always be a whole number, then we can declare it to be of type INTEGER.)

To separate the declare section from the action part of the program, we'll write the word BEGIN to tell the computer that it has completed the setup tasks and that it is time to start executing the main part of the program. Finally, at the conclusion of the program we'll use the word END to tell the computer that it is finished with the program and can take a rest.

The complete program looks like:

```
PROGRAM taxcalc (INPUT, OUTPUT);
VAR
   tax, price: REAL;
BEGIN
   READ(price);
   tax := 0.0675 * price;
WRITE(tax)
END.
```

Here are some notes about the punctuation. At the end of the program we will put a period instead of a semicolon to tell the computer that there are no more statements coming. Also, we will not put a semicolon at the end of the last statement before the END command. The rules for semicolons in Pascal will be discussed more later.

Now we've written our first program in Pascal. However, we still need to figure out how to get the computer to execute the program. The computer can't understand the instructions when they are written on a piece of paper (at least today's computers can't), so we will need a better way to feed the program in to the computer.

Computers

Let's take a look at an actual computer. Assume that we've just bought a brand new computer and we're now taking it out of the box. The computer looks like a television screen attached to a typewriter keyboard. The keyboard has keys for letters, numbers, and some special symbols. The screen is a cathode ray tube (CRT) screen. The screen will be used by the computer to display messages to us. Somewhere in the middle of the computer is the actual brain, that is, the *central processing unit* (CPU). It is the CPU that controls the operations of the computer. However, the CPU doesn't understand Pascal. It only understands an even stranger coded language called *machine language.* Our Pascal program needs to be translated into machine language before the computer can execute it. (To execute a program merely means to have a computer do what the instructions say to do.)

There are several steps involved in arranging for the computer to execute the program. At first this procedure will seem confusing, but you will soon become used to it after you have written several Pascal programs. (See the section at the end of this book called "How Do I Run Pascal on My Computer?" for some hints on using some of the popular Pascal versions.) First, you must type the program on the keyboard that comes with the computer. While you are typing, the CPU will be obeying a special program called a *text editor.* A text editor is simply a program that allows you to type in words and then edit (change) them. You may have an editor called Ed the Editor with your computer. (Ed comes with computers that use the *CP/M operating system.*) Or you may have a *word processing* text editor, such as *Wordstar,* that you may be able to use. In any case, you will have to learn to use the editor that comes with your computer and then type your program. The typing process will be similar to typing on a regular typewriter. The main difference is that you will see what you type on the screen. The fun part is that you will be able to change what you have typed easily if you make a mistake.

Second, once you have typed your program, you need to store it somewhere where you will be able to get to it again. When you first type your program, it is stored inside the computer's *main memory.* However, anything stored in the main memory normally disappears when you turn the power to the computer off, and so you need a more permanent place to store your program. (Otherwise you would need to type the program in again every time you want to use it. That would defeat the whole purpose of the computer. Remember that the only reason to write a computer program is to reduce the amount of work that you need to do.) Fortunately, most computers allow you to store programs (and other information) on small plastic *disks* (also known as *floppy disks*). A floppy disk is a bit like a small phonograph record usually either 5 or 8 inches across. The surface of the disk is covered with magnetic material similar to tape recorder tape, and the disk is covered with a protective covering. Some computers use ordinary cassette tapes to store information, but tapes are more awkward to use because it takes the computer longer to transfer information to or from a tape. To use a disk, you need to insert it into a slot in the side of the computer called a *disk drive*. (On some computers, such as the Apple II, the disk drive is a separate unit that you connect to the computer.) After you have put the disk in the disk drive, you will need to follow the instructions that came with your computer to learn how to store the program on the disk. You will need to give your program a *filename*. For example, we might give our program the filename TAXCALC.SRC. In this case TAXCALC is the name of the file, and SRC is an example of a *file extension*. A file extension is a three-letter code that tells a bit about what type of file this is. Here the three letters SRC stand for "source." The original Pascal program sent to a computer is called the *source program*. If you have a CP/M operating system computer, then you will need to put a period . between the file name and the file extension.

Now that the program is stored on the disk, we need to begin the process of translating the Pascal program into machine language. We must obtain a disk that contains a program called a Pascal *compiler*. A compiler program is like a translator program: It translates our Pascal program into machine language. Usually we will put the disk with the compiler in drive A and the disk containing our program in drive B, and then type in the command that causes the compiler to be executed. Once the compiler is finished, it will have created a new program called an *object program*, written in machine language. (In some cases you may have to perform one more intermediate step: you may need to use a program called a *linkage editor* to connect the compiler output to other support programs that the computer will need in order to execute your program.)

Now we're just about ready to see the program run! Let's suppose that our computer uses the CP/M operating system. (The DOS operating system for the IBM PC is very similar to CP/M.) When the computer is ready for us to type a command, it will display the message:

    A>

Running Programs

The "A>" message is called the *prompt.* Let's suppose that the compiler has created an object program file with the name TAXCALC.COM. (Note that the file name is the same as our original file, but the file extension is different. The file extension COM means that the file is a COMmand file.) Suppose that the disk containing this file is in drive A. To execute the program, we merely need to type the command TAXCALC—and the computer will work on our program!

After we type TAXCALC, the screen will look like this:

    A>TAXCALC
    –

The computer suddenly stops. It is not out to lunch. Instead, it is waiting for us to type in the value of the price. The first action command in our program is the statement READ(price);. When we are using a microcomputer (or when we are logged on to a big computer in interactive mode), a READ statement tells the computer to wait for the user to type in the value at the keyboard.

The small blinking dash on the screen is called the *cursor.* It tells us where on the screen the next item we type will appear. Let's type in the value 100.00 for the price. The screen looks like this:

```
A>TAXCALC
100.00
```

After we have typed the number, we must type the RETURN (or ENTER) key on the right side of the keyboard. The RETURN key tells the computer that we're done typing a line. After we type the RETURN key, the screen will suddenly look like this:

```
A>TAXCALC
100.00
   6.74999E+00
```

And that's the answer!

The answer does look a bit strange. It is written in *exponential notation.* The capital E stands for exponent. The number after the E (+00 in this case) represents the power of 10 by which we must multiply the first part of the number. So, 6.7499E+00 means $6.7499 \times 10^0 = 6.7499$ (since $10^0 = 1$). Here are some more examples of numbers in exponential notation:

$2.5E+01$ means $2.5 \times 10^1 = 2.5 \times 10 = 25.$

$6.78E+03$ means $6.78 \times 10^3 = 6.78 \times 1,000 = 6,780.$

$6.45E-01$ means $6.45 \times 10^{-1} = \frac{6.45}{10} = 0.645.$

$3E-02$ means $3 \times 10^{-2} = \frac{3}{100} = 0.03.$

Exponential notation is also known as *scientific notation.* It is especially helpful for writing very large or very small numbers. For example, $602,000,000,000,000,000,000,000 = 6.02 \times 10^{23} = 6.02E+23$ and $0.0000001 = 1 \times 10^{-7} = 1E-07.$

It is an annoying feature of Pascal that real numbers are always written in exponential notation unless you tell it otherwise. In the next chapter we will see how to make the output easier to read.

We have now reached an important milestone: We have written a complete Pascal program and watched it being executed. Admittedly, the tax calculation problem is so simple that we could have solved the problem just as easily without a computer. However, in the next few chapters we will develop some more of the Pascal language, and we will see what a versatile tool a computer can be.

Notes to Chapter 1

■   You can give variables almost any name that you choose. However, there are some restrictions. Variable names normally cannot be longer than 31 characters, and they should contain only letters or digits. The first character of a name must be a letter. And there is one other very important restriction. You cannot give a variable a name that is the same as one of the words used in the Pascal language. For example, you cannot name a variable var, const, begin, or end. These words are called *reserved words* because they have a special meaning reserved for them and therefore cannot be used as variable names. The list of Pascal reserved words is included at the end of the book. In the programs written in this book, the reserved words will always be written in capital letters.

■   There will be times when you would like the output from your programs to be printed out, in addition to appearing on the screen. If you are using a CP/M computer, hold down the control key and then type P. This command will cause everything appearing on the screen to be printed on the printer as well. Then type the command filename to execute the program. If you would like a printed version of your program, then type the command TYPE *filename*. When you no longer want all of the screen display to appear on the printer, type control-P again.

Chapter 1 Exercises

1. Write a program that reads in a number n and calculates $12n$.

2. Write a program that reads in two numbers and multiplies them together.

3. Must every program include the words INPUT and OUTPUT as a part of the first line?

4. Write the following in scientific notation:
   (a) 4,739.26
   (b) .000450
   (c) 160,000,000
   (d) .1049
   (e) 300,000

CHAPTER 2

Input and Output

We've now written a full-fledged Pascal program. However, after we have run the program a few times, the screen will be full of a confusing long list of numbers:

```
A>TAXCALC
100
  6.7499E+00

A>TAXCALC
6.95
  4.69124E-01

A>TAXCALC
24.55
  1.65712E+00
```

We know that 100 represents a sales amount and that 6.74999E+00 represents a tax amount. 6.95 is another sales amount, and 4.69124E-01 is another tax amount. However, we know that because we just wrote the program 5 minutes ago. The meaning of the numbers is not at all obvious just by looking at them. So let's figure out some new output commands so that we will have more control over the appearance of the output.

The Need for Labels

It would help a lot if we could include labels above each number explaining what it means. Let's add a command to our computer that orders the computer to display the word "tax". We could try the command WRITE(tax), but we know that won't work. The command WRITE(tax) tells the computer to print the value of the variable *tax,* not the word "tax". When we want the computer to print out a word just as we have written it, we will enclose the word in single quotation marks. For example, the command WRITE('tax') causes the output:

```
tax
```

In general, when we enclose a line of characters between two quotation marks in a WRITE statement, the computer will print out the characters exactly as they are, with no questions asked.

General form: The command

```
WRITE('characters')
```

causes the output:

```
characters
```

Now we can write the tax program so that it labels the output. There is another useful feature we can add: We can have the computer display a message telling us what number we need to type in. So far, we've only written one program, and that program only asks us to type in one number. When the computer stops and asks us for the input, we have no problem remembering what number we should type in. However, you can imagine what a nightmare we would face if the computer suddenly stopped in the middle of the program, asked us to type in a number, and we forgot what we were supposed to type in!

We'll add one further modification. When we run our program several times, the screen fills up fairly fast. In some cases it would be helpful if we could put more than one output item on a single line. For example, it would be convenient to have the output look like this:

```
The tax is 6.74999E+00
```

rather than this:

```
The tax is
  6.74999E+00
```

We can do this easily just by making it possible to include more than one item in a single WRITE statement. The items need to be separated by commas. For example, the command:

```
WRITE ('The tax is',1.03);
```

will cause the output:

```
The tax is 1.03000E+00
```

If the variable *tax* has the value 4.69124E−01, then the command

```
WRITE ('The tax is ',tax);
```

causes the output:

```
The tax is 4.69124E−01
```

READLN and WRITELN

There are two more Pascal input/output commands we must learn. So far we have used the READ and WRITE statements to accept data and display data. There are two other statements which operate similarly to the READ and WRITE statements. These are the READLN and WRITELN statements (the "LN" part of each statement stands for line—WRITELN means "write line" and READLN means "read line").

  The difference between the READ and READLN statements is in the way the *next* READ or READLN statement is handled. After executing a READ statement, the program will get the data for the next input statement from the current data line. A READLN statement, however, will force the next input statement to get its data from the *next* data line. For example, the sequence of statements

```
READ(a); {a,b,c are integers}
READLN(b);
READ(c);
```

with the data lines typed in as

```
2 -4 6
10
```

will assign the value 2 to a and −4 to b. After b is assigned the value −4, the next READ statement will get its data from the next data line, and so c will equal 10. Notice that data items on the same line are separated by one or more blank spaces.

  A WRITELN statement will force the *next* line of output to be printed on a new line. A simple WRITE statement will allow the contents of the next output statement to be printed on the same line. The printing of a series of WRITE statements is forced by a WRITELN statement (and on some systems also when input is expected or at the end of the program). To print a blank line, use a WRITELN with no output message. If no WRITEs are waiting to be printed, a blank line will be output. The following illustrates the use of the WRITELN:

```
WRITE('Hello, ');
WRITELN('how are you?');
WRITELN; {prints a blank line}
WRITELN('I am fine, ');
WRITELN('thank you.');
```

The output will look like:

```
Hello, how are you?

I am fine,
thank you.
```

  Here's the new version of the tax program that puts labels on both the input and output:

```
PROGRAM taxcalc (INPUT, OUTPUT);
  VAR
    price, tax : REAL;
  BEGIN
    WRITELN('Input the price: ');
    READLN(price);
    tax := 0.0675 * price;
    WRITELN('The tax is: ', tax)
  END.
```

  Now, after we run the program several times, we can see that the screen is much more meaningful:

```
A>TAXCALC
Input the price:
100
The tax is: 6.74999E+00

A>TAXCALC
Input the price:
6.95
The tax is: 4.69124E-01

A>TAXCALC
Input the price:
24.55
The tax is: 1.65712E+00
```

Controlling the Format of Output

We still have one more problem. It is very annoying to have the answers always written in exponential notation. So, we need to think of a Pascal command to tell the computer that we don't want the answer written that way. We need a command that controls the *format* of a number when it appears on the screen. Let's tell the computer two things: how many columns we want the number to fill and how many digits we would like to the right of the decimal point. For example, here's how the number 33.3333 looks under some different formats:

Output	No. of columns	No. of decimal digits
33.	3	0
33.3	4	1
33.33	5	2
33.333	6	3
33.3333	7	4
_33.3	5	1
___33.3	7	1
_____33.333	11	3

The number of columns that a number fills when it is printed out is called the *field width* of the number. Note that the decimal point also counts for one space. In the listing above, an underline, _ represents one blank space. On your screen, of course, you will only see a blank instead of a _ .

In Pascal, the two format numbers need to be written immediately after the number in the output statement, separated from it by colons (:). The field width number is listed first, and then the number of decimal digits. For example, the statement WRITE(x:6:2); will cause the value of *x* to be output with a field width of 6 with two digits to the right of the decimal point.

Here is an example of a simple program that illustrates formatting:

```
PROGRAM formatdemo (INPUT, OUTPUT);
VAR
  y: REAL;
```

```
BEGIN
  y : = 33.3333;
  WRITELN(y);
  WRITELN(y:3:0);
  WRITELN(y:4:1);
  WRITELN(y:5:2);
  WRITELN(y:6:3);
  WRITELN(y:7:4);
  WRITELN(y:5:1);
  WRITELN(y:6:1);
  WRITELN(y:7:1);
  WRITELN(y:8:1);
  WRITELN(y:8:2);
  WRITELN(y:8:3);
  WRITELN(y:11:3)
END.
```

The output from this program looks like this:

```
  3.33333E+01
33.
33.3
33.33
33.333
33.3333
 33.3
  33.3
   33.3
  33.33
 33.333
    33.333
```

The general form of the format for real numbers is:

WRITE(*expression:field width:decimal digits*);

(You don't need to worry about what happens if the number is too big to fit in the specified field length. Pascal will simply expand the field width to make room.)

Now we can rewrite the tax calculation program. For dollar amounts we would like two decimal digits printed out. Let's use the format 7:2.

```
PROGRAM taxcalc (INPUT, OUTPUT);
VAR
  tax, price: REAL;
BEGIN
  WRITELN('Input the price: ');
  READ(price);
  tax : = 0.0675 * price;
  WRITELN('The tax is: ', tax:7:2)
END.
```

The output from this program looks like:

```
A>TAXCALC
Input the price:
100
The tax is 6.75
```

```
A>TAXCALC
Input the price:
6.95
The tax is 0.47

A>TAXCALC
Input the price:
24.55
The tax is 1.66
```

The numbers are now much easier to read.

Here is an example of a program that allows you to read in the amount of gasoline that you have purchased, measured in liters, and then converts that amount into the equivalent amount measured in gallons:

```
PROGRAM gallonconvert (INPUT, OUTPUT);
VAR
  gallons, liters :REAL;
BEGIN
  WRITELN('Enter the amount of gasoline in liters');
  READLN(liters);
  gallons := 0.2642 * liters;
  WRITELN('The amount of gasoline in gallons is ',gallons:5:2)
END.
```

Here is a sample output from this program:

```
Enter the amount of gasoline in liters:
30.0
The amount of gasoline in gallons is 7.93
```

Comments Explain What Is Happening

Now we've written two complete programs, and in the course of this book we will write many more programs. To make it easier to keep track of all those programs, it would help to include a brief word of explanation with each program. At the very least, it would help to include a sentence that describes what the program does. The computer itself doesn't care what it's doing or why, and so there's no need to include an explanation for the computer's benefit. However, we do need an explanation for the benefit of the people that read the program. An explanation included in a program is called a *comment.* In order to include a comment in a program, all we need to do is figure out a symbol that tells the computer to ignore a few words. (The computer would become very confused if it tried to execute an explanation.) In Pascal, a comment begins with a left brace { and it ends with a right brace }. [On some systems, a left parenthesis followed by an asterisk (* is used to mark the beginning of a comment, and an asterisk followed by a right parentheses *) is used to mark the end of a comment.] Here is an example of the liters-to-gallons conversion program that includes a few comments:

```
PROGRAM gallonconvert (INPUT, OUTPUT);
    {This program converts liters to gallons. The user will supply
    the liter amount.}
VAR
  gallons, liters :REAL;
BEGIN
  WRITELN('Enter the amount of gasoline in liters');
  READLN(liters);
  gallons := 0.2642 * liters;
  WRITELN('The amount of gasoline in gallons is ',gallons:5:2)
END.
```

Note that you can include any kind of information that you like in a comment. The computer won't mind. Often it is useful to include your name and the date that the program was written. Also include any other information that would be helpful to you while you are reading the program. And of course you should remember that the names you give to the variables used in the program make a big difference in how understandable the program is. Make sure to use variable names that indicate what the variables mean, and also make sure that the name of the program gives a clue as to what the program does.

Here's another trick that makes a big difference as to how understandable your programs are. In Pascal you can cram as many statements as you want on one line, or you can make one statement cover several lines, and you can indent lines however you want. The computer doesn't care at all about how the program looks on the page; it always ignores all the blank spaces anyway. However, the appearance of the program makes a big difference to a human reader. For example, here is an example of the gasoline program where all of the statements have been crammed together as tightly as possible:

```
PROGRAM gallonconv (INPUT, OUTPUT);VAR
gallons,liters:REAL;BEGIN WRITELN('Enter the amount of gasoline
in liters');READLN (liters);
gallons:=0.2642*liters;WRITELN('Amount of gasoline in gallons
is',gallons:4:2) END.
```

Here is another example of the gasoline program, where the program has been spread out to cover as many lines as possible:

```
PROGRAM
gallonconv
 (INPUT, OUTPUT)
;   VAR
gallons
, liters:            REAL      ;
     BEGIN
WRITELN               (
 'Enter the amount of gasoline in liters'
);
                     READLN      (liters);
gallons
:= 0.2642            *liters;
WRITELN
('The amount of gasoline in gallons is',
      gallons:4 :2 )
                    END.
```

Both of these last two versions of the program are very difficult for people to read, although they are both perfectly intelligible to the computer. The program is much easier for people to read if it is spaced out normally.

Here is an example of a program that will help you if you are planning a trip to Great Britain. You will need to convert your dollars into pounds; so the program tells you how many pounds you can receive in exchange for a given amount of dollars. First, the program asks you to type in the current exchange rate. Then type in the dollar amount that you want to convert.

```
PROGRAM currencyconv (INPUT, OUTPUT);
VAR
 rate, dollars, pounds: REAL;
BEGIN
 WRITELN('Enter current exchange rate');
```

```
    READLN(rate);
    WRITELN('Enter the dollar amount');
    READLN(dollars);
    pounds := rate * dollars;
    WRITELN;
    WRITELN('The pound amount is ', pounds:5:2)
  END.
```

(Try running this program yourself.)

You will need some practice working with assigning values to variables so that you understand how the process works. For example, let's suppose that we want to write a program that performs a trivial operation: read in two numbers *a* and *b*, and then switch their values (in other words, give the value of *a* to *b*, and give the value of *b* to *a*). Here is a sample program that we think might work:

```
PROGRAM switch (INPUT, OUTPUT);
  VAR
    a, b: REAL;
  BEGIN
    READLN(a);
    READLN(b);
    WRITELN('a = ',a:4:0,'b = ',B:4:0);
    a := b;
    b := a;
    WRITELN('a = ',a:4:0,'b = ',b:4:0)
  END.
```

Now, let's try to run this program, using the initial values *a* = 25 and *b* = 10. The output is

```
a = 25. b = 10.
a = 10. b = 10.
```

Something clearly didn't work. The value of 10 was assigned to *a* all right, but how come the statement b := a did not assign the value of 25 to *b*? If we look closely at the program, we can see what is going on. After the first WRITELN statement, *a* has the value of 25 and *b* has the value 10. After the statement a := b; then *a* acquires the value 10. When you assign a new value to a variable, then the old value of that variable is lost and gone forever. All the statement b := a does is take the new value of *a* (which is now 10) and assign it to *b*.

Here is a new version of the switch program that will work:

```
PROGRAM switch (INPUT, OUTPUT);
  VAR
    a, b, temp: REAL;
  BEGIN
    READLN(a);
    READLN(b);
    WRITELN('a = ',a:4:0,'b = ',b:4:0);
    temp := a;
    a := b;
    b := temp;
    WRITELN ('a = ',a:4:0,'b = ',b:4:0)
  END.
```

Now let's run this program:

```
a = 25. b = 10.
a = 10. b = 25.
```

The variable "temp" acts as a temporary storage location to help us successfully execute the switch. First, we store the original value of *a* (which is 25) under the name temp. Then, we assign the value of *b* to *a*. This time, however, we do not lose all of the information about the original value of *a*, because we have stored that value under the name temp. To complete the program, all we need to do is assign to *b* the value that is currently being stored under the name temp.

You can also use the *old* value of a variable to calculate the new value of the variable. For example, these statements:

```
a: = 10;
WRITELN(a);
a: = a+1;
WRITELN(a);
a: = 2 * a;
WRITELN(a);
```

cause the output:

```
10
11
22
```

Note to Chapter 2

■ Here is another program that illustrates the difference between READ and READLN.

```
PROGRAM formatdemo (INPUT, OUTPUT);
{This program demonstrates the difference between READ and
READLN}
VAR
x, y : INTEGER;
BEGIN
WRITELN('*Enter integer value for x');
READ(x);
WRITELN('*Enter integer value for y');
READLN(y);
WRITELN('*x = ',x,' y = ',y);
WRITELN('*Enter integer values for x and y on separate lines');
READLN(x);
READLN(y);
WRITELN('*x = ',x,' y = ',y);
WRITELN('*Enter values for x and y on the same line');
READ(x);
READLN(y);
WRITELN('*x = ',x,' y = ',y)
END.
```

After we execute this program, the screen looks like this:

```
*Enter integer value for x
16
*Enter integer value for y
23
*x =   16 y=   23
*Enter integer values for x and y on separate lines
44
118
*x =   44 y =   118
```

```
*Enter values for x and y on the same line
33   44
*x =   33 y =   44
```

Note that asterisks have been added in front of all the lines that the computer typed. Let's run the program again:

```
*Enter integer value for x
22
*Enter integer value for y
7
*x =   22 y =   7
*Enter integer values for x and y on separate lines
16 44 55 28 11
33
*x = 16 y = 33
*Enter values for x and y on the same line
24 77 88 99 34
*x = 24 y = 77
```

(Note that if you type more numbers on a line than the computer is looking for, it will ignore all the surplus numbers.)

Chapter 2 Exercises

1. What will be assigned to the variables a, b, c, and d given the following sequence of READ and READLN statements?

    ```
    READ(a);
    READLN(b);
    READLN(c);
    READ(d);
    ```

    Data is typed in as

    ```
    -4        61        10
    34         7
    -22        5
    13
    9        -83
    ```

2. Given the following sequence of WRITE and WRITELN statements, what will the output look like?

    ```
    WRITE('Hello');
    WRITE('How are you');
    WRITE('Today?');
    WRITELN('Fine thank you');
    WRITELN;
    WRITE('Goodbye');
    WRITE('Goodbye');
    ```

3. Given the number 16.89, what will the output look like with the following output formats:
    (a) 4:0   (c) 6:2   (e) 3:2
    (b) 6:1   (d) 7:3   (f) 5:1

4. When are comments needed?

CHAPTER 3

Arithmetic Operations

We'll want our computer to do a lot more than multiply, and so we'll add some other arithmetic operations to our language's repertoire. We will develop several different types of mathematical expressions in this chapter. Normally, a mathematical expression will appear in one of two places: in an assignment statement:

> *variable* := *expression*;

or in an output statement:

> writeln(*expression*);

Adding, Subtracting, Multiplying, Dividing

To make things as easy as possible, we will use familiar symbols for most operations. We will use a + symbol to stand for addition, and a − symbol to stand for subtraction. For example, the expression 2 + 2 means "two plus two," and the expression 64 − 16 means "sixty-four minus sixteen." We'll use the symbol / to stand for division for real numbers, because the expression 12/4 looks a little bit like the fraction $^{12}/_4$. For example, the expression $^{100}/_{20}$ means "one hundred divided by twenty." Here are some more examples of arithmetic expressions and their values:

10.06 + 26.115

36.175

    34.1 * 26.3

896.83

    16.5/14.1

1.1702

    5/8

0.625

Integers

So far we have only discussed numbers that are real numbers. Remember that a real number is a number that may contain a fractional part, such as 1.75, 3.3333, or −6.7618. In Pascal a numerical value will be considered to be a real number if it contains a decimal point, such as 5.0, 16.35, 0.467. There will also be times when we will want to use variables that are integers—that is, whole numbers such as 1, 2, 10, 15, 100, or the negatives of whole numbers, such as −1, −2, −10, −15, or −100. An integer variable must be declared to be of type INTEGER in the declaration section. The arithmetic operations of addition (+), subtraction (−), and multiplication (*) work the same for integers as they do for real numbers. However, the operation of division is different. Here is an example of a division problem with real numbers. Suppose we set out on a trip of 14.0 miles and it takes us 5.0 hours to reach the destination. Then we can say that our average speed during the trip was 14.0 ÷ 5.0 = 14.0/5.0 = 2.8 miles per hour.

    Here is an integer division problem that uses the same numbers. Suppose you have 14 people going on a car trip. Suppose each car can carry 5 people. To calculate the number of cars you will need, you must perform the division calculation 14 ÷ 5. However, it makes no sense to say that you need 2.8 cars. When we divide integers, we need two parts of the answer: the quotient (in this case 2) and the remainder (in this case 4). So if you take 2 cars, there will be 4 people left over. If you want to fit everyone in, then you will need to take 3 cars.

    In Pascal there are two commands used for integer division. The expression a DIV b is the quotient when a is divided by b. The expression a MOD b is the remainder when a is divided by b (MOD is short for the technical mathematical term *modulus*).

    Here are some examples:

      30 DIV 5 is 6; 30 MOD 5 is 0

      42 DIV 10 is 4; 42 MOD 10 is 2

      16 DIV 3 is 5; 16 MOD 3 is 1

       5 DIV 8 is 0; 5 MOD 8 is 5

    We can also calculate what your bank balance will be if you put $100 in the bank today and the bank pays 5% interest per year. After n years the total amount of money you will have in the bank will be $100 \times (1.05)^n$. We use two asterisks ** to represent exponentiation. For example, the computer will interpret 10 ** 3 to mean 10 = 10 × 10 × 10. The formula 100 * 1.05 ** 10 has the result: 162.89. [However, note that some versions of Pascal don't include an exponentiation operator at all. You will need to check with your local version. If you don't have an exponentiation operator, then the expression a^x can be written like this: exp(x * ln(a)).]

The Order Matters

As soon as we put two different operations on the same line, we have another problem. How does the computer know that the formula is $100 \times (1.05)^n$ and not $(100 \times 1.05)^n$? If the computer does the operations in order from left to right, it will do the multiplication first and the exponentiation second, and it won't give us the answer we want. Fortunately, we can give the computer some rules of precedence so it will do the operations in the order that corresponds most closely to ordinary algebraic notation. In Pascal, whenever the computer comes to an arithmetic instruction, it will do the exponentiations first, it will do the multiplications and divisions next, and it will do the additions and subtractions last.

For example, $5 + 10 * 6 ** 2$ means $5 + 10 * 36$, which means $5 + 360$, which is 365. In this case the computer will do $6 ** 2$ first, it will do $10 * 36$ next, and it will do $5 + 360$ last.

The next question we should ask is: What should we have the computer do if there are two multiplications on the same line? For example, suppose the computer faces the expression $6 * 3 + 2 * 6$. Whenever there are two operations of the same level of precedence, we may as well have the computer do them in the order in which they appear, that is, from left to right. In the expression above, first the computer will do $6 * 3$, then it will do $2 * 6$, and finally it will do $18 + 12$, to give 30. (Try some more sample problems involving arithmetic expressions to make sure that you understand the precedence rules clearly. See the exercises.)

What if we don't want to have the operations done in the order in which the computer wants to do them? Suppose we need to convert the algebraic expression $5(6 + 10)$ into computer notation. We can't write $5 * 6 + 10$, because we would get $30 + 10$, which isn't what we want. Therefore we'll need to add a new instruction to tell the computer to override its normal precedence rule. We can use ordinary parentheses for this purpose. The keyboard has a left parenthesis (and a right parenthesis), so we can make the rule that any operation within a pair of parentheses will be done first. Then our expression can be written as

$$5 * (6 + 10)$$

The result is 80 (since $5 * 16 = 80$).

Here is an example of a program that reads in a temperature measured in degrees fahrenheit and then converts it to the equivalent temperature measured in degrees celsius:

```
PROGRAM tempconv (INPUT, OUTPUT);
VAR
   far, cel : REAL;
BEGIN
   WRITELN('Enter the degrees fahrenheit');
   READLN(far);
   cel := (5/9) * (far - 32);
   WRITELN('Degrees celsius is ',cel:4:1)
END.
```

If necessary, we can have one pair of parentheses inside another pair of parentheses:

$$3 * (5 + (3 + 1) ** 2)$$

The computer does the operation inside the innermost pair of parentheses first:

$$3 * (5 + 4 ** 2)$$

There are two operations inside the outer pair of parentheses. The addition sign comes first, but the exponentiation has higher precedence so it is done before the addition:

    3 * (5 + 16)

The addition is done next:

    3 * 21

and the final result is

    63

If you try enough examples, you will inevitably make a mistake. For example, suppose your program contains this arithmetic expression:

    (((10 + 5)/3) ** 2

When you attempt to compile the program, the computer screen will suddenly start acting strange and will display the word ERROR (or some equivalent). Fortunately, the computer will soon return to normal. However, the computer will give you an error message whenever your program contains an instruction that it can't handle. In this case, the computer was trying to figure out in what order to evaluate your expression, and it found more left parentheses than right parentheses. Since it didn't know what you really meant, it had to give you an error message. Computers are usually not smart enough to figure out what you mean if you say something different from what you really mean.

Type in the corrected version:

    ((10 + 5)/3) ** 2

You'll have to remember the parentheses rule.

In any arithmetic expression, the number of left parentheses (must be exactly the same as the number of right parentheses).

Suppose you throw a baseball straight up, and you need to know how high it will be at any time. The height of an object thrown straight up can be found from the formula

$$h = -\frac{1}{2} gt^2 + v_0 t + h_0$$

where t is the time (in seconds) since the object was thrown, v_0 is the speed (in meters per second) at which it was initially thrown, g is the acceleration of gravity, which equals 9.8, and h_0 is the height of the object (in meters) at the moment it is being thrown. In our case, suppose $v_0 = 100$ and $h_0 = 15$. The expression for the height when $t = 2$ is

    -0.5 * 9.8 * 2 ** 2 + 100 * 2 + 15

and the answer is

    195.4

Check this expression carefully to make sure that it follows the rules of precedence correctly. We know that the computer first will do the exponentiation 2 ** 2, then it will do the three multiplications from left to right, and finally it will do the two additions.

We can also calculate the height 6 seconds after the throw:

$$-0.5 * 9.8 * 6 ** 2 + 100 * 6 + 15$$

438.6

Built-In Mathematical Functions

In addition to the ordinary arithmetic functions we've used up to now, it will be useful to add some special mathematical functions to our computer. Don't worry if these are unfamiliar to you. You can skip over any functions that you haven't heard of. In this case, as the adage says, what you don't know can't hurt you.

First, it will help you to have a square root function. In algebra a square root is symbolized by a radical sign $\sqrt{}$. For example, $\sqrt{25} = 5$, because $5 \times 5 = 25$. In PASCAL, the square root of 25 is written SQRT(25). Some other examples are as follows:

SQRT(36)

6

SQRT(121)

11

If $x = 144$, then

SQRT(x)

12

You should note that the quantity for which you're calculating the square root always needs to be surrounded by parentheses.

Pascal also contains a function that automatically calculates the square of a number: SQR(X). For example, SQR(3) is 9, SQR(10) is 100, and SQR(6) is 36. (Make sure that you don't confuse the SQR function with the SQRT function!)

For another example, suppose you want to know the diagonal distance across a field that is 100 yards long and 30 yards wide (see Figure 3-1). From the pythagorean theorem, the distance will be

$$\sqrt{100^2 + 30^2}$$

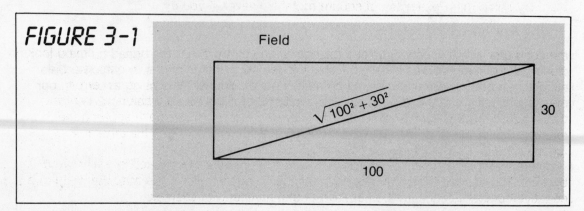

FIGURE 3-1

Field

$\sqrt{100^2 + 30^2}$

30

100

In Pascal this expression can be written as

```
SQRT(100 ** 2 + 30 ** 2)
```
104.4030651

There are some cases where it is helpful to ignore all the decimal places in a real number. We can add a function to eliminate all the decimal digits; we'll call it TRUNC (short for TRUNCation). Try some examples:

```
TRUNC(5.6)
```
5
```
TRUNC(2.0345)
```
2
```
TRUNC(109)
```
109
```
TRUNC(6.999)
```
6
```
TRUNC(104.651)
```
104
```
TRUNC(-0.5)
```
0
```
TRUNC(-10.7)
```
-10
```
TRUNC(-18)
```
-18

Another useful function is the ROUND function. It calculates the integer that is nearest to a particular number. Here are some examples:

```
ROUND(6.6)
```
7
```
ROUND(6.4)
```
6
```
ROUND(-1.54)
```
-2
```
ROUND(-3.04)
```
-3
```
ROUND(6.5)
```
7

We can even put one built-in function inside another:

```
TRUNC(SQRT(100 ** 2 + 30 ** 2))
```
104

Try some more examples of square roots. However, if you try

```
SQRT(4 ** 2 - 5 ** 2)
```

the computer will give you an error message when you try to run the program. If you look closely at the expression, you will see that you're asking the computer to calculate the square root of a negative number, and it can't do that. You will always get an error message if you try to use a function on a number that is not an allowable argument for that function. [The argument of a function is the number to which you're applying the function. For example, in the expression SQRT(25) the number 25 is the argument of the function SQRT.]

Another simple function we can include is the absolute value function, symbolized by ABS. The absolute value of a positive number is equal to itself; the absolute value of a negative number is equal to the negative of that number. For example:

```
        ABS(16)
16
        ABS(-10)
10
        ABS(-165.42)
165.42
        ABS(0)
 0
```

Now we can calculate:

```
        SQRT(ABS(4 ** 2 - 5 ** 2))
3
```

If you are familiar with trigonometry, you may like to have the computer do some trigonometric functions. That will be much easier than having to look up the values of the trigonometric functions in a table. We can use SIN and COS to stand for sine and cosine, respectively, and we can use ARCTAN to stand for the inverse trigonometric function arctan.

Suppose you need to measure the distance to a rock that is located in the middle of a river. You can't very well swim across the river with a tape measure, but you can calculate the distance if you know some trigonometry. First, stand along the river bank directly opposite the rock (point *A* on Figure 3-2). Then go to a point 10 yards away (point *B* on Figure 3-2), and observe the rock from there. Next, measure the angle between the rock and point *A*.

Suppose this angle turns out to be 65°, which is the same as 1.13446 radians. Then the distance *d* can be found from the formula:

$$d = 10 \tan 1.13446$$

FIGURE 3-2

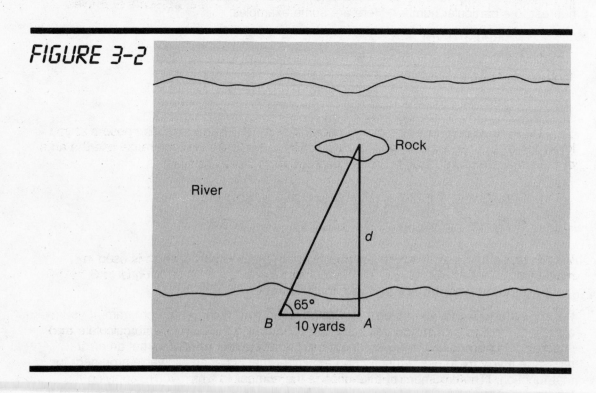

To calculate this expression in Pascal, we need to use the fact that $\tan x = \sin x / \cos x$. Here is a sample program segment:

```
angle := 1.13446;
distance := 10*SIN(angle)/COS(angle);
```

The result is 21.445; so the rock is 21.445 yards away from the shore. Here are some other examples of trigonometric functions:

```
    SIN(0)
0
    SIN(1)
0.8415
    SIN(0.5236)
0.5000
    COS(0.5236)
0.8660
    COS(0)
1
```

Two more useful mathematical functions are the *exponential* function and the *natural logarithm* function. In Pascal the function EXP(x) means e^x, where e is a very special number approximately equal to 2.71828. Here are some examples:

```
    EXP(0)
1
    EXP(1)
2.71828
    EXP(2)
7.3891
    EXP(30)
1.06865E+13
```

The natural logarithm of a number is the power to which you must raise e to get that number. In other words, if $y = $ EXP(x), then $x = $ LN(y). Here are some examples:

```
    LN(1)
0
    LN(2.71828)
1
    LN(10)
2.3026
```

Let's try another example of an important arithmetic calculation. Suppose that you know the radius r of a circle, and you would like to know the circumference and the area of the circle. We can calculate these quantities from these formulas:

Circumference $= 2\pi r$

Area $= \pi r^2$

In these formulas, the funny symbol π is the greek letter *pi,* which is used in mathematics to represent a very special number that is approximately equal to 3.14159. Here is one version of a program that will work:

```
PROGRAM circle (INPUT, OUTPUT);
    {This program reads in the value of the radius of a circle and
    then calculates the circumference and area.}
    VAR
        radius, circumference, area, pi: REAL;
    BEGIN
        WRITELN('Input the value of the radius: ');
        READLN(radius);
        pi := 3.14159;
        circumference := 2 * pi * radius;
```

```
          area := pi * radius ** 2;
          WRITELN('The circumference is ',circumference);
          WRITELN('The area is ',area)
     END.
```

Constants

However, note that pi is not really a variable at all. The three variables *radius,*
circumference, and *area* quite definitely are variables, because they will have different
values whenever we choose a different circle. But pi will always have the value 3.14159,
no matter what. When something steadfastly maintains the same value all of the time like
that, we will call it a *constant* instead of a variable. It will be quite useful to be able to
treat constants differently from variables, and so we will add a new command that allows
a particular name to represent a constant. Constants are declared at the beginning of the
program along with the variable declarations. (However, note that you do *not* give a value
to a variable when you declare it, but you do give a value to a constant when it is
declared.) The command

```
     CONST
        pi = 3.14159
```

declares that the name pi will represent a constant that will always have the value
3.14159. We do not need to tell the computer what type of number pi is, since the
computer can tell by looking at the assignment statement that pi must be a real number,
since 3.14159 is a real value. And another quirk to note about Pascal: When you assign
a value to a constant, you use a regular equals sign = (unlike the := symbol that you use
when you are assigning a value to a variable.)
     Here is a new version of the circle program:

```
     PROGRAM circle (INPUT,OUTPUT);
          {This program reads in a value for the radius of a circle and
          then calculates the circumference and the area.}
        CONST
          pi = 3.14159;
        VAR
          radius, circumference, area : REAL;
        BEGIN
          WRITELN('Input the value of the radius: ');
          READLN(radius);
          circumference := 2 * pi * radius;
          area := pi * radius ** 2;
          WRITELN('The circumference is ',circumference:8:3);
          WRITELN('The area is ',area:8:3)
        END.
```

Here is an example of the output from this program:

```
     Input the value of the radius:
     10
     The circumference is 62.832
     The area is 314.159
```

The general form for a constant declaration is:

```
     CONST
     name=value;
```

Name can be any legal variable name, and *value* must be either a real number value or an integer value (or, as we will see later, a character value or a boolean value). After it has been declared, a constant can be used in exactly the same way as you use a variable, except for the obvious exception that you cannot ever put it on the left-hand side of an assignment statement. If you did that, then you would change its value and it would no longer be a constant.

You can include more than one constant in a constant declaration. Here is an example:

```
CONST
    pi = 3.14159, count = 10;
```

As you become more familiar with programming, you will come across things with varying degrees of constancy. The least constant items are regular variables, which might change their value frequently during the program execution. Slightly more constant are items that will keep the same value during the entire time that the program is running, but might have a different value when the program is run again. You will have to decide for yourself whether these items are constant enough to warrant being declared as constants. Then there are some items that will keep the same value for many runs of the program. These items should be declared as constants. However, these might need to be changed one day. For example, suppose you wrote a program to calculate per-game average statistics for NFL teams. Prior to 1978, you could declare a constant to represent the number of games per season:

```
CONST numgames = 14;
```

However, in 1978 the NFL changed its schedule to be 16 games long. All you would have to do is change the constant section of your program:

```
CONST numgames = 16;
```

The fact that all the constants are declared at the beginning of the program makes it easy to change the value of a constant if the situation requires it. Finally, there are a few absolute rock solid constants that will never ever change their value, such as π.

Notes to Chapter 3

■ When people write numbers, such as 1,345,656, they like to insert commas in the numbers to make them easier to read. However, you cannot insert commas in the middle of a number in a Pascal program.

■ Note that you must assign a value to a variable before it is allowed to appear in an expression.

■ You cannot assign a real value to an integer variable. An error condition will result if you attempt that.

Chapter 3 Exercises

1. Write a program that converts a number of inches into feet and inches. For example, 18 inches becomes 1 foot 6 inches.

2. Write a program that converts a number of seconds into minutes and seconds.

3. Write a program that reads in the number of earned runs a pitcher has given up (ER), the number of whole innings he has pitched (IP), and the number of extra thirds of innings (TI) he has pitched, and then calculates the earned run average (ERA) from the formula

$$ERA = 9 \cdot \frac{ER}{IP + TI/3}$$

4. Write a program that reads in put-outs (PO), assists (A), and errors (E), and then calculates the fielding average (FA), from the formula:

$$FA = \frac{PO + A}{PO + A + E}$$

5. Write a program that calculates slugging average from the formula:

$$SA = \frac{4HR + 3TR + 20B + SI}{AB}$$

where HR = home runs, TR = triples, DB = doubles, SI = singles, and AB = times at bat.

6. Write a program that reads in an integer N and then prints the rightmost b digits of N.

7. Write a program that reads in a number X and then prints the value of $f(X)$, where $f(X) = X$ if $X > 0$, and $f(X) = 0$ if $X < 0$.

* 8. Write a program that reads in a, b, c, d, and e and then calculates $ax^4 + bx^3 + cx^2 + dx + e$. (Can you write this program without using the exponentiation operator? Don't type x more than four times in the program.)

9. Write a program that reads in the distance to a star d in parsecs, and the absolute magnitude of the star M, and then calculates the apparent magnitude (that is, the brightness of the star as seen from earth). Use the formula:

$$\text{Magnitude} = M + 5 \log \frac{d}{10}$$

*10. Write a program that reads in an angle in radians and converts it into an angle in degrees.

11. Write a program that reads in a distance in kilometers and converts it into a distance in miles.

12. Write a program that reads in the two coordinates (x,y) of a point and an angle T and then calculates the new coordinates (x_2,y_2) of the same point when measured in the coordinate system formed by rotating the original x and y axes by an angle T. Use the formulas

$$x_2 = x \cos T + y \sin T$$

$$y_2 = y \cos T - x \sin T$$

13. Write a program that reads in a number x and then calculates the hyperbolic cosine of x, using the formula:

$$\cosh x = \frac{1}{2}(e^x + e^{-x})$$

14 Write a program that reads in two sides (a and b) of a triangle, as well as the angle between those two sides C, and then calculates the length of the third side c from the law of cosines:

$$c^2 = a^2 + b^2 - 2ab \cos C$$

Convert these mathematical expressions to Pascal notation:

15. $\dfrac{11/8}{7/3}$

16. $\dfrac{1}{1 - a}$

17. $\dfrac{1}{1 + a^2}$

18. $\dfrac{1}{1/x + 1/y}$

19. $\sqrt{(x - h)^2 + (y - k)^2}$

20. $\dfrac{-b + \sqrt{b^2 - 4ac}}{2a}$

21. $r \sin A \cos B$

CHAPTER 4

The IF and CASE commands

Calculating a Payroll

Suppose you have the job of computing the amount of pay earned by each of a large group of workers. To do that, you will need to write a program that reads in the number of hours a worker has worked during a particular week and then multiplies that number by the wage rate. If the wage is $7.00 per hour, the program might look like this:

```
PROGRAM payroll (INPUT, OUTPUT);
    {This program reads in the value of the number of hours for a
    worker and then calculates pay for this week, assuming that the
    worker is paid $7 per hour.}
VAR
    hours, pay : REAL;
BEGIN
    WRITELN('Input the number of hours: ');
    READLN(hours);
    pay : = 7 * hours;
    WRITELN('Pay is: ',pay:7:2)
END.
```

This program works fine, except for one complication. When an employee works more than 40 hours per week, he or she gets overtime pay at 1½ times the regular rate. However, you can write a new program that will calculate the pay for the workers that work overtime:

```
PROGRAM payroll (INPUT, OUTPUT);
  {This program calculates the payroll for workers who work
   overtime. Each worker is paid $7 per hour for the first 40 hours,
   and then 1.5 * 7 for each hour over 40.}
  VAR
    hours, pay: REAL;
  BEGIN
    WRITELN('Input the number of hours: ');
    READLN(hours);
    pay := 7 * 40 + 1.5 * 7 * (hours - 40);
    WRITELN('Pay is: ', pay: 7: 2)
  END.
```

In order to know which program to use, all we have to do is look at the number of hours worked. If *hours* is greater than 40, we use the overtime program; otherwise we use the regular program. This method is a bit cumbersome, though. It would be nice to find some way to write *one* program that handles both situations. To do this, all we need is a statement that checks to see whether *hours* is greater than 40. If it is, then the computer calculates the overtime pay; otherwise it calculates regular pay.

The IF Command

We will use the keyword IF when we want the computer to make a choice like this. An IF command looks like this:

IF *test condition is true*

    THEN *do something*

    ELSE *do something else;*

In this case, the test condition we want to check is whether *hours* < 40. Fortunately, our keyboard comes equipped with a less than sign (<).
Here is a new version of the payroll program:

```
PROGRAM payroll (INPUT, OUTPUT);
  {This program calculates the payroll for both overtime
   and nonovertime workers. Each worker is paid $7 per
   hour up to 40 hours, and then 1.5 * 7 for each hour
   after 40 hours.}
  VAR
    hours, pay: REAL;
  BEGIN
    WRITELN('Input the number of hours: ');
    READLN(hours);
    IF hours <= 40
      THEN pay := 7 * hours
      ELSE pay := 7 * 40 + 1.5 * 7 * (hours - 40);
    WRITELN('Pay is: ', pay: 7: 2)
  END.
```

The general form of an IF command is:

IF *condition*

    THEN *statement1*

    ELSE *statement2;*

The *condition* must be an expression that is either true or false. If the *condition* is true, then *statement1* is executed; otherwise *statement2* is executed.

Here are some examples of possible conditions that we might want to check:

A = B	Does A equal B?
	(Note that when we use an = sign in a condition, we do not put a : in front of it.)
A > B	Is A greater than B?
A < B	Is A less than B?
A >= B	Is A greater than or equal to B?
A <= B	Is A less than or equal to B?
A <> B	Is A greater than or less than B?
	(In other words, is A not equal to B?
	Written mathematically, does A $\neq$ B?)

We'll see later that the condition in an IF statement can also be a compound condition, consisting of two or more simple conditions joined by the words AND or OR. Also, the condition can be a special type of variable called a *boolean variable,* which can have one of two possible values: true or false.

We can, of course, leave out the ELSE part of the IF statement if we want. We can tell the computer to perform a specific instruction if the condition is true, but do nothing and skip to the next instruction if the condition is false.

For example, suppose we want to have the computer print a special message to identify those workers who have worked less than 20 hours.

```
PROGRAM payroll (INPUT, OUTPUT);
    {This program calculates the payroll for overtime
    and regular workers. A special message is printed
    if the worker has worked less than 20 hours per week.}
    VAR
      hours, pay : REAL;
    BEGIN
      WRITELN ('Input the number of hours: ');
      READLN (hours);
      IF hours < 20
        THEN WRITELN ('This worker worked < 20 hours. ');
      IF hours <= 40
        THEN pay : = 7 * hours
        ELSE pay : = 7 * 40 + 1.5 * 7 * (hours − 40);
      WRITELN ('Pay is: ', pay: 7: 2)
    END.
```

Here is a sample of the output from this program:

```
Input the number of hours:
16
This worker worked < 20 hours.
Pay is: 112.00

Input the number of hours:
38
Pay is: 266.00

Input the number of hours:
45
Pay is: 332.50
```

Now, suppose that workers who work more than 50 hours per week are paid double time for every hour in excess of 50. For example, a worker who works 53 hours will be paid for 40 hours at $7, 10 hours at $10.50, and 3 hours at $14 per hour. We need to figure out a way to have the computer perform this calculation. All we need to do is include another IF statement as part of the action clause of the first IF statement.

```
PROGRAM payroll (INPUT, OUTPUT);
   {This payroll program pays workers at 1.5 times the
   normal rate for every hour over 40 and 2 times the
   normal rate for every hour over 50 hours.}
VAR
   hours, pay: REAL;
BEGIN
   WRITELN('Input the number of hours: ');
   READLN(hours);
   IF hours > 50
      THEN pay : = 7 * 40 + 10 * 10.5 + 2 * 7 * (hours − 50)
      ELSE IF hours > 40
          THEN pay : = 7 * 40 + 1.5 * 7 * (hours − 40)
          ELSE pay : = 7 * hours;
   WRITELN('Pay is: ', pay: 7: 2)
END.
```

The principle of IF/THEN/ELSE statements is quite simple, but, as you can see, the statements themselves can become quite complicated if we start combining them. For example, suppose that the number 75 is read in as the number of hours. However, we know that this value must be wrong, because no worker can work more than 70 hours per week at our company. We can write a new payroll program that uses three nested IF statements that first checks to make sure that the number of hours read in is less than 70:

```
PROGRAM payroll (INPUT, OUTPUT);
   {This program prints an error message if the number
   of hours read in is greater than 70.}
   VAR
   hours, pay : REAL;
BEGIN
   WRITELN('Input the number of hours: ');
   READLN(hours);
   IF hours > 70
     THEN WRITELN('Hours cannot be > 70')
     ELSE IF hours > 50
             THEN pay : = 7 * 40 + 10 * 10.5 + 2 * 7 * (hours − 50)
             ELSE IF hours > 40
                  THEN pay : = 7 * 40 + 1.5 * 7 * (hours − 40)
                  ELSE pay : = 7 * hours;
   WRITELN('Pay is: ', pay: 7: 2)
   END.
```

Now, suppose that we want to do more than one thing if the condition in the IF statement is true. For example, suppose we want to do two things for nonovertime workers:

1. Calculate their pay: pay := 7 * hours.

2. Write the message: "No overtime wages paid."

Likewise, for overtime workers we will like to do two things:

1. Calculate their pay: pay := 280 + 1.5 * 7 * (hours − 40).
2. Write the message: "Overtime wages paid."

Compound Statements

We cannot do this task using only simple IF statements. However, we can group two or more statements together and treat them as one statement. Such a statement is called a *compound statement.* A compound statement consists of a group of statements that are treated as a unit. A compound statement begins with the word BEGIN and ends with the word END, and it can consist of as many statements as you want in the middle. Here is an example of a compound statement:

```
BEGIN
  pay : = 280 + 1.5 * 7 * (hours − 40);
  WRITELN ('Overtime wages paid. ')
END;
```

This compound statement contains two simple statements. The first statement calculates the pay for overtime workers, and the second statement writes the message, "Overtime wages paid."

Here is a payroll program that uses compound statements:

```
PROGRAM payroll (INPUT, OUTPUT);
  {This program prints an appropriate message for
  overtime workers and regular workers.}
  VAR
    hours, pay : REAL;
BEGIN
  WRITELN ('Input the number of hours: ');
  READLN (hours);
  IF hours > 40
    THEN BEGIN
        pay : = 280 + 1.5 * 7 * (hours − 40);
        WRITELN ('Overtime wages paid')
      END
    ELSE BEGIN
        pay : = 7 * hours;

        WRITELN ('No overtime wages paid. ')
      END;
  WRITELN ('Pay is: ', pay: 7: 2)
END.
```

There is another feature of the payroll programs that we have done so far that is unrealistic. We have assumed that all the workers are paid the same standard wage rate of $7 per hour. Now, let's suppose that there are four different groups of workers classified by their skill level. Let's suppose that workers in class 1 earn $4.10 per hour, workers in class 2 earn $5.36 per hour, workers in class 3 earn $7.36 per hour, and workers in class 4 earn $8.75 per hour. Now, in order to run the payroll program, we first need to read in the classification level and then the number of hours. Here is a way to solve this problem using IF statements:

```
PROGRAM payroll (INPUT, OUTPUT);
  {This program calculates the payroll for four different
  classes of workers.}
  VAR
    hours, pay, wage : REAL;
```

```
      class : INTEGER;
    BEGIN
      WRITELN('Input the classification number: ');
      READLN(class);
      IF class = 1
      THEN wage : = 4.10
      ELSE IF class = 2
         THEN wage : = 5.36
         ELSE IF class = 3
         THEN wage : = 7.36
            ELSE wage : = 8.75;
      WRITELN('Input the number of hours: ');
      READLN(hours);
      IF hours > 40
         THEN pay : = 40 * wage + 1.5 * wage * (hours − 40)
         ELSE pay : = hours * wage;
      WRITELN ('Pay is: ', pay: 7: 2)
    END.
```

The CASE Command

However, it is very awkward to have all of those IFs, THENs, and ELSEs jumbled together in the middle of the program like that. So, let's make up a new command that allows us to easily select from among one of several possible courses of action. (Note that the IF command only lets us select between two possible courses of action.) We'll call our command the CASE command. The CASE command needs to work like this:

in CASE *class* = 1 then wage := 4.1

in CASE *class* = 2 then wage := 5.36

and so on. The exact form of the Pascal CASE command is illustrated in the following payroll program.

```
      PROGRAM payroll (INPUT, OUTPUT);
        {This program calculates the payroll for four
        different classes of workers.}
        VAR
          wage, hours, pay : REAL;
          class : INTEGER;
        BEGIN
          WRITELN('Input classification level: ');
          READLN(class);
          CASE class OF
            1: wage : = 4.1;
            2: wage : = 5.36;
            3: wage : = 7.36;
            4: wage : = 8.75
          END;
          WRITELN('Input the number of hours: ');
          READLN(hours);
          IF hours > 40
            THEN pay : = 280 * wage + 1.5 * wage * (hours − 40)
            ELSE pay : = hours * wage;
          WRITELN('Pay is: ', pay: 7: 2)
        END.
```

Here is a sample of the output from this program:

```
Input classification level:
1
Input the number of hours:
26
Pay is: 106.60

Input classification level:
4
Input the number of hours:
39
Pay is: 341.25
```

The general form of the CASE command is as follows:

CASE *variable* OF

value1: *statement1*;

value2: *statement2*;

.

.

.

The *variable* must be an integer variable, and *value1, value2,* and so on, must all be integer values. (We will see later that the CASE variable may be of any type other than type REAL.) If *variable* has the value *value1*, then *statement1* is executed. If *variable* has the value *value2*, then *statement2* is executed, and so on.

You may be asking: What if the *variable* does not have *any* of the possible values? In this situation the result depends on your system. In some systems, an error message is printed if the CASE variable does not have any of the listed values. In other systems, you are allowed to include a last-minute desperation escape clause that the computer will execute if the variable does not have any of the listed values. Here is an example of such a clause:

```
CASE class OF
    1: wage : = 4.1;
    2: wage : = 5.36;
    3: wage : = 7.36;
    4: wage : = 8.75
    ELSE WRITELN('You typed an invalid class number.')
END;
```

Here is a very simple example of the CASE command:

```
PROGRAM message (INPUT, OUTPUT);
    {This program reads in the value of your place in a race,
    first place, second place, or third place, and then prints
    an appropriate message.}
    VAR
      place : INTEGER;
    BEGIN
    WRITELN('Type in your place: ');
    READLN(place);
    CASE place OF
        1: WRITELN(' ********** FIRST PLACE!!!!! ');
        2: WRITELN(' *** Second Place!! ***');
        3: WRITELN(' Third place ')
    END
END.
```

Chapter 4 Exercises

1. Write a program that compares the unit prices of three types of cereals in different sized boxes. For each type of cereal have the program read in the price of the box and the number of grams of cereal contained in that box. After all the items have been read in, have the computer print the price of the item with the lowest price per gram.

2. Write a program that reads in the win-loss record of the first-place team, then reads in the win-loss record of another team, and then prints out how many games the other team is behind the first-place team.

3. Write a program that reads in the win-loss records of the first-place team and the second-place team, then reads in the number of games remaining for each team, and then calculates the first-place team's clinching number. In other words, how many first-place-team wins plus second-place-team losses will be required until the first-place team has clinched first place?

*4. Write a program that solves the quadratic equation

   $$ax^2 + bx + c = 0$$

   for any possible real values of the constants *a, b,* and *c.* In particular, if $a = 0$ and $b \neq 0$, the equation is a linear equation; if $a = 0$, $b = 0$, and $c \neq 0$, the equation has no solutions; and if $a = 0$, $b = 0$, and $c = 0$, any value of *x* will be a solution.

5. Write a program that calculates a sales tax on an item, assuming a tax rate of 0.065. However, if the item costs less than 10 cents, then no tax is charged.

6. Write a program that reads in a number and calculates its square root. However, if the number typed in is negative, print a message explaining that you cannot take the square root of a negative number.

7. What is the main difference between an IF and a CASE statement?

8. Is this legal? Assume that hours is an integer.

```
CASE hours > 40 OF
  TRUE: WRITELN('Worked overtime');
  FALSE: WRITELN('No overtime')
END;
```

CHAPTER 5

The WHILE and REPEAT Commands

The REPEAT Command

One feature of our payroll program is still very awkward. Whenever we want to calculate the pay for a different worker, we need to run the entire program again. It would be much easier if we could set up the program so that it could calculate the pay for several different workers. What we need to have it do is repeat the payroll commands several times. So, we will add the REPEAT command to our language. However, we don't want the computer to continue repeating the commands indefinitely. Eventually we will have completed the calculations for the last workers, and then we would like to stop. We will use the keyword UNTIL to indicate when to stop repeating. The REPEAT/UNTIL command works like this:

> REPEAT
>
> > *a bunch of actions*
>
> UNTIL *stopping condition is true.*

Once the stopping condition is true, then we will stop repeating the commands.

Now we face the question: How will we tell the computer that we are done typing in values for the hours worked? If we type in a negative number for the hours, then the computer will use that as a signal that it is time to stop. We know that no worker will ever really have worked a negative number of hours.

Here is an example of the program:

```
PROGRAM payroll (INPUT, OUTPUT);
{This program will continue calculating pay for the workers. In
order to stop the program, type in a negative value for the hours
worked.}
  CONST
    wage = 7.0;   {Note that the wage rate is being defined as a real
                   number constant in this example.}
  VAR
    hours, pay : REAL;
  BEGIN
    REPEAT
     WRITELN('Input the number of hours.');
     READLN(hours);
     IF hours > 40
        THEN pay : = wage * 40 + 1.5 * wage * (hours − 40)
        ELSE pay : = wage * hours;
     WRITELN('Pay is: ',pay:7:2);
    UNTIL hours < 0
  END.
```

Here is a sample of the output from this program:

```
Input the number of hours.
35
Pay is: 245.00

Input the number of hours.
42
Pay is : 301.00

Input the number of hours.
−1

Pay is: −7.00
```

The general form of the REPEAT/UNTIL command is:

REPEAT

   statements

UNTIL *condition*;

First, the computer will execute the *statements*. Then, it will check to see if the *condition* is true. If the condition is true, then the computer will continue on to the next instruction. If the condition is false, then the computer will return to the first statement immediately following the REPEAT command.

You need to remember two important features of the REPEAT command: (1) The statements in the middle will always be executed at least once, because the computer does not check the condition until after completing the first pass through the middle. (2) The computer will *stop* repeating the statements when the condition becomes *true*. It will continue repeating the statements as long as the condition is false.

Here is another simple example of a program with a REPEAT command:

```
PROGRAM printnumbers (INPUT, OUTPUT);
  VAR
    number : INTEGER;
  BEGIN
    number : = 1;
    REPEAT
```

```
        WRITELN(number);
        number := number + 1;
      UNTIL number = 8
    END.
```

The output from this program looks like:

```
1
2
3
4
5
6
7
```

However, you do have to be careful when using the REPEAT command. You must make sure that the stopping condition eventually becomes true. Here is another example of a program with a repeat command:

```
PROGRAM endlessloop (INPUT, OUTPUT);
  VAR
    number : INTEGER;
  BEGIN
    number := 1;
    REPEAT
      WRITELN(number);
    UNTIL number = 8
END.
```

This program has the output:

```
1
1
1
1
```

Trapped in an Endless Loop

If you watch the screen, all you will see will be an endless stream of 1s flowing past you. You will become pretty tired of 1s, but the program as it is written now will never stop. The variable *number* starts out with the value 1, but this time its value never changes—it always stays at 1. Since *number* never becomes equal to 8, the stopping condition after the UNTIL command is never met, and so the computer endlessly repeats the command WRITELN(number);. In computer programming this type of situation is called an *endless loop*. However, don't panic. Every computer will have some key that you can push to escape the clutches of the endless loop. You might have a key labeled BREAK on your computer, or you might have to hold down the CONTROL key and then press the C key. After you have found out how to escape the endless loop, you can fix the program and run it again.

Whenever you use a REPEAT command, you must make sure that the stopping condition depends on a variable that is changed during the execution of the statements in the middle. Otherwise, the variable in the stopping condition will always retain the same value, and the stopping condition will never become true (unless it happened to be true in the first place, in which case the statements in the middle will be executed once before the computer passes on to the next instruction).

The WHILE Command

The REPEAT command is essentially a negative sort of command. It says, "Keep repeating this action UNTIL a stopping condition is true." There are also times when we would like a command that looks at things in a more positive light: "Keep doing this action WHILE a continuing condition is true." We will add a WHILE command to our language. Here is an example of a payroll program written with a WHILE command:

```
PROGRAM payroll (INPUT, OUTPUT);
{This program uses a WHILE command to calculate the payroll for
several workers. The program will stop when a negative value is
typed in for the number of hours.}
CONST
  wage = 7.0;
VAR
  hours, pay : REAL;
BEGIN
  WRITELN('Input the number of hours: ');
  READLN(hours);
  WHILE hours > 0 DO
    BEGIN {Start of WHILE loop}
      IF hours > 40
        THEN pay := wage * 40 + 1.5 * wage * (hours - 40)
        ELSE pay := wage * hours;
      WRITELN('Pay is: ', pay:7:20);
      WRITELN('Input the number of hours: ');
      READLN(hours)
    END {End of WHILE loop.}
END.
```

As long as the condition *hours* > 0 is true, the computer will continue to execute the statements in the middle of the WHILE loop. However, as soon as the command *hours* > 0 becomes false (which will happen as soon as you type a negative number), the computer will jump to the next instruction after the WHILE loop (which is the end of the program in this case).

Here is a sample of the output from this program:

```
Input the number of hours:
21
Pay is: 147.00

Input the number of hours:
50
Pay is: 385.00

Input the number of hours:
-1
```

Note that this program has one advantage over the version of the program that used the REPEAT command. In the REPEAT version, after we typed in −1 for the number hours, the machine printed out −7 as the value of the pay. In the version using the WHILE command, the computer will not print out that result. However, the WHILE command version does have the slight disadvantage that it forces us to write the command WRITELN(hours) twice, once before the WHILE loop and once in the middle of the WHILE loop. Suppose you had tried to write the program like this:

```
PROGRAM incorrect (INPUT, OUTPUT);
  VAR
   hours, pay: REAL;
  BEGIN
  WHILE hours > 0 DO  {No value has been assigned to the variable
                       hours before it reaches this WHILE command,
                       and so an error condition will result.}
      BEGIN
        READLN('hours');
        IF hours > 40
           THEN pay : = 7 * 40 + 1.5 * 7 * (hours - 40)
           ELSE pay : = 7 * hours;
        WRITELN('Pay is ', pay: 7: 2)
      END
  END.
```

This program would not work because it asks you to check the condition *hours* < 0 before a value has been assigned to the variable *hours*.

The general form of the WHILE command is:

WHILE *condition* DO

BEGIN

  statements in middle of loop

END;

When the computer comes to the WHILE command, it will first check to see if the *condition* is true. If it is, then the computer will execute the statements in the middle of the loop. After passing through the loop, the computer will return to check the *condition* again. The computer will keep executing the statements in the middle of the loop until the *condition* becomes false, in which case the computer will skip to the first statement after the WHILE loop.

Here is a simple example of a program with a while loop:

```
PROGRAM demo (INPUT, OUTPUT);
  {This program is an example of the WHILE command.}
VAR
  number : INTEGER;
BEGIN
  number : = 1024;
  WHILE number > 0 DO
    BEGIN
     WRITE(number: 6);
     number : = number DIV 2
    END
END.
```

The output from this program looks like:

```
1024    512    256    128    64    32    16    8    4    2    1
```

Here is another example:

```
PROGRAM average (INPUT, OUTPUT);
  {This program will accept an integer value from the user, sum the
   integers up to that value, and then print the average.}
VAR
  max : INTEGER;
```

```
        av, sum, number : REAL;
    BEGIN
      WRITELN('Enter an integer: ');
      READLN(max);
      number := 1.0;
      sum := 0.0;
      WHILE number <= max DO
        BEGIN
          sum := sum + number;
          number := number + 1.0
        END; {end WHILE loop}
      av := sum/max;
      WRITELN:
      WRITELN('The sum of the first ',max:1,' integers is ',
            sum:5:0);
      WRITELN('The average of the first ',max:1,' integers is ',
            av:4:2)
    END.
```

Note that the computer checks the condition before it executes the loop the first time. If the condition is false the first time it is checked, the computer will not execute the loop at all. This is different from a REPEAT loop. The statements in the middle of a REPEAT loop will always be executed at least once, because the condition is not checked until after the loop is completed.

You also have to be careful to avoid endless loop programs, such as this one:

```
    PROGRAM endless (INPUT, OUTPUT);
    VAR
      number : INTEGER;
      root : REAL;
    BEGIN
      WRITELN('Enter an integer ');
      READLN(number);
      IF number < 0 THEN number := ABS(number);
      WHILE number >= 0 DO
        BEGIN
          root := SQRT(number);
        WRITELN('Square root is ',root:4:2);
        WRITELN:
        WRITELN('Enter an integer ');
        READLN(number);
        IF number < 0 THEN number := ABS(number)
      END
    END.
```

This program is designed so that the variable *number* is always nonnegative, and so the continuing condition is always true. Therefore the program will never stop.

Prime Factors

Here is another example of a program using the WHILE command. Any whole number can be expressed as the product of a group of prime numbers. These numbers are called the *prime factors* of that number. For example:

6 = 3 * 2

5 = 5

$$12 = 2 * 2 * 3$$
$$9 = 3 * 3$$
$$20 = 2 * 2 * 5$$
$$30 = 2 * 3 * 5$$

To calculate prime factors of a number *n,* we need to find out which prime numbers evenly divide *n.* Once we have found such a prime number (call it *k*) then we set n := n div k, print out the value of *k,* and then look for more prime numbers that evenly divide the new value of *n.* Once *n* has been divided down to 1, then we can stop. Here is the program:

```
PROGRAM prmfct (INPUT, OUTPUT);
  {This program prints a list of the prime factors of a number.}
  VAR
    divisor, adder, n : INTEGER;
  BEGIN
    READLN(n);
        WRITELN;
        WRITELN('Prime Factors of ',n); WRITELN;
        divisor := 2;
        adder := 1;
        WHILE n > 1 DO
          BEGIN
            IF (n MOD divisor) = 0
              THEN BEGIN
                n := n DIV divisor;
                WRITE(divisor, ' ')
              END
            ELSE BEGIN
              divisor := divisor + adder;
              adder := 2
            END
          END {WHILE loop}
  END.
```

(Note that, instead of dividing by all the prime numbers, we first divide by 2 and then by all the odd numbers greater than 2.)

Here is a sample of the output of this program:

```
72
Prime Factors of 72
2   2   2   3   3

60
Prime Factors of 60
2   2   3   5

7
Prime Factors of 7
7
```

Chapter 5 Exercises

1. Write a program that will calculate the average of a series of positive integers entered by the user. When the user enters a negative number, use that as a signal to mean that all the numbers have been read in. Use a WHILE loop.

2. Rewrite Exercise 1 using a REPEAT loop.

3. What are the two main differences between a REPEAT and a WHILE loop?

4. Will these do the same things:

```
WRITELN ('Enter a number');
READLN (number);
WHILE number > 0 DO
BEGIN
   sum : = sum + number;
   WRITELN ('Enter number');
   READLN (number)
END;
```

and

```
WRITELN ('Enter a number');
READLN (number);
REPEAT
   sum : = sum + number;
   WRITELN ('Enter number');
   READLN (number);
UNTIL number < 0;
```

5. Write a program that will print out a table of the square and square roots of a series of numbers. When the user enters a zero, use that as a signal to stop the program.

The measurement conversion programs listed in Chapters 2 and 3 will convert only one value at a time. To make another conversion, you must run the program again. It would be much better if we could print a table which lists all the desired conversions without having to rerun the program. Keeping this in mind, rewrite the following conversion programs, using first a WHILE loop and then using a REPEAT loop.

6. Liter to gallon conversion

7. Program which converts degrees celsius to degrees fahrenheit

8. Program which converts an amount of money expressed in one currency to the equivalent amount expressed in a different currency.

9. Write a program that reads in a number N and then determines whether it is a prime number.

10. Write a program that prints all the prime factors of a number. For example, the prime factors of 12 are $2 \times 2 \times 3$, and the prime factors of 60 are $2 \times 2 \times 3 \times 5$.

11. Write a program that calculates the number of trailing zeros in an integer. For example, 55 has no trailing zeros, whereas 10500 has two trailing zeros.

*12. Write a program that reads in a number less than 64 and then prints the five digits of the binary representation of that number.

*13. Write a program that uses Newton's method to solve the third-degree equation

$$ax^3 + bx^2 + cx + d = 0$$

First, have the computer read in values for a, b, c, and d. Next, have the computer read in an initial guess for the solution (x_1). Then calculate a closer guess from the formula

$$x_2 = x_1 - \frac{ax_1{}^3 + bx_1{}^2 + cx_1 + d}{3ax_1{}^2 + 2bx_1 + c}$$

Keep repeating the process. Each time you will have a closer approximation to the true solution. Continue until the solution you find for x satisfies

$$| ax^3 + bx^2 + cx + d | < 0.01$$

CHAPTER 6

FOR Loops

Calculating the Average

Suppose you are trying to calculate your average expenditures on groceries each week for the last 2 months. For example, suppose that the expenditure numbers for the last 2 months are 14, 12, 16, 45, 12, 19, 21, 30. It would be convenient to write a program that can automatically calculate the average of eight numbers:

```
PROGRAM average (INPUT, OUTPUT);
{This program reads in 8 numbers and then calculates their
average.}
VAR
   amount, total, average : REAL
BEGIN
   total : = 0;
   READLN(amount);
   total : = total + amount;
   READLN(amount);
   total : = total + amount;
   READLN(amount);
   total : = total + amount;
   READLN(amount);
   total : = total + amount;
```

```
        READLN(amount);
        total := total + amount;
        READLN(amount);
        total := total + amount;
        READLN(amount);
        total := total + amount;
        READLN(amount);
        total := total + amount;
        average := total/8;
        WRITELN('The average is: ',average:8:3);
    END.
```

At first you should be suspicious of the statement *total := total + amount,* since *total* can't be equal to *total + amount* unless *amount* happens to equal 0. However, remember that the statement is not an equation. It's a computer assignment statement. This is the way it works. First, it calculates the value of the expression on the right. Then it stores that value in the box labeled by the variable name on the left side. There's no reason why you can't use the old value of a variable to help calculate its new value.

The main problem with that program is that it is too long. We shouldn't have to type the instruction READLN(amount) eight times. After all, remember that the sole purpose of getting a computer is to save work for us. Fortunately, we can write the same program using a WHILE loop:

```
    PROGRAM average (INPUT, OUTPUT);
    {This program calculates the average of 8 numbers. The variable
    count tells how many times the computer has gone around the
    loop.}
      VAR
        amount, total, average : REAL;
        count : INTEGER;
      BEGIN
        total := 0.0;
        count := 1;

        WHILE count <= 8 DO
          BEGIN
            READLN(amount);
            total := total + amount;
            count := count + 1
          END;
      average := total/8;
      WRITELN('The average is: ',average)
    END.
```

FOR Loops

The WHILE loop in this program works exactly like the WHILE loops in the programs in Chapter 5. However, there is one important difference. In this case, we know that the statements in the middle of the loop will always be executed exactly eight times. In the previous examples of WHILE loops, we did not know in advance how many times the loop would be executed before the continuing condition became false. In cases where the loop will always be executed the same number of times, it would help to have a more convenient way of expressing that command to the computer. So, we will add a FOR loop to our computer. If we want the FOR loop to be executed exactly eight times, we will put the statement FOR count := 1 TO 8 DO BEGIN at the start of the loop. We will simply put the command END at the end of the loop. Here is an example of the average calculation program using a FOR loop:

```
PROGRAM average (INPUT, OUTPUT);
{This program reads in eight numbers and then calculates their
average, using a FOR loop.}
VAR
   amount, total, average : REAL;
   count : INTEGER;
BEGIN
   total : = 0.0;
   FOR count : = 1 TO 8 DO
     BEGIN
       READLN(amount);
       total : = total + amount
     END;
   average : = total/8;
   WRITELN('The average is: ', average: 8:3)
END.
```

Here is an example of running this program:

```
16
23
11
12
34
 9
10
45
The average is: 20.000
```

The general form of a FOR loop is:

FOR *counter* := *start* TO *stop* DO

　　BEGIN

　　　　statements in middle of loop

　　END;

Here *counter* is the variable that will be increased by 1 each time; *start* is the initial value of the counter variable; and *stop* is the final value of the counter variable. (In the program shown above to calculate averages, *counter* is the variable named count, *start* is 1, and *stop* is 8. The variable *counter* will normally be an INTEGER, although it can also be any simple type except REAL. *start* and *stop* can be numbers, variable names, or expressions. The first time that the statements in the middle are executed, *counter* will have the value *start*. The second time the loop is executed, *counter* will have the value *start* + 1; then the next time it will have the value *start* + 2, and so on. Once *counter* becomes greater than *stop*, then the computer will stop executing the loop and will skip to the first instruction following the loop.

For another simple example of a loop, here's a program that prints a table of the numbers from 1 to 10 with their squares and square roots:

```
PROGRAM sqrtable (INPUT, OUTPUT);
{This program prints a table of the numbers from 1 to 10 and their
squares and square roots.}
VAR
 n : INTEGER;
BEGIN
```

```
WRITELN (' Number Square Sqr Rt');
FOR n : = 1 TO 10 DO
    WRITELN (n: 8, SQR (n) : 8, SQRT (n) : 8: 4)
END.
```

In this case there is only one statement that we need to have executed during the loop, and so we don't need a BEGIN and an END to mark the beginning and the end of the loop. The output from this program looks like this:

Number	Square	Sqr Rt
1	1	1.0000
2	4	1.4142
3	9	1.7321
4	16	2.0000
5	25	2.2361
6	36	2.4495
7	49	2.6458
8	64	2.8284
9	81	3.0000
10	100	3.1623

DOWNTO

In the previous program, we started at 1 and went up to 10. There might also be times when we would like to start at 10 and go DOWNTO 1. In Pascal we can use the command DOWNTO instead of TO. Here is another version of the square root table program:

```
PROGRAM sqrtable (INPUT, OUTPUT);
    {This program prints a table of the numbers from 1 to 10 and
    their squares and square roots.}
    VAR
      n : INTEGER;
    BEGIN
      WRITELN (' Number Square Sqr Rt');
      FOR n : = 10 DOWNTO 1 DO
        WRITELN (n: 8, SQR (n) : 8, SQRT (n) : 8: 4)
      END.
```

Here is the output from this program:

Number	Square	Sqr Rt
10	100	3.1623
9	81	3.0000
8	64	2.8284
7	49	2.6458
6	36	2.4495
5	25	2.2361
4	16	2.0000
3	9	1.7321
2	4	1.4142
1	1	1.0000

When you use DOWNTO, then you must of course make sure that the final value is smaller than the initial value.

Calculating Areas

Suppose you are interested in the areas of different sized circles. We can write a program that prints a table of the area of several circles with different radii:

```
PROGRAM areacalc (INPUT, OUTPUT);
  {This program prints a table of the area of different sized
  circles using a FOR loop.}
VAR
    radius: INTEGER;
    area: REAL;
CONST
    pi = 3.14159;
BEGIN
  WRITELN ('Radius':10, 'Area':10);
    {Note that you can also specify the field width for a series of
    letters, such as 'radius' or 'area'. In this case we have
    specified that each heading word will be printed with a field
    width of 10 so that the headings line up with the output.}
  WRITELN;
  FOR radius := 1 TO 10 DO
    BEGIN
      area := radius * radius * pi;
      WRITELN (radius:10, area:10:4);
      WRITELN
    END
END.
```

There is another way that we could find the area of a circle that works even if we don't know the formula area $= \pi r^2$. Let's consider a circle with radius of 1. We can approximate the area of the quarter circle by a collection of n little rectangles (see Figure 6-1). By adding together the area of all the rectangles, we can find the approximate area of the circle. Let's let x represent the x coordinate of the midpoint of one of the rectangles. Then the height of the rectangle is $y = \sqrt{1 - x^2}$. The width of the rectangle is $1/n$. Here is the program:

```
PROGRAM circle (INPUT, OUTPUT);
    {This program calculates the approximate area of a circle of
    radius 1 by finding the sum of the areas of rectangles. The
    mathematical name for this procedure is numerical
    integration.}
VAR
  area, x, y: REAL;
  i, n: INTEGER;
BEGIN
  area := 0;
  WRITELN ('Input the number of rectangles: ');
  READLN (n);
  x := -1/(2*n);
  FOR i := 1 TO n DO
      BEGIN
          x := x + 1/n;
          y := SQRT (1 - SQR (x));
          area := area + y
      END;
  area := area/n;
```

```
    WRITELN('Area of quarter circle is: ',area:8:5);
    WRITELN('Area of whole circle is: ',4*area:8:5)
END.
```

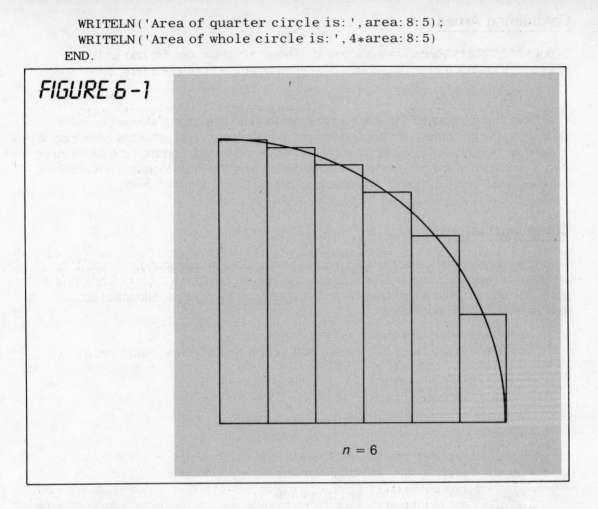

FIGURE 6-1

$n = 6$

Nested Loops

We can also put one loop inside of another loop. Such a loop is called a *nested loop.*
Here is a simple example of a program with a nested loop:

```
PROGRAM nest (INPUT,OUTPUT);
   {This program contains an example of a nested loop.}
VAR
   i, j: INTEGER;
BEGIN
  FOR i : = 1 TO 2 DO
     BEGIN
        WRITELN ('***********');
        FOR j : = 1 TO 3 DO
          BEGIN
             WRITE ('<');
             WRITE (i,j:5);
             WRITELN ('>')
          END {End of j loop}
     END {End of i loop}
  END. {end of program}
```

The output from this program looks like this:

```
***********
<1    1>
```

```
<1     2>
<1     3>
**********
<2     1>
<2     2>
<2     3>
```

Note that the counter variable for the outer loop (in this case *i*) stays at its initial value while the computer runs through the entire inner loop. Then, after the inner loop is completed, the value of the outer counter variable is increased, and then the entire inner loop is run again. If the outer loop has *m* repetitions and the inner loop has *n* repetitions, the statements in the middle of the inner loop will be executed $m \times n$ times.

Compound Interest

Here is a program that uses a nested loop to print a table of compound interest. The program considers seven possible values of the interest rate (from 0.03 to 0.09), and it prints the total account balance at the end of each year for 8 years. The initial account balance was $100 in each case.

```
PROGRAM interesttable (INPUT, OUTPUT);
    {This program uses nested FOR loops to calculate and print out
    interest tables.}
VAR
    rate, balance: REAL;
    years, counter: INTEGER;
CONST
    init = 100;
BEGIN
WRITE ('Rate ');
FOR years : = 1 TO 8 DO WRITE (years:9);
WRITELN;
FOR counter : = 3 TO 9 DO
    BEGIN
        rate : = counter/100;
        balance : = init;
        WRITE (rate:6:2);
        FOR years : = 1 TO 8 DO
            BEGIN
                balance : = balance * (1 + rate);
                WRITE (balance:9:2);
            END; {years FOR loop}
        WRITELN;
        WRITELN
    END {counter FOR loop}
END.
```

The output from this program looks like this:

Rate	1	2	3	4	5	6	7	8
0.03	103.00	106.09	109.27	112.55	115.93	119.40	122.99	126.68
0.04	104.00	108.16	112.49	116.99	121.67	126.53	131.59	136.86
0.05	105.00	110.25	115.76	121.55	127.63	134.01	140.71	147.75
0.06	106.00	112.36	119.10	126.25	133.82	141.85	150.36	159.38
0.07	107.00	114.49	122.50	131.08	140.25	150.07	160.58	171.82
0.08	108.00	116.64	125.97	136.05	146.93	158.69	171.38	185.09
0.09	109.00	118.81	129.50	141.16	153.86	167.71	182.80	199.26

Chapter 6 Exercises

1. Write a program that reads in a value for n, then reads in n numbers, and then prints the average of the n numbers.

2. The Tourist Trap Souvenir Manufacturing Firm, Inc. is a monopolist. There is the following relationship between the price it charges p and the quantity q of output it can sell:

$$q = 100 - \frac{1}{2}p$$

   The cost c of making each souvenir is given by

$$c = \frac{1}{2}q^2 + 10$$

   Write a program that calculates the firm's profits for each possible value of the price from $p = 0$ to $p = 200$. Have the program identify the price that leads to the maximum profits.

3. Suppose p is the principal amount currently owed on a home mortgage. If s is the monthly payment on the mortgage and r is the monthly interest rate, then the amount rp is the amount of interest paid in a given month and $s - rp$ is the amount that is subtracted from the principal that month. Write a program that reads in the initial value of the principal, the interest rate, and the monthly payment amount. Then, for each month, have the program print out the principal amount remaining after that month. Finally, have the computer tell how many months it will take until the principal amount is reduced to zero, that is, until the house is paid for.

4. An error message will be printed if a computer is asked to find tan 90°. Write a program that prints out a table of sin, cos, and tan for the angles 0°, 10°, 20°, . . . , 90° without generating any error messages. Have the computer print "INFINITY" as the value for tan 90°.

5. Print a table listing the areas and circumferences of circles that have radii of 1, 2, 3, 4, . . . , 20.

6. Write a program that reads in at-bat totals and the number of hits for nine baseball players and then prints their batting averages.

7. Write a program that prints a list of all the prime numbers from 2 to 75.

8. For teams that have played 1, 2, 3, 4, . . . , 20 games, print a table showing their winning percentages for every possible value of their won-loss records.

Use rectangles to find approximations for the areas of the regions in Exercises 9 to 11.

* 9. The area under the curve $y = \sin x$ from $x = 0$ to $x = \pi/2$

*10. The area of the ellipse $\dfrac{x^2}{9} + \dfrac{y^2}{16} = 1$

*11. The area under the curve $y = e^{-x^2}$ from $x = 0$ to $x = 2$

*12. Make a table that gives the area under the curve $y = \dfrac{1}{\sqrt{2\pi}}e^{-(1/2)x^2}$,

   to the right of the line $x = 0$, and to the left of the line $x = x$, for these 100 values of x, : 0.01, 0.02, 0.03, 0.04, . . . , 1. (This area is very important because this curve is the standard normal probability curve.)

*13. Find the approximate volume of the ellipsoid formed by rotating the ellipse $\frac{x^2}{25} + \frac{y^2}{9}$ about the x axis. (Use nested loops.)

*14. Approximate the curve $y = \sin x$ from $x = 0$ to $x = \pi/2$ by a series of small straight segments. Then add up the lengths of all the straight segments to find an approximation for the total length of the curve.

15. Write a program that reads in a number n and then calculates $n!$ (n factorial), which is equal to

$$n! = n \times (n - 1) \times (n - 2) \times (n - 3) \times \cdots \times 4 \times 3 \times 2 \times 1$$

*16. Write a program that reads in a number x and then calculates an approximation for e^x, using the formula

$$e^x = 1 + x + \frac{x^2}{2!} + \frac{x^3}{3!} \times \frac{x^4}{4!} + \cdots$$

*17. Write a program that reads in a number x and then calculates an approximation for $\sin x$, using the formula

$$\sin x = x - \frac{x^3}{3!} + \frac{x^5}{5!} - \frac{x^7}{7!} + \frac{x^9}{9!} - \cdots$$

*18. Write a program that reads in a number x and then calculates an approximation for $\cos x$, using the formula

$$\cos x = 1 - \frac{x^2}{2!} + \frac{x^4}{4!} - \frac{x^6}{6!} + \cdots$$

*19. Write a program that calculates an approximate value for π, using the formula

$$\frac{\pi}{4} = 1 - \frac{1}{3} + \frac{1}{5} - \frac{1}{7} \cdots$$

(*Warning:* It takes a long time for this series to come up with a close approximation for π.)

20. Write a program that (1) reads in a value for n; (2) reads in n numbers (call them $x_1, x_2, \ldots, x_n$); (3) calculates the expected value of x: $E(x) = (x_1 + x_2 + \ldots + x_n)/n$; (4) calculates $E(x^2) = (x_1^2 + x_2^2 + \ldots + x_n^2)$; and (5) calculates an estimate of the standard deviation (σ) from the formula

$$\sigma = \sqrt{E(x^2) - E(x)^2}$$

21. Suppose you are planning to save s dollars every year for n years. If the interest rate is r, what will be the balance in your account at the end of the n years?

CHAPTER 7

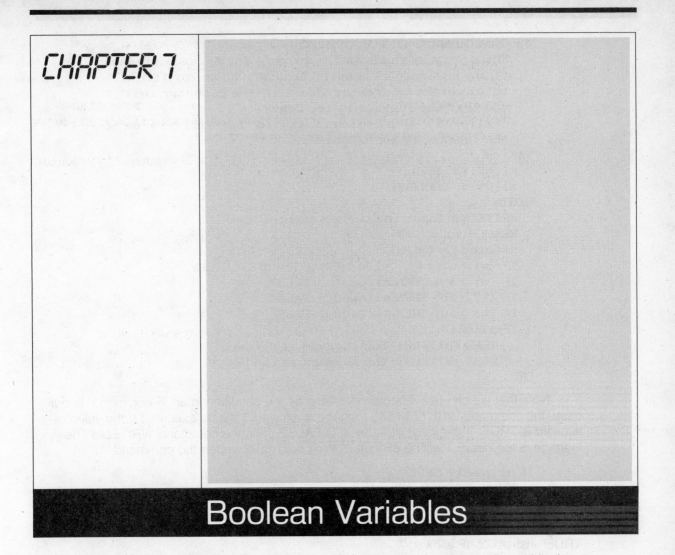

Boolean Variables

Suppose we are taking an airline trip. We must make sure that our luggage fits within the airline weight limitation. Let's say that our particular airline allows each passenger to check three suitcases. The total weight of all the suitcases must be less than 100 pounds, and none of the suitcases can weigh more than 50 pounds. We'll write a simple program to check whether our luggage meets the weight limitation. The output of the program will be very simple, since there are only two possible outcomes. Either our luggage will be allowed, or it will be too heavy.

In computer programming we frequently encounter this type of either/or decision, and so we will make up a new type of variable to make it easier to represent this situation on the computer. This new type of variable will be called a *boolean variable.* Boolean variables are named after George Boole, a nineteenth century English mathematician who studied the rules of logic. A boolean variable can have only one of two possible values: true or false. A boolean variable must be declared in the declare section along with the integer and real variables.

TRUE or FALSE?

In our case, we will use a boolean variable called *allowed.* The value of *allowed* will be TRUE if the luggage meets the weight limitation. Otherwise it will have the value FALSE. At the start of the program, we will set the value of *allowed* to be TRUE. We will assume that it is innocent until proven false. Then we will check each of the conditions, and if any condition is not met, then we will set the value of *allowed* to false. Here is the program:

```
PROGRAM luggage (INPUT, OUTPUT);
    {This program reads in the weights for three suitcases.
     If any suitcase is heavier than 50 pounds, or if the
     total weight is greater than 100, the computer tells
     you that the luggage is too heavy.
     ''allowed'' is a boolean variable that will be true if
     the luggage is acceptable.}
VAR
    w1,w2,w3: REAL;
    allowed: BOOLEAN;
BEGIN
    WRITELN('Input the three weights: ');
    READLN(w1,w2,w3);
    allowed := TRUE;
    IF (w1 + w2 + w3) > 100 THEN allowed := FALSE;
    IF (w1 > 50) THEN allowed :=FALSE;
    IF (w2 > 50) THEN allowed :=FALSE;
    IF (w3 > 50) THEN allowed :=FALSE;
    IF allowed
        THEN WRITELN('The luggage is allowed. ')
        ELSE WRITELN('The luggage is too heavy. ')
END.
```

Note that we can use a boolean variable as the condition in an IF command. In our case, the command WRITELN('The luggage is allowed.') will be executed if the value of *allowed* is TRUE. If the value of *allowed* is FALSE, then the command WRITELN('The luggage is too heavy.') will be executed. We could have written the command:

```
IF allowed = TRUE
    THEN WRITELN('The luggage is allowed. ')
    ELSE WRITELN('The luggage is too heavy. ')
```

This sequence will work just as well, but it is a bit redundant to write "IF allowed = TRUE" instead of "IF allowed."

Here is a sample of the output from three runs of this program:

```
Input the three weights:
33
30
29
The luggage is allowed.

Input the three weights:
64
12
9
The luggage is too heavy.

Input the three weights:
45
42
23
The luggage is too heavy.
```

Here is another example of a program with a boolean variable. Suppose we are considering buying some triangular shaped pieces of land. We are given the lengths of the three sides, but we would like to know the area of each triangle. Let *a*, *b*, and *c* represent the lengths of the three sides. We can calculate the area from an interesting formula known as *Hero's formula:*

$$\text{Area} = \sqrt{s\,(s-a)(s-b)(s-c)}$$

where $s = (a+b+c)/2$.

However, suppose that someone tries to sell you a triangle with these dimensions: 2, 4, and 7 miles. It is impossible for a triangle to have these dimensions. In any triangle, the sum of the lengths of any two sides must be greater than the third side. In this case, $2 + 4$ is less than 7; so these three numbers cannot represent a triangle.

Our program will first check to see if the three numbers can represent a triangle. If they can't, then it will set a boolean variable called *triangle* to FALSE. Here is the program:

```
PROGRAM tritest (INPUT, OUTPUT);
    {This program reads in three numbers representing
    the lengths of the three sides of a triangle. Then
    it calculates the area of the triangle. However,
    if it is impossible for the three numbers to represent
    a triangle, then a message is printed.}
VAR
    a, b, c, s, area : REAL;
    triangle : BOOLEAN;
BEGIN
    WRITELN ('Type in the lengths of the three sides of the
        triangle. ');
    READLN (a, b, c);
    triangle : = TRUE;
    IF (a+c) <= b THEN triangle : = FALSE;
    IF (a+b) <= c THEN triangle : = FALSE;
    IF (b+c) <= a THEN triangle : = FALSE;

    IF triangle
        THEN BEGIN
            s : = (a + b + c) /2;
            area : = SQRT (s*(s-a) *(s-b) *(s-c)) ; {Hero's formula}
            WRITELN ('The area is: ', area: 7: 3)
            END
        ELSE WRITELN ('These three numbers cannot represent a
            triangle. ')
    END.
```

Here is a sample of the output:

```
Type in the lengths of the three sides of the triangle.
6
8
10
The area is: 24.000

Type in the lengths of the three sides of the triangle.
5
12
13
The area is: 30.000

Type in the lengths of the three sides of the triangle.
1
1
1
The area is: 0.433
```

```
Type in the lengths of the three sides of the triangle.
2
4
7
These three numbers cannot represent a triangle.
Type in the lengths of the three sides of the triangle.
5
10
5
These three numbers cannot represent a triangle.
```

Leap Years

Here is an example of a program that uses a series of cascaded IF statements. Suppose we need to determine whether or not a particular year is a leap year. We'll create a boolean variable called *leap*. First, we need to check to see if the year is divisible by 4. If it is not, then we know immediately that the year is not a leap year. However, if the year is divisible by 4, then we need to check to see if it is divisible by 100. A year that is divisible by 100 is *not* a leap year, unless it also happens to be divisible by 400. This rule is so complicated because the amount of time it takes for the earth to go around the sun (365 days, 6 hours, 9 minutes, 9.5 seconds) does not fit into a whole number of days.

Here is the program:

```
PROGRAM leaptest (INPUT, OUTPUT);
    {This program reads in a number
     representing a year and then determines
     whether or not it is a leap year.}
VAR
    year : INTEGER;
    leap : BOOLEAN;
BEGIN
  WRITELN('Type in the year.');
  READLN(year);
  IF (year MOD 4) <> 0
     THEN leap : = FALSE
     ELSE IF (year MOD 100) <> 0
             THEN leap : = TRUE
             ELSE IF (year MOD 400) = 0
                     THEN leap : = TRUE
                     ELSE leap : = FALSE;
  IF leap
     THEN WRITELN('This year is a leap year.')
     ELSE WRITELN('This year is not a leap year.')
END.
```

The output is

```
Type in the year.
1984
This year is a leap year.


Type in the year.
1987
This year is not a leap year.
```

Type in the year.
1900
This year is not a leap year.

Type in the year.
2000
This year is a leap year.

Boolean variables are also useful when a program can be run in either of two modes. For example, let's consider a compound interest program that gives you two choices. You may select the detail option and see the balance in the account at the end of every month, or you may select the summary option and only see the balance at the end of each year. We will use a boolean variable called *detail*. At the start of the program, the user will choose whether *detail* should be set to TRUE or FALSE. Here is the program:

```
PROGRAM interest (INPUT, OUTPUT);
    {This program calculates compound interest.
    You have your choice whether you would like
    the balance printed at the end of each month
    or only at the end of each year.}
CONST
    rate = 0.005; {Monthly interest rate}
VAR
    month, year, n, query : INTEGER;
    balance : REAL;
    detail : BOOLEAN;
BEGIN
    WRITELN('Type in the number of years.');
    READLN(n);
    WRITELN('Type in the initial balance.');
    READLN(balance);
    WRITELN('Type 1 if you would like output every month.');
    WRITELN('Otherwise, type 0.');
    READLN(query);
    IF query = 1
        THEN detail := TRUE
        ELSE detail := FALSE;
    IF detail
        THEN WRITELN('Year Month  Balance')
        ELSE WRITELN('Year  Balance');
    year := 0;
    REPEAT
        year := year + 1;
        FOR month := 1 TO 12 DO
          BEGIN
            balance := balance * (1 + rate);
            IF detail THEN WRITELN(year:4, month:6, balance:10:2)
          END;
        IF detail
            THEN WRITELN('********************')
            ELSE WRITELN(year:4, balance:9:2);
    UNTIL year >= n
END.
```

Here is the output of the program when you select the summary mode (detail = FALSE):

```
Type in the number of years.
5
Type in the initial balance.
100
Type 1 if you would like output every month.
Otherwise, type 0.
0
Year   Balance
   1   106.17
   2   112.72
   3   119.67
   4   127.05
   5   134.88
```

Here is the output of the program when you select the detail mode (detail = TRUE):

```
Type in the number of years.
5
Type in the initial balance.
100
Type 1 if you would like output every month.
Otherwise, type 0.
1
Year  Month  Balance
   1     1   100.50
   1     2   101.00
   1     3   101.51
   1     4   102.01
   1     5   102.52
   1     6   103.04
   1     7   103.55
   1     8   104.07
   1     9   104.59
   1    10   150.11
   1    12   106.17

*********************
   2     1   106.70
   2     2   107.23
   2     3   107.77
   2     4   108.31
   2     5   108.85
   2     6   109.39
   2     7   109.94
   2     8   110.49
   2     9   111.04
   2    10   111.60
   2    11   112.15
   2    12   112.72
*********************
   3     1   113.28
   3     2   113.84
   3     3   114.41
   3     4   114.99
   3     5   115.56
   3     6   116.14
   3     7   116.72
```

```
        3         8      117.30
        3         9      117.89
        3        10      118.48
        3        11      119.07
        3        12      119.67
*********************
        4         1      120.26
        4         2      120.87
        4         3      121.47
        4         4      122.08
        4         5      122.69
        4         6      123.30
        4         7      123.92
        4         8      124.54
        4         9      125.16
        4        10      125.79
        4        11      126.41
        4        12      127.05
*********************
        5         1      127.68
        5         2      128.32
        5         3      128.96
        5         4      129.61
        5         5      130.25
        5         6      130.91
        5         7      131.56
        5         8      132.22
        5         9      132.88
        5        10      133.54
        5        11      134.21
        5        12      134.88
*********************
```

Logical Operators : AND, OR, NOT

Boolean variables cannot be added or multiplied like real or integer variables. However, boolean variables can be used with logical operators. The three logical operators are NOT, AND, and OR. The NOT operation is very simple. It makes a TRUE boolean variable become FALSE, and a FALSE boolean variable become TRUE. For example, if a is TRUE and b is FALSE, then NOT a is FALSE and NOT b is TRUE.

Suppose you have two TRUE statements:

Statement 1: "The sky is blue."

Statement 2: "The sun rises in the east."

If you combine them into one statement with the word AND, like this:

Combined statement: "The sky is blue and the sun rises in the east."

then clearly the combined statement is true. Therefore, if a and b are both TRUE, then a AND b is TRUE. However, if you link one false statement and one true statement together with *and,* like this:

"The sky is blue and the sun rises in the west."

then the combined statement is false.

On the other hand, if you link one false statement and one true statement together with *or*, then the combined statement is true:

"The sky is blue or the sky is purple."

Therefore, we can make a table that tells how to combine boolean variables with AND and OR:

The AND operation:

TRUE AND TRUE   is TRUE

TRUE AND FALSE   is FALSE

FALSE AND FALSE is FALSE

(In other words, *a* AND *b* is TRUE only if both *a* and *b* are TRUE.)

The OR operation:

TRUE OR TRUE   is TRUE

TRUE OR FALSE   is TRUE

FALSE OR FALSE is FALSE

(*a* OR *b* is TRUE if either *a* or *b* is TRUE.)

Here is a sample program using these logic functions:

```
PROGRAM example (INPUT, OUTPUT);
    {This program is an example of the boolean
    logic functions: NOT, AND, and OR.}
BEGIN
    WRITELN('Examples of NOT function: ');
    WRITELN('NOT TRUE: ', NOT TRUE);
    WRITELN('NOT FALSE: ', NOT FALSE);
    WRITELN('Examples of AND function: ');
    WRITELN('TRUE AND TRUE: ', TRUE AND TRUE);
    WRITELN('TRUE AND FALSE: ', TRUE AND FALSE);
    WRITELN('FALSE AND FALSE: ', FALSE AND FALSE);
    WRITELN('Examples of OR function: ')
    WRITELN('TRUE OR TRUE: ', TRUE OR TRUE);
    WRITELN('TRUE OR FALSE: ', TRUE OR FALSE);
    WRITELN('FALSE OR FALSE: ', FALSE OR FALSE);
    WRITELN('Examples of parentheses: ');
    WRITELN('NOT TRUE AND FALSE: ', NOT TRUE AND FALSE);
    WRITELN('NOT (TRUE AND FALSE): ', NOT (TRUE AND FALSE));
    WRITELN('NOT TRUE AND FALSE OR TRUE AND FALSE: ');
    WRITELN(NOT TRUE AND FALSE OR TRUE AND FALSE)
END.
```

The output from this program is:

```
Examples of NOT function:
NOT TRUE: FALSE
NOT FALSE: TRUE
Examples of AND function:
TRUE AND TRUE: TRUE
TRUE AND FALSE: FALSE
```

```
FALSE AND FALSE: FALSE
Examples of OR function:
TRUE OR TRUE: TRUE
TRUE OR FALSE: TRUE
FALSE OR FALSE: FALSE
Examples of parentheses:
NOT TRUE AND FALSE: FALSE
NOT (TRUE AND FALSE) : TRUE
NOT TRUE AND FALSE OR TRUE AND FALSE:
FALSE
```

Believe it or not, computers are made up of lots of simpleminded electronic devices that represent these types of logical operations. In computers, information is stored by devices that can be in two states. Note that boolean variables can also be one of two states. Many people find it boring to design complicated logic circuits containing millions of ANDs and ORs. Fortunately, you don't need to do any of that to use a computer. You only need to use boolean variables if you find them convenient. If you don't intend to write complicated boolean expressions, you may skip over the next few paragraphs.

Once we start putting more than one logical operation on the same line, we need to decide on some rules of precedence. For example, in the expression NOT TRUE AND FALSE, is the NOT done first, or is the AND done first? IF the NOT is done first, then the result is FALSE AND FALSE, which is FALSE. We will decide that, in general, a NOT will be done before any other logical operation. ANDs will be done next, and ORs will be done last. However, you may override the normal precedence rule by using parentheses. If you want the AND done first in the expression NOT TRUE AND FALSE, then write it like this:

NOT (TRUE AND FALSE)

which has the result NOT FALSE, which is TRUE. See the example in the program above.

Let's look at this monster expression:

NOT TRUE AND FALSE OR TRUE AND FALSE

There are no parentheses; so the computer will follow its normal procedence rules. First, the computer will do the NOT:

(NOT TRUE) AND FALSE OR TRUE AND FALSE

giving the result:

FALSE AND FALSE OR TRUE AND FALSE

Next, the computer will do the two ANDs:

(FALSE AND FALSE) OR (TRUE AND FALSE)

giving the result:

FALSE OR FALSE

Therefore, the final result is FALSE.

Here's a program that illustrates the AND command. Suppose that we are told a team's score in a football game, but we need to know how many touchdowns and field goals the team made. In general, we cannot tell that information from the score alone. However, we can perform the calculation if we make these assumptions: (1) no safeties;

(2) no missed extra points; (3) no 2-point conversions; and (4) less than seven field goals. This program reads in the score and assigns it to an integer variable *s*. If *s* is divisible by 7, then we know that the score consists solely of touchdowns. We will keep subtracting by 7, counting the number of touchdowns each time, until we reach 0. If *s* is not divisible by 7, then we will keep subtracting by 3 until *s* is divisible by 7. The boolean variable *continue* will become FALSE when *s* becomes 0, which means that we can stop.

```
PROGRAM football (INPUT, OUTPUT);
    {This program reads in a football score and then calculates
    the number of field goals and touchdowns. Assume no safeties,
    no missed extra points, no 2-point conversions, and less than
    seven field goals.}
VAR
    td, fg, s, score : INTEGER;
    continue : BOOLEAN;
BEGIN
REPEAT
    td := 0;
    fg := 0;
    WRITELN('Type in the score: ');
    READLN(score);
    s := score;
    continue := (s>0);
    WHILE continue DO
      BEGIN
        WHILE (continue) AND ((s MOD 7) = 0) DO
          BEGIN
                {This section will be executed when s is divisible
                by 7.}
            td := td + 1;
            s := s - 7;
            continue := (s>0)
          END;
        IF continue
          THEN BEGIN
                {This section will be executed when s is not
                divisible by 7.}
            fg := fg + 1;
            s := s - 3;
            continue := (s>0)
          END
      END;
    WRITELN('Score: ', score);
    WRITELN(td, ' touchdowns ', fg, ' field goals');
UNTIL score>100     {The program will stop when you type in a
                    score that is greater than 100.}
END.
```

Here is a sample of the output from this program:

```
Type in the score:
0
Score: 0
0 touchdowns 0 field goals

Type in the score:
20
```

2 touchdowns 2 field goals

Type in the score:
34
4 touchdowns 2 field goals

Type in the score:
120
15 touchdowns 5 field goals

(Note that there are some scores, such as 2, 8, and 11, that cannot possibly result if you score only touchdowns and field goals. The program will give an incorrect result if you type in one of these impossible scores.)

Note to Chapter 7

■ Pascal provides a useful function that tests whether an integer is an odd or even number. The function ODD(x) produces the boolean value TRUE if x is odd; otherwise it produces the value FALSE.

Chapter 7 Exercises

1. What's wrong with the following portion of a program?

```
VAR
   avg, sum, count : INTEGER;
   correct : BOOLEAN;
BEGIN
   sum: =0;
   count: =0;
   WRITELN ('Enter a value');
   READLN (number);
   WHILE correct DO
     BEGIN
       sum: =sum + number;
       count: =count + 1;
       WRITELN ('Enter a number');
       READLN (number)
     END;
   avg: =sum/count;
```

2. Is the following legal?

```
VAR
   legal: BOOLEAN;
BEGIN
   legal: =TRUE
   WHILE legal = TRUE DO
     BEGIN
       {statements}
     END;
```

For the following problems determine the outcome of the given boolean expressions. Assume that A is true, B is false, and C is true.

3. NOT A OR B AND NOT C

4. NOT A OR A

5. A AND (C OR NOT B)

6. NOT (A OR (B AND NOT C))

7. B AND (NOT (A OR B AND C))

CHAPTER 8

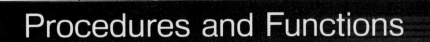

Procedures and Functions

Procedures

Let's look at a payroll program similar to the ones that we used in Chapter 5:

```
PROGRAM payroll (INPUT, OUTPUT);
    {This program uses a WHILE command to calculate the payroll
    for several workers. The program will stop when a negative
    value is typed in for the number of hours.}
CONST
    wage = 7.0;
VAR
    hours, pay : REAL;
BEGIN
    WRITELIN ('Input the number of hours: ');
    READLN (hours);
    IF (hours > 70)
       THEN WRITELN ('Hours are greater than 70. ');
    WHILE hours > 0 DO
       BEGIN
          IF hours > 40
             THEN pay : = wage * 40 + 1.5 * wage * (hours − 40)
             ELSE pay : = wage * hours;
          WRITELN ('Pay is =', pay: 7: 2);
          WRITELN ('Input the number of hours: ');
```

```
        READLN(hours);
        IF (hours > 70)
            THEN WRITELN('Hours are greater than 70.')
    END
END.
```

This program works fine. However, it has one highly annoying feature. The sequence of statements, "WRITELN ('Input the number of hours:'); READLIN(hours); IF (hours > 70) THEN WRITELN ('Hours are greater than 70.') " needs to be typed twice. It would save us a big chunk of typing if we could find a way to tell the computer to execute the same set of instructions more than once.

We'll develop a way that allows the computer to execute a little subblock of instructions on demand. The little subblock is called a *procedure.* A procedure looks like a mini Pascal program. A procedure always starts with the word PROCEDURE followed by the name of the procedure. (Remember that a Pascal program always starts with the word PROGRAM followed by the name of the program.) A procedure might have some variable declarations. Then it has the word BEGIN, followed by some action statements. The procedure ends with the word END.

We'll write a procedure to read in the number of hours in the payroll program. We'll call the procedure "readhours." Here is what the procedure looks like:

```
PROCEDURE readhours;
    BEGIN
        WRITELN('Input the number of hours: ');
        READLN(hours);
        IF (hours > 70)
            THEN WRITELN('Hours are greater than 70.')
    END;
```

Now we need to type our procedure into the Pascal program "payroll". In a Pascal program, the procedures need to be typed after the variable declarations but before the BEGIN command that marks the beginning of the action part of the program. (We'll call that part of the program the *main program block.*) When we want to have the procedure "readhours" executed, all we need to do is type the word "readhours". When the computer reaches the word readhours, it will pretend that it had really come across the three commands:

```
WRITELN('Input the number of hours: ');
READLN(hours);
IF (hours > 70)
    THEN WRITELN('Hours are greater than 70.');
```

Here is the way that the complete program looks:

```
PROGRAM payroll (INPUT, OUTPUT);
    {This program uses a WHILE command to calculate the payroll
    for several workers. The program will stop when a negative
    value is typed in for the number of hours.}
CONST
    wage = 7.0;
VAR
    hours, pay : REAL;

PROCEDURE readhours;
    BEGIN
        WRITELN('Input the number of hours: ');
        READLN(hours);
        IF (hours > 70)
            THEN WRITELN('Hours are greater than 70.')
```

```
      END;
  {This is now the main program block.}
  BEGIN
      readhours;
      WHILE hours > 0 DO
          BEGIN
            IF hours > 40
                THEN pay : = wage * 40 + 1.5 * wage * (hours - 40)
                ELSE pay : = wage * hours;
              WRITELN('Pay is =',pay:7:2);
              readhours
          END
  END.
```

Here is a sample of the output from this program:

```
Input the number of hours:
10
Pay is = 70.00
Input the number of hours:
73
Hours are greater than 70.
Pay is = 626.50
Input the number of hours:
42
Pay is = 301.00
Input the number of hours:
-1
```

The advantage of using procedures is clear when a block of instructions needs to be used more than once. However, there is an even more important reason to use procedures in a Pascal program. When you have a complicated problem, it is much easier to understand the problem if you break it up into smaller, more manageable pieces. The idea is to follow a "divide and conquer" strategy. Write a procedure to handle each little part of the problem. Then the final program is easy to write. The main program block only needs to consist of a series of commands telling the computer to execute the different procedures. (When the name of a procedure appears in the main program block, it is called a *procedure call*.) We will discuss this strategy for writing complicated programs more later in the book. From now on we will use procedures in many of the programs we write.

Here is the general form for a procedure declaration:

PROCEDURE *procedure-name* (*parameter1,parameter2*, . . . :*type*)

   declaration section

   BEGIN

      statement 1;

      statement 2;

      .

      .

      .

      last statement

   END;

The parameter list is included if you will need to feed some values into the procedure. Our procedure readhours has no parameter. A procedure may have one, two, or more parameters. We will give some examples of procedures with parameters later. (As we will see later, a parameter list may include parameters of more than one type.)

We can now write out the general form for a Pascal program:

PROGRAM *program-name* (INPUT,OUTPUT);

    constant declarations;

    type declarations {discussed in Chapter 10}

    variable declarations;

    procedure declarations;

BEGIN

    main program block

END.

Functions

Here is another application that will lead us to develop a new kind of program block, called a *function*. If you're at a crucial point in a card game, it helps to know what the probability is that a particular hand will arise. One way to calculate this probability is to deal out millions of hands and count how many times the hand you're interested in turns up. A faster method is to learn a little probability theory. You'll need to know how many possible hands can be dealt from the deck. If there are *n* cards in the deck and *j* cards in each hand, then there are

$$\frac{n!}{j!(n-j)!}$$

ways of dealing out the hands. (The exclamation mark stands for *factorial*; *m* factorial is equal to the product of all the numbers from 1 up to *m*. For example, $5! = 5 \times 4 \times 3 \times 2 \times 1 = 120$, and $7! = 7 \times 6 \times 5 \times 4 \times 3 \times 2 \times 1 = 5040$.)

This sounds like a problem for the computer. It's easy to write a little program that calculates *m*!, since all it needs to do is multiply together all the numbers from 1 to *m*:

```
z : = 1;
i : = 1;
REPEAT
    z : = z * i;
    i : = i + 1;
UNTIL i > m;
```

After executing this program segment, the variable *z* will have the value *m*!. To calculate a value for the complicated formula $n!/[j!(n-j)!]$, we merely need to write a program that uses this little segment three times:

```
PROGRAM hands (INPUT, OUTPUT);
    {This program calculates the number of possible hands
    of ''j'' cards that can be drawn from a deck of ''n'' cards.}
VAR
    n, j, z, i, a, b, c, number : REAL;
BEGIN
    WRITELN ('Input the values of n and j: ');
```

```
      READLN(n,j);
      {Calculate n! and store the result as a.}
      z := 1;
      i := 1;
      REPEAT
          z := z * i;
          i := i + 1;
      UNTIL i > n;
      a := z;
      {Calculate j! and store the result as b.}
      z := 1;
      i := 1;
      REPEAT
          z := z * i;
          i := i + 1;
      UNTIL i > j;
      b := z;
      {Calculate (n − j)! and store the results as c.}
      z := 1;
      i := 1;
      REPEAT
          z := z * i;
          i := i + 1;
      UNTIL i > (n − j);
      c := c;
      number := a/(b * c);
      WRITELN('The number of hands is,' number)
   END.
```

Once again, you should protest the thought of having to type the instructions for the factorial routine three times. Remember, the computer is supposed to save us work. We'll create a new kind of program block called a function. A function is a program block that takes on an output value after it is given an input value. Note that a function in Pascal is quite similar to the mathematical functions you may have studied in a math class. Here is a table that describes some of the behavior of the factorial function (we'll call it *fact*):

FACT FUNCTION

Input number	Output number
1	fact(1) = 1
2	fact(2) = 2
3	fact(3) = 6
4	fact(4) = 24
5	fact(5) = 120

Arguments

Now we have to write the factorial function in Pascal. The first word of a function is always FUNCTION. Next comes the function name (in this case "fact"). Then, we have to include a list of *arguments*. The arguments to a function are the input numbers that are fed into it. The factorial function only has one argument, but we will later see that a function can have several arguments. (The arguments of a function are also called its *parameters*.) The first line of the fact function looks like this:

```
FUNCTION fact (x: REAL) : REAL;
```

In this case we are using *x* to stand for the name of the argument. We need to include the word REAL after the *x* to tell the computer that the argument will be of type REAL. Finally, we need to include the word REAL after the argument list to tell the computer that the result of the function will be of type REAL. The letter *x* in this case is called a *dummy argument* because it doesn't matter what name you use for the dummy argument in the declaration of the function. The exact same function could be declared by using *y* or q173 instead. However, you have to make sure that you use the same name for the dummy argument all through the function. (You may point out that the argument and the result of the factorial function will always be integers. However, we will declare them both to be real numbers because we can handle larger numbers that way.)

The complete factorial function looks like this:

```
FUNCTION fact (x: REAL) : REAL;
      {This function calculates the factorial
      of the number x.}
VAR i, z: REAL;
BEGIN
    z := 1.0;
    IF x > 1.0
        THEN BEGIN
                i := 1.0;
                REPEAT
                  z := z * i;
                  i := i + 1.0;
                UNTIL i > x
             END;
    fact := z
END;
```

Note that we can include a declaration section after the function heading line if we like. In this case we are declaring two variables (*i* and *z*). If variables are used only inside the function, it is a good idea to declare them in the function itself instead of in the main declaration section (more on this later). After the variables are declared, we must put the word BEGIN, followed by the action statements of the function. Sometime before the end of the function, the function name itself must be assigned to the value that it is supposed to have. The statement fact := z fulfills this requirement. After the REPEAT loop is completed, the variable z will be equal to x factorial.

When we're in the main program block, it's easy to tell the computer to execute the function. The expression fact(5) will have the value 5! (that's 5 factorial, not 5 exclamation point). It's that easy. We can use the expression fact(5) just the same as we could use a regular variable name. For example, we could include it in an expression:

```
n := fact (5) /2;
```

or in an output statement:

```
WRITELN ('The factorial of 5 is ', fact (5));
```

Or, of course, we could use the expression fact(4), fact(8), or any other argument value that we might choose,

Here is the complete program to calculate the number of card hands. The program is named *combin*, because the number of *j* card hands that can be dealt from an *n* card deck is also called the number of *combinations* of *n* things taken *j* at a time.

```
PROGRAM combin (INPUT, OUTPUT);
      {This program reads in two numbers, n and j, and
      then calculates the number of combinations of
      n objects taken j at a time.}
```

```
VAR
  number, n, j: REAL;

FUNCTION fact (x: REAL) : REAL;
    {This function calculates the factorial
    of the number x. }
  VAR i, z: REAL;
  BEGIN
      z := 1.0;
      IF x > 1.0
        THEN BEGIN
                i := 1.0;
                REPEAT
                  z := z * i;
                  i := i + 1.0;
                UNTIL i > x
              END;
      fact := z
  END;
  {Main program block: }
  BEGIN
    WRITELN('Input the number of cards in deck (n): ');
    READLN(n);
    WRITELN('Input the number of cards in hand (j): ');
    READLN(j);
    number := fact(n) / (fact(j) * (fact(n-j)));
        {Notice how we can use the fact function in
        expressions. }
    WRITELN('There are ', number, ' possible hands. ')
  END.
```

Here are some samples of the output of this program:

```
Input the number of cards in deck (n):
20
Input the number of cards in hand (j):
4
There are 4.84500E+03 possible hands.

Input the number of cards in deck (n):
20
Input the number of cards in hand (j):
5
There are 1.55040E+04 possible hands.

Input the number of cards in deck (n):
10
Input the number of cards in hand (j):
3
There are 1.20000E+02 possible hands.
```

For example, there are 4,845 possible four-card hands you can deal from a deck of 20 cards. You probably would be interested in the number of hands you can deal from a 52-card deck, since standard decks have 52 cards. If you try to run this program for $n =$ 52, the computer will tell you that it has encountered an overflow error. An overflow error occurs when the computer is asked to calculate a number that is too big for it to handle. The value of 52! is about 8×10^{67}; so you can see how large the values of the factorial function become. (We will later write a program that can handle the number of hands that can be dealt from a 52-card deck.)

Useful Functions

Now we'll create some more of our own functions. If you think of a function that you wish Pascal had included, you can add it yourself. For example, suppose you would like a function that doubles a number. We can define that function like this:

```
FUNCTION double (x: REAL) : REAL;
BEGIN
    double : = 2 * x
END;
```

Because *x* is a dummy argument, the function would behave exactly the same if it had been declared like this:

```
FUNCTION double (y: REAL) : REAL;
BEGIN
    double : = 2 * y
END;
```

Think of it this way. The inner workings of the function are completely invisible to someone in the main program block. The person in the main program block only sees the number that goes into the function and the result that comes out of the function.

Here are some more examples of user-defined functions that will appeal to the more mathematically inclined readers. (If you're not mathematically inclined, you may skip the next few functions.) Suppose that our local version of Pascal does not include an exponentiation operator (**). In that case it would be very useful to define our own power function, such that power(x,n) = x^n. Here is the function declaration for the power function:

```
FUNCTION power (x,n : REAL) : REAL;
BEGIN
    power : = EXP (n * LN (x))
END;
```

For example, power(2,5) is 32 since $2^5 = 32$; power(30,0.5) is 5.4772 since $30^{0.5} = \sqrt{30} = 5.4772$.

We'll also modify the sin function. The standard sin function calculates the value of sin *x* when *x* is measured in radians. However, there are often times when it is convenient to calculate sin *x* when *x* is measured in degrees. Since 180 degrees is equal to 3.14159 radians, we can write the function sind, which calculates the sin of an angle measured in degrees:

```
FUNCTION sind (x : REAL) : REAL;
CONST pi = 3.141593;
    BEGIN
      sind : = SIN(pi * x/180.0)
    END;
```

For example, sind(30) is 0.5.

We'll also create a new logarithm function. The function LN(x) calculates the natural logarithm of *x*, which is the logarithm of *x* to the base *e* (*e* is an irrational number that is approximately equal to 2.71828 . . .). It is often convenient to be able to calculate the common logarithm of *x*, which is the logarithm to the base 10, written log *x*. We can use the formula: log *x* = (log *e*)(ln *x*) = 0.4342945 × ln *x*.

```
FUNCTION log (x : REAL) : REAL;
    BEGIN
      log : = 0.4342945 * LN (x)
    END;
```

For example, log(5) is 0.699.

We can also easily add a tangent function, since $\tan x = (\sin x)/(\cos x)$.

```
FUNCTION tan (x : REAL) : REAL;
   BEGIN
    tan : = SIN(x)/COS(x)
   END;
```

For example, tan (0.7845) is 1.

By now you should be getting the idea of how user-defined functions are created. Note that all these functions, except the power function, have just one argument. We will create one more function with two arguments. Suppose we know the coordinates (x,y) of a point and we would like to know the angle between the x axis and the line connecting

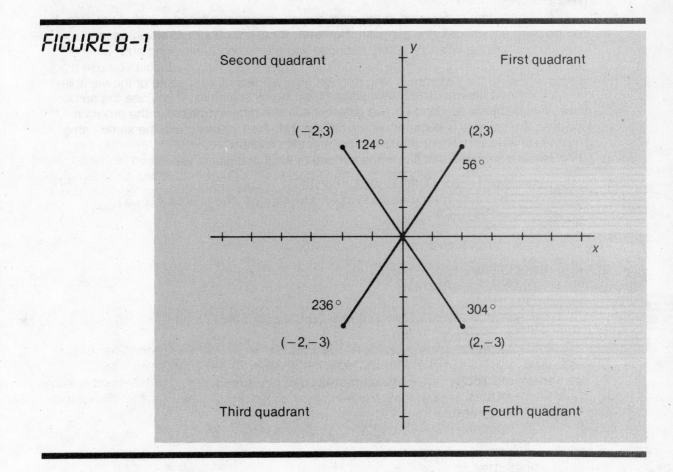

FIGURE 8-1

the origin to that point (see Figure 8-1). Pascal comes equipped with the ARCTAN function, and so we can calculate ARCTAN(y/x). However, suppose we have one point in the first quadrant, such as (2,3), and the corresponding point in the third quadrant, (−2,−3). In both cases the ARCTAN function will give the result 0.9828 radian (56 degrees). However, these two points are in reality quite different. It will be useful to create a modified arctan function [we'll call it atn(x,y)] that calculates arctan(y/x) and places the result in the correct quadrant:

```
FUNCTION atn (x,y : REAL) : REAL;
   CONST pi = 3.14159;
   VAR z : REAL;
   BEGIN
      z : = ARCTAN(y/x);
      IF x < 0 THEN z : = z + pi;
```

```
        IF z < 0 THEN z : = z + 2 * pi;
    atn : = z
    END;
```

Local and Global Variables

We mentioned earlier that a variable that is used only within a particular function or procedure should be declared within that procedure. There are some important reasons for doing that. A variable declared within a procedure is called a *local variable*. A local variable is only valid within its own procedure. If you try to use a local variable outside its own neighborhood, the computer will pretend that it had never heard of that variable before.

A variable that is declared in the main declaration area is called a *global variable*. It can be used anywhere in the program. However, there are important advantages to using local variables when possible. Suppose you are writing a very long and complicated program. It would be very difficult to give every single variable you use a distinct name. (If the program is long enough, you will likely forget some of the variable names you have already used.) It would probably wreck something if you use the same global variable name to stand for two different items at different points in the program. However, if a variable is declared as a local variable, then you may use the same name to mean something different at another point in the program.

Here is a program that illustrates the use of local and global variables:

```
PROGRAM local (INPUT, OUTPUT);
    {This program demonstrates the use of local and global
    variables.}
VAR
    x, y, z, : INTEGER;

PROCEDURE p1;
    VAR x, y: INTEGER;
    BEGIN
        WRITELN ('**** We are now in procedure p1. ');
        x : = 20; y : = 30;
        WRITELN ('x = ', x, ' y = ', y, ' z = ', z);
        p2;
        WRITELN ('**** We are back in procedure p1. ');
        WRITELN ('x = ', x, ' y = ', y, ' z = ', z);
        x : = 200; y : = 300;
        WRITELN ('x = ', x, ' y = ', y, ' z = ', z)
    END;

PROCEDURE p2;
    VAR x : INTEGER;
    BEGIN
        WRITELN ('***** We are now in procedure p2. ');
        x : = 15;
        WRITELN ('x = ', x, ' y = ', y, ' z = ', z);
        z : = 50;
        WRITELN ('x = ', x, ' y = ', y, ' z = ', z)
    END;

{Main program block}
BEGIN
    WRITELN ('***** This is the main program block. ');
    x : = 1; y : = 2; z : = 3;
    WRITELN ('x = ', x, ' y = ', y, ' z = ', z);
```

```
    p1;
    WRITELN('**** We are back in the main program block.');
    WRITELN('x = ',x,' y = ',y,' z = ',z)
END.
```

The output from this program looks like:

```
***** This is the main program block.
x = 1 y = 2 z = 3
**** We are now in procedure p1.
x = 20 y = 30 z = 3
***** We are now in procedure p2.
x = 15 y = 2 z = 3
x = 15 y = 2 z = 50
**** We are back in procedure p1.
x = 20 y = 30 z = 50
x = 200 y = 300 z = 50
**** We are back in the main program block.
x = 1 y = 2 z = 50
```

In this program note that z is used only as a global variable. Therefore, when the value of z is changed in p2, the change is valid both in p1 and in the main program block. y is declared as both a global variable and as a local variable inside procedure p1. Therefore, when the variable name y is used inside p1, it means something completely different from when it is used elsewhere in the program. Initially y is given the value 2 in the main block. Then, in p1, the local version of y is given the value of 30. When you enter p2, then the name y once again refers to the global variable y, which has the value 2. Upon returning to p1, y once again becomes the local variable whose value is changed from 30 to 300. However, once you return to the main program, the name y once again refers to the global variable which has the value 2. See if you can trace the history of the values for the variable name x. Note that the name x has three meanings in this program: as a global variable, as a local variable inside procedure p1, and as a different local variable inside procedure p2.

Parameters for Procedures

In a function declaration, the dummy parameters used are local to that function. There also are times when you would like to feed parameter values to a procedure. To do that, you need to include a list of parameters after the procedure name. Here is an example of a simple procedure with two parameters:

```
PROCEDURE percent (x, t : REAL);
    {This procedure calculates x/t and then expresses the result
    as a percent.}
BEGIN
    WRITELN((100*x/t):6:1,'%')
END;
```

We can call this procedure with a statement like this in the main block:

```
percent(2.4, 3.6);
```

The computer will pretend that it had really come across the statement:

```
WRITELN((100*2.4/3.6):6:1,'%');
```

causing the output:

```
  66.7%
```

When the computer executes the procedure, the computer will fill in the value 2.4 in the place of the dummy parameter *x* and the value 3.6 in place of the dummy parameter *t*.

You could also write the procedure call by supplying variable names for the parameters:

```
percent(a, b);
```

The computer will pretend that it had really come across the statement

```
WRITELN((100*a/b):6:1,'%');
```

In these cases the parameters are called *value parameters* because only the values of the parameters are passed to the procedure.

There might be times when you would like a procedure to assign a value *to* a variable of your choice. In that case you need to use a different type of parameter called a *variable parameter*. Here is a new version of the percent procedure:

```
PROCEDURE percent (x, y: REAL; VAR result : REAL);
   BEGIN
    result : = 100 * x/y
   END;
```

In this case *x* and *y* are value parameters. The word VAR indicates that *result* is a variable parameter. Now we can use this procedure call:

```
percent(2.4, 3.6, p);
```

The computer will pretend that it had come across this statement:

```
p : = 100 * 2.4/3.6;
```

and the variable *p* will be assigned the value 100 * 2.4/3.6.

In the procedure call you must, of course, use a variable in the place of the variable parameter. It would cause an error to write this procedure call:

```
percent(2.4, 3.6, 10.0);
```

because then the computer would pretend that it had come across this statement:

```
10.0 : = 100 * 2.4/3.6
```

and of course it cannot execute that statement.

Notes to Chapter 8

■ It is possible to put the declaration for one procedure inside the declaration section of another procedure. For example:

```
PROCEDURE outer;
VAR x : REAL;
      PROCEDURE inner;
           BEGIN x : = 100 * x END;
BEGIN
     READLN(x);
     inner;
     WRITELN(x)
END;
```

In this case the inner procedure is called a *nested procedure*. A nested procedure can only be called from within the procedure in which it is declared. It will not be recognized elsewhere in the program.

■ Some Pascal compilers do not allow a procedure or function to call another procedure unless the called procedure is defined before the calling procedure. If you expect a procedure will need to be called by a procedure defined later, you can add the word FORWARD to its declaration.

Chapter 8 Exercises

Write functions that perform the following transformations, along with the reverse transformations:

1. Inches to meters

2. Gallons to liters

3. Acres to hectares

4. Miles to kilometers

5. Miles to light years

6. Pounds to kilograms

7. Parallax to distance in parsecs

8. Volts RMS to volts peak to peak

9. Degrees to radians

10. Write a function that converts a monthly inflation rate into an annual inflation rate.

11. Write a function that rounds a number off to n decimal places.

12. Write a function that calculates the hyperbolic cosine of x, defined by $\cosh x = \frac{1}{2}(e^x + e^{-x})$.

Suppose your computer had no built-in functions and no exponentiation operation. Write functions that perform the following tasks:

*13. Calculate the square root of a number.

*14. Calculate the sine of a number. (See Chapter 6, Exercise 17.)

15. The quantity

$$\frac{n!}{j!(n-j)!}$$

is called the binomial coefficient. It is often symbolized by $\binom{n}{j}$. The program in the chapter calculates $\binom{n}{j}$ by calling the factorial procedure three times. This method is not very efficient. Write a function that calculates $\binom{n}{j}$ in a more efficient manner.

16. Suppose you need to conduct an opinion poll from a population of n people. Of these people, r approve the President's performance and the rest disapprove. If you question a total of b people and x number of people in the poll approve of the President's performance, the probability that x will equal a particular number j is given by the expression

$$Pr\,(x = j) = \frac{\binom{r}{j}\binom{n-r}{b-j}}{\binom{n}{b}}$$

where x is said to be a random variable with the hypergeometric distribution. Write a program that reads in the values for n, r, and b and then prints $Pr(x = j)$ for $j = 0$ to $j = b$. Use the function from Exercise 15 three times. You will have a good poll if the probability is high that x will be about equal to rb/n. You will have a very poor poll if the probability is high that x will equal 0 or b.

*17. Write a more efficient version of the program in Exercise 16. (The program's longest loop should contain no more than either j or $b - j$ iterations.)

18. Suppose you are going to roll a pair of dice n times, and the probability of rolling doubles is p ($p = 1/6$). The probability that you will roll k doubles in the n rolls is

$$\binom{n}{k} p^k (1 - p)^{n-k}$$

(This is an example of a random variable with a binomial distribution.) Suppose you roll the dice 20 times. Use the function from Exercise 15 in a program that calculates the probability that you will roll k doubles for $k = 0, 1, 2, 3, 4, \ldots,$ 20.

19. If you're with a group of s people, the probability that no two people in the group will have the same birthday is given by

$$\frac{\frac{365!}{(365-s)!}}{365^s}$$

Write a program that calculates this probability for $s = 2, 5, 10, 15, 20, \ldots,$ 50.

20. Write a function that reads in a point (x, y) and an angle A and then calculates the coordinates of the point in the new coordinate system formed by rotating the axes by an angle A. (See Chapter 3, Exercise 12.)

CHAPTER 9

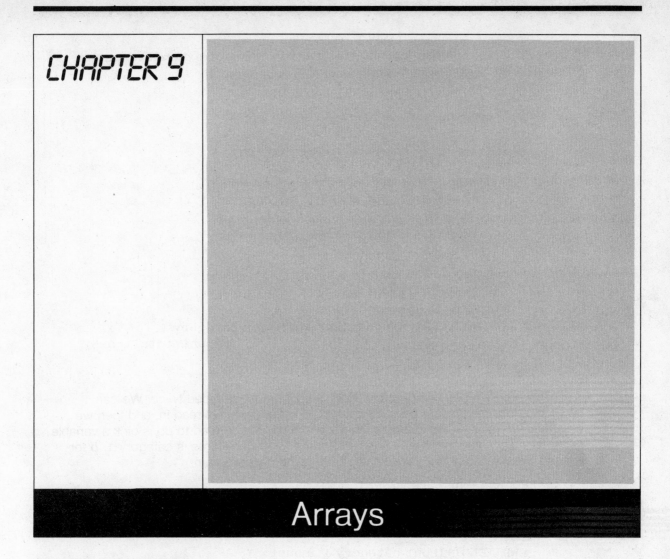

Arrays

Spending Categories

Computers can be very useful for keeping track of financial data. Suppose that you divide your expenditures into six broad categories, and the following table tells you how much you spent on each category last week:

	Category	Amount spent
(food)	1	34.26
(clothing)	2	12.00
(books)	3	14.95
(transportation)	4	56.95
(housing)	5	112.00
(other)	6	2.07

It would be useful to know what fraction of the total expenditures goes to each of the six categories.

Here is one possible program:

```
PROGRAM expshare (INPUT, OUTPUT);
   {This program calculates the fraction of expenditures for
   each of six categories.}
VAR
   total, amount: REAL;
   i: INTEGER;
BEGIN
   total := 0;
   FOR i := 1 TO 6 DO
      BEGIN
         WRITELN('Input amount for category ', i);
         READLN(amount);
         total := total + amount
      END;
   FOR i := 1 TO 6 DO
      BEGIN
         WRITELN('Input amount for category ', i);
         READLN(amount);
         WRITELN('Expenditure share for category ', i, ' is: ',
                                       (amount/total):5:3)
      END
END.
```

This program has one problem: Each amount must be typed twice. We can, however, store the amount for each category the first time it is read in, and then we won't have to input all the amounts the second time. All we need to do is pick a variable name for each category. We can use *a* to stand for expenditures in category 1, *b* for expenditures in category 2, and so on. Here is the new program:

```
PROGRAM expshare (INPUT, OUTPUT);
VAR
   a, b, c, d, e, f, total : REAL;
BEGIN
   WRITELN('Input category 1 amount: ');
   READLN(a);
   WRITELN('Input category 2 amount: ');
   READLN(b);
   WRITELN('Input category 3 amount: ');
   READLN(c);
   WRITELN('Input category 4 amount: ');
   READLN(d);
   WRITELN('Input category 5 amount: ');
   READLN(e);
   WRITELN('Input category 6 amount: ');
   READLN(f);
   total := a + b + c + d + e + f;
   WRITELN('Category 1 share is: ', (a/total));
   WRITELN('Category 2 share is: ', (b/total));
   WRITELN('Category 3 share is: ', (c/total));
   WRITELN('Category 4 share is: ', (d/total));
   WRITELN('Category 5 share is: ', (e/total));
   WRITELN('Category 6 share is: ', (f/total))
END.
```

It's good that each number has to be typed in only once with this program. But look at how long the program itself is! And suppose you ever want to add more categories. You would then have to make the program longer than it is now.

Subscripts

There must be a better way. We need some way that will allow us to store six values other than the cumbersome method of using a different name for each value. Perhaps we can think of a way where we can use *one* letter to stand for six values. However, we will have to find some way to tell the different values apart. (Think how confusing it would be if everyone in your family had the same name.) Therefore, we'll identify each value by its own number. For example, suppose we decide to use the name *spend* to stand for the six expenditure values. Then we can say that $spend_1 = 34.26$, $spend_2 = 12.00$, $spend_3 = 14.95$, $spend_4 = 56.95$, $spend_5 = 112.00$, and $spend_6 = 2.07$. The small numbers written below the line are called *subscripts*. We can't actually display subscripts on the screen, but we can enclose the subscripts in brackets []. For example, the computer can represent the expenditure data as follows:

```
spend[1] is 34.26
spend[2] is 12.00
spend[3] is 14.95
spend[4] is 56.95
spend[5] is 112.00
spend[6] is 2.07
```

We'll still call the number in the brackets a subscript, even though it is not actually written below the main line. On some computers the subscripts in an array are enclosed between a parenthesis-period (. and a period-parenthesis .)

We can use a variable name in place of the number in the subscript. For example, the two statements

```
i := 3 ;
a[i] := 11;
```

will do exactly the same thing as the one statement:

```
a[3] := 11 ;
```

Arrays

We'll call a variable name that stands for more than one value an *array*. Each particular value in the array is called an *element* of the array. If each element of the array can be identified with only one subscript, as is the case with the array *spend,* we call it a *one-dimensional array*. A one-dimensional array is also sometimes called a *list* or *vector*. (We'll later use arrays that have more than one dimension.) Before we use an array in a program, we must tell the computer what type of array it is supposed to be. In the expenditure share program, we must tell the computer that *spend* is supposed to be a one-dimensional array with six elements, numbered from 1 to 6. The declaration section for the array spend looks like this:

```
VAR
    spend : ARRAY [1..6] OF REAL;
```

The expression 1 . . 6 tells the computer that the smallest allowable subscript for *spend* is 1, and the highest allowable subscript is 6. The word REAL is there, of course, to tell the computer that spend is an array consisting of real numbers. Here is the final version of the expenditure share program:

```
PROGRAM expshare (INPUT,OUTPUT);
    {This program reads in the total amount that was spent in each
    of six categories and then calculates the fraction spent in
    each category.}
```

```
VAR
   i : INTEGER;
   total : REAL;
   spend : ARRAY [1..6] OF REAL;
BEGIN
   total := 0;
   FOR i := 1 TO 6 DO
     BEGIN
       WRITELN('Input amount for category ',i);
       READLN(spend[i]);
       total := total + spend[i]
     END;
   FOR i := 1 to 6 DO
     WRITELN('Expenditure share for category ',i,' is: ',
                                        (spend[i]/total):5:3)
END.
```

The output from the program looks like:

```
Input amount for category 1
34.26
Input amount for category 2

12.00
Input amount for category 3
14.95
Input amount for category 4
56.95
Input amount for category 5
112.00
Input amount for category 6
2.07
  Expenditure share for category 1 is: 0.148
  Expenditure share for category 2 is: 0.052
  Expenditure share for category 3 is: 0.064
  Expenditure share for category 4 is: 0.245
  Expenditure share for category 5 is: 0.482
  Expenditure share for category 6 is: 0.009
```

The general form of an array declaration statement for a one-dimensional array is:

arrayname : ARRAY [*lowsub* .. *highsub*] OF *type*

arrayname is the name of the array being declared. *lowsub* is the lowest allowable subscript value. In many cases *lowsub* will be 1. However, there will be some cases where *lowsub* will have the value 0 or some other value. *highsub* is the highest allowable subscript value.

The development of arrays greatly increases our capabilities for handling and processing data. Now we can write a more complicated program to take care of personal finances.

Suppose you have decided that your expenditures can be classified into 30 different categories. Here are some possible categories:

Category 1: Food

Category 2: Fun books

Category 3: Boring books

Category 4: Charity donations, etc.

Every time you spend any money, you should keep track of the amount and the category number on which it was spent. Then you'll have a record that looks like this:

Date	Category	Amount
2/4	5	6.95
2/5	12	.54
2/8	20	56.45

The list will go on for several more pages as you add to your expenses each month.

We can use spend as an array for the amount spent in each category. Since there are 30 categories, spend must contain 30 elements. At the start of the program all the elements of spend must be set to zero. When the program is being run, first we'll type in the category number. Then we'll type in the amount spent in that category. The computer will then add the amount to the appropriate element in the array spend. We have only one problem: How do we tell the computer to stop? We cannot use a FOR loop since we don't know how many items there will be in the list (and since the number of items will probably change next month anyway). If 0 is typed in for the category number, the computer will use that as a signal that it is time to stop and print the output. The full program looks like this:

```
PROGRAM finance (INPUT, OUTPUT);
    {This program reads in a list of expenditure items and their
    categories, and then presents the total for each of the
    30 categories.}
CONST
  numcat = 30; {number of categories}
VAR
  categ : INTEGER;
  amount : REAL;
  spend : ARRAY[1..numcat] OF REAL;
BEGIN
  FOR categ := 1 TO numcat DO spend[categ] := 0;
  REPEAT
    WRITELN('Input category number: ');
    READLN(categ);
    IF categ <> 0
      THEN BEGIN
            WRITELN('Input amount: ');
            READLN(amount);
            spend[categ] := spend[categ] + amount
          END;
  UNTIL categ = 0;
    {Now the output is printed:}
  WRITELN(' Category Amount');
  FOR categ := 1 TO numcat DO
      WRITELN(categ:9, spend[categ]:9:2)
END.
```

Sorting

There will often be times when it will be useful to put the numbers in a list in order. For example, you might like to know which category had the highest spending total, which had the second highest, and so on. Here is a simple program designed to sort the numbers in an array. The method is called the *bubble sort* method. Although it is not the fastest sorting method, the bubble sort method is not difficult to program. The method works like this. First, examine the first two numbers in the list. If they are in order, leave them alone; if not, interchange them. Do the same thing with the second and third numbers, then with the third and fourth numbers, until finally you have reached the last number. At this point you are guaranteed that the largest number in the list has "bubbled" up the list so that it is now the last number in the list. Next, repeat the same procedure for the first $n - 1$ numbers. After doing that, you will be guaranteed that the second largest number will be in the second to last place. Keep repeating the procedure until eventually all the numbers are in order.

Here is a Pascal program to perform a bubble sort:

```
PROGRAM sort (INPUT, OUTPUT);
    {This program reads in a series of numbers and then
    uses a bubble sort to put them in order.}
VAR
  n : INTEGER;
  a : ARRAY[1..500] OF REAL;    {This program assumes that you
                                will sort less than 500 numbers.}

PROCEDURE readin;
    {This procedure reads elements in to the array a.}
VAR
    i : INTEGER;
BEGIN
    WRITELN('Input the number of numbers in the list:');
    READLN(n);
    FOR i := 1 TO n DO
        BEGIN
            WRITELN('Input number ', i);
            READLN(a[i])
        END
END;

PROCEDURE printout;
VAR i : INTEGER;
BEGIN
    FOR i := 1 TO n DO WRITELN(i:6, a[i]:9:2)
END;

PROCEDURE swap(i, j: INTEGER);
    {This procedure swaps a[i] and a[j].}
VAR
    temp : REAL,
BEGIN
    temp := a[j];
    a[j] := a[i];
    a[i] := temp
END;

PROCEDURE bubsort;
VAR
    i, j: INTEGER;
```

```
BEGIN
   FOR i : = 1 TO n DO
      BEGIN
         FOR j : = 1 TO (n − i) DO
            IF a[j] > a[j+1] THEN swap(j,j+1)
      END
END;
BEGIN   {Main program block}
   readin;
   bubsort;
   printout
END.
```

Note that this program has been divided into four procedures. One procedure handles the input and one procedure handles the output. The procedure *swap* will swap two elements in the array *a* when it is called. The procedure *bubsort* performs the actual bubble sort routine. Note that the main block of the program consists only of procedure calls.

Here is a sample output from this program:

```
Input the number of numbers in the list:
12
Input number 1
12.3
Input number 2
33.3
Input number 3
4.5
Input number 4
19.8
Input number 5
76.3
Input number 6
2
Input number 7
33
Input number 8
11.4
Input number 9
9.7
Input number 10
16.33
Input number 11
2.04
Input number 12
9.1
       1        2.00
       2        2.04
       3        4.50
       4        9.10
       5        9.70
       6       11.40
       7       12.30
       8       16.33
       9       19.80
      10       33.00
      11       33.30
      12       76.30
```

Binary Search

There also will be times when we would like to search through a list to see if a particular number is contained in the list. If the list is not in order, then trying to find one particular number would be like trying to find a needle in a haystack. However, if the list has already been put in order, then we can use a fast method called a *binary search*. To execute a binary search, look at the number that is in the exact middle of the list. If the number you're looking for is smaller than the midpoint number, then you know that your number is in the first half of the list. Otherwise it is in the second half of the list. Once you've determined which half of the list your number is in, repeat the procedure to determine which quarter, then which eighth, and so on, until you've finally found the exact position of the number you're looking for.

Here is a Pascal program to perform a binary search:

```
PROGRAM binsearch (INPUT, OUTPUT);
    {This program executes a binary search to determine if a
    number x is contained in the array a.}
VAR
  n : INTEGER;
  x : REAL;
  a : ARRAY[1..500] OF REAL;

PROCEDURE readin;
    {This procedure reads elements in to the array a.}
VAR
  i : INTEGER;
BEGIN
  WRITELN('Input the number of numbers in the list: ');
  READLN(n);
  FOR I : = 1 TO n DO
        BEGIN
            WRITELN('Input number ',i);
            READLN(a[i])
        END
END;

PROCEDURE binsearch;
VAR
  lowbound, upbound, position : INTEGER;
  continue : BOOLEAN;
BEGIN
  lowbound : = 1;
  upbound : = n;
  continue : = TRUE;
  WHILE continue DO
    BEGIN
        position : = (lowbound + upbound) DIV 2;
        IF a[position] = x
            THEN BEGIN
                    WRITELN('In list at position ',position);
                    continue : = false
                END
            ELSE BEGIN
                    IF a[position] > x
                        THEN upbound : = position
                        ELSE lowbound : = position;
                    IF (upbound - lowbound) = 1
```

```
                    THEN BEGIN
                         IF a [upbound] = x
                         THEN WRITELN ('In list at position ',
                         upbound)
                         ELSE IF a [lowbound]=x
                         THEN WRITELN ('In list at posiition ',
                            lowbound)
                          ELSE WRITELN ('Not in list. ');
                          continue : = FALSE
                       END
             END
END   {end of WHILE loop.}
END;

BEGIN {Main program block}
    readin;
REPEAT
    WRITELN ('Type in the number you are looking for: ');
    READLN (x);
    binsearch;
  UNTIL x= -1 {The program stops when you type in -1.}
  END.
```

Note that we can use the same readin procedure that we used before. That is another advantage of breaking your programs up into procedures—often you will find that you can use the same procedure in more than one program. So why should you have to write it again each time?

Here is a sample of the output of this program:

```
Input the number of numbers in the list:
10
Input number 1
16
Input number 2
18
Input number 3
34
Input number 4
41
Input number 5
58
Input number 6
61
Input number 7
62
Input number 8
63
Input number 9
72
Input number 10
76
Type in the number you are looking for:
16
In list at position 1
Type in the number you are looking for:
34
In list at position 3
```

```
Type in the number you are looking for:
63
In list at position 8
Type in the number you are looking for:
33
Not in list.
Type in the number you are looking for:
12
Not in list.
Type in the number you are looking for:
100
Not in list.
Type in the number you are looking for:
-1
Not in list.
```

Basketball Statistics

We can also use the computer to keep track of the statistics for our favorite basketball team. If there are eight players on the team, we can store all their point totals in a one-dimensional array with eight components called scores:

```
VAR
    scores : ARRAY[1..8] OF INTEGER;
```

Then scores[1] will be the point total for player 1, scores[2] will be the point total for player 2, and so forth. However, we don't want to keep track of just points. We also want to keep track of field goals, field goal attempts, free throws, free throw attempts, and rebounds. This will be more difficult, because we can't store all the statistics in one one-dimensional array. We can use eight arrays. We can say that s1 is the array that stores statistics for player 1, s2 stores statistics for player 2, and so forth. That means that the statistics for one game can be represented on the computer as follows:

Statistic:	FG	FGA	FT	FTA	Reb
Player 1:	s1(1)=5	s1(2)=13	s1(3)=4	s1(4)=4	s1(5)=10
Player 2:	s2(1)=5	s2(2)=8	s2(3)=0	s2(4)=1	s2(5)=9
Player 3:	s3(1)=6	s3(2)=10	s3(3)=2	s3(4)=3	s3(5)=11
Player 4:	s4(1)=9	s4(2)=16	s4(3)=5	s4(4)=8	s4(5)=1
Player 5:	s5(1)=8	s5(2)=12	s5(3)=2	s5(4)=2	s5(5)=3
Player 6:	s6(1)=3	s6(2)=4	s6(3)=2	s6(4)=2	s6(5)=1
Player 7:	s7(1)=4	s7(2)=6	s7(3)=0	s7(4)=0	s7(5)=2
Player 8:	s8(1)=3	s8(2)=7	s8(3)=0	s8(4)=0	s8(5)=0

Two-Dimensional Arrays

This method will work, but it will be a bit cumbersome. And if we look closely at the statistics, we will notice an interesting pattern. We can use an array called scores to stand for all the statistics, and then use *two* subscripts to identify the element we need. To do that, we need to declare scores to be a two-dimensional array. The general form for a two-dimensional array declaration is:

```
VAR
    arrayname : ARRAY[m1 .. m2,n1 .. n2] OF type;
```

This command tells the computer to treat *arrayname* as a two-dimensional array. An element in *arrayname* must be identified with two subscripts, The first subscript must be between m1 and m2, and the second subscript must be between n1 and n2.

A two-dimensional array is also called a *matrix* or a *table.* For example, if we define the array scores with this declaration statement:

```
VAR
   scores : ARRAY[1..9,1..8] OF REAL;
```

then we are declaring that scores will be an array with 9 rows and 8 columns. (It is traditional to write the row subscript in a matrix before the column subscript.) The first subscript in our array will identify the player number. (Note that it is very important that you always write the two subscripts in the correct order.) The statistic numbers are defined by this list:

Column 1 : Field goals (FG)

Column 2 : Field goal attempts (FGA)

Column 3 : Free throws (FT)

Column 4 : Free throw attempts (FTA)

Column 5 : Rebounds (Reb)

Column 6 : Field goal percent (FG%)

Column 7 : Free throw percent (FT%)

Column 8 : Total points (Pts)

We will have to type in the statistics in columns 1 to 5. The statistics in columns 6 to 8 will be calculated by the computer.

There are three main parts for the basketball program. First, we must read in the statistics. Second, we will have to perform the calculations for field goal percent, free throw percent, total points, and then calculate the total statistics for the team. Finally, we will have to have the output printed. Each of these three tasks will be written as a separate procedure. Here is the program:

```
PROGRAM team (INPUT, OUTPUT);
    {This program keeps track of the statistics for eight players
    on a basketball team.}
CONST
    numplayers = 8; numrows = 9;
       {The number of rows in the array ''scores'' is equal to one
       more than the number of players to allow for the row
       containing the totals.}
VAR
    scores: ARRAY [1..numrows,1..8] OF REAL;
          {Note that you may use an integer constant in the
          declaration of an array.}

PROCEDURE readin;
    {This procedure reads in field goals, field goal attempts,
    free throws, free throw attempts, and rebounds for the 8
    players.}
VAR
 player,stat : INTEGER;
BEGIN
  FOR player := 1 TO numplayers DO
        BEGIN
```

```
                WRITELN ('Input statistics for player ',player);
                FOR stat := 1 TO 5 DO
                    BEGIN
                        CASE stat OF
                            1 : WRITELN ('FG');
                            2 : WRITELN ('FGA');
                            3 : WRITELN ('FT');
                            4 : WRITELN ('FTA');
                            5 : WRITELN ('REB').
                        END;
                        READLN (scores[player,stat])
                    END
            END
END;

PROCEDURE calculate;
    {This procedure calculates the totals for the team as well as
    field goal percent, free throw percent, and total points.}
VAR
    player, stat : INTEGER;
    total : REAL;
BEGIN
FOR stat := 1 TO 5 DO
    BEGIN
        total := 0;
        FOR player := 1 TO numplayers DO
                total := total + scores[player, stat];
        scores[numrows, stat] := total
    END;
FOR player := 1 TO numrows DO
    BEGIN
        {Field goal percent:}
        IF scores[player, 2] <> 0
          THEN scores[player, 6] :=
            scores[player, 1]/scores[player, 2]
          ELSE scores[player, 6] := 0;
        {Free throw percent:}
        IF scores[player, 4] <> 0
          THEN scores[player, 7] :=
            scores[player, 3]/scores[player, 4]
          ELSE scores[player, 7] := 0;
        {Total points:}
        scores[player, 8] := 2 * scores[player, 1] +
            scores[player, 3]
    END
END;

PROCEDURE printout;
    {This procedure prints the output from
    the basketball program.}
VAR
    player, stat : INTEGER;
BEGIN
    WRITELN('Player    FG FGA FT FTA Reb    FG%    FT%    Pts');
    FOR player := 1 TO numrows DO
        BEGIN
```

```
            IF player < numrows
                 THEN WRITE (player: 7)
                 ELSE WRITE ('Total');
            FOR stat : = 1 TO 5 DO
                 WRITE (TRUNC (scores [player, stat]) : 5);
            WRITE (scores [player, 6] : 7: 3, scores [player, 7] : 7: 3);
            WRITE (TRUNC (scores [player, 8]) : 6);
            WRITELN
        END
   END;

   BEGIN {Main program block}
      readin;
      calculate;
      printout
   END.
```

Following is a sample of the output from this program. (*Note*: This time we will not show the appearance of the screen while you are typing in the numbers.)

Player	FG	FGA	FT	FTA	Reb	FG%	FT%	Pts
1	5	13	4	4	10	0.385	1.000	14
2	5	8	0	1	9	0.625	0.000	10
3	6	10	2	3	11	0.600	0.667	14
4	9	16	5	8	1	0.562	0.625	23
5	8	12	2	2	3	0.667	1.000	18
6	3	4	2	2	1	0.750	1.000	8
7	4	6	0	0	2	0.667	0.000	8
8	3	7	0	0	0	0.429	0.000	6
Total	43	76	15	20	37	0.566	0.750	101

There is one problem with this program. It doesn't print out the player's names! We will see how to do that in Chapter 11.

If you want to record statistics for several games, then you may declare scores to be a three-dimensional array. In that case the first subscript identifies the game number, the second subscript identifies the player number, and the third subscript identifies the statistic number. You may declare arrays to have as many dimensions as you wish (subject to the limitations of your available memory). However, you are likely to find that arrays with one or two dimensions will be the most useful. In any case, you must make sure that you always use exactly as many subscripts as there are dimensions in the array.

Calendar Program

We will look at one more program in this chapter. In complicated practical programs you will frequently have to keep track of dates. For example, the computer may calculate that a particular event occurs on the 194th day of the year. However, before you output that result, you would like to have it converted into the month and day. That will make the result much more understandable. It is a slightly tricky problem to convert a year date (that is, the number of days that have elapsed since the start of the year) into the appropriate month and day. The problem arises because months are not all of the same length. However, by using an array we can accomplish the task:

```
PROGRAM calendar (INPUT, OUTPUT);
    {This program reads in a number from 1 to 365 and then
    determines what month and day correspond to that
    year date. Assume that this year is not a leap year.}
VAR
    yd, month, day: INTEGER;

PROCEDURE date (yeardate: INTEGER);
VAR
    stop : BOOLEAN;
    m : ARRAY [1..13] OF INTEGER;
BEGIN
    m[1]:= 0; m[2]:= 31; m[3]:= 59; m[4]:= 90; m[5]:= 120;
    m[6]:= 151; m[7]:= 181; m[8]:= 212; m[9]:= 243; m[10]:= 273;
    m[11]:= 304; m[12]:= 334; m[13]:= 365;

    month := 0;
    stop := FALSE;
    REPEAT
        month := month + 1;
        IF yeardate < (m[month+1]+1)
            THEN BEGIN
                    day := yeardate − m[month];
                    stop := TRUE
                END
    UNTIL stop
END;

BEGIN {Main program block}
    REPEAT
        WRITELN ('Input year date: ');
        READLN (yd);
        date (yd);
        WRITELN ('Month: ', month, ' Day: ', day);
    UNTIL yd = 0        {The program stops when you type in 0.}
END.
```

Here is a sample output:

```
Input year date:
194
Month: 7 Day: 13
Input year date:
35
Month: 2 Day: 4
Input year date:
1
Month: 1 Day: 1
Input year date:
365
Month: 12 Day: 31
Input year date:
0
Month: 1 Day: 0
```

It would look nicer to have the computer print January instead of Month:1. We will develop a way to have the computer do that in Chapter 11.

Chapter 9 Exercises

1. Write a procedure that reads in a value for *N* and then reads in *N* values for the one-dimensional array *A*. (Assume *N* < 50.)

2. Write a procedure that reads in values for N1 and N2 and then reads in N1 × N2 values for the two-dimensional array B. Read in the first row first, then the second row, and so on. (Assume that N1 < 50 and N2 < 50.)

In all the exercises that follow, assume that the necessary arrays have already been read into the computer.

3. Write a program that checks to see whether a list of numbers is arranged in ascending order.

4. Write a program that prints all the elements of a list *A* in the opposite order from the order in which they are contained in *A*.

5. *H* is a 162-element list consisting of the number of hits by a major league baseball player in each game during the season. Write a program that calculates the longest consecutive string of games during which the player had at least one hit during each game. (If the result is larger than 56, have the computer print: "This player has just broken Joe DiMaggio's record hitting streak.")

6. *N* is a list containing the digits 0, 1, 2, 3, . . . , 9. Write a program that calculates how many times each digit occurs in *N*.

7. *M* is a list of arbitrary numbers. Write a program that prints each number that occurs in *M* and then prints how many times that number occurs in *M*.

8. Write a new version of the date conversion program that works for leap years.

9. Write a program that does the opposite of the program in Exercise 8, that is, it reads in a month-number and day-number and then calculates the year-date for that date.

10. Write a program that reads in the year, month, and date for a day between 1801 and 2099 and then determines the day of the week corresponding to that date.

11. *A* is a list of *n* integers. Write a program that tests to see whether *A* contains every integer from 1 to *n*.

12. Write a program that removes all the zeros from a list of numbers but leaves all the nonzero elements of the list in the same order.

13. Consider an 8 by 6 array *D*. Write a program that prints out all the elements of *D*, with the sum of each row being printed to the right of that row and the sum of each column being printed below that column.

14. *S* is a 20 by 2 array. The first column consists of the score for your team in the big football game each year for the past 20 years. The second column contains the scores for your arch rival each year. Write a program that calculates how many games your team has won, how many games the arch rivals have won, and how many games have been ties.

15. Consider two lists, *A* and *B*, each with *n* elements. Each list is sorted in numerical order. Write a program that merges *A* and *B* into a new array *C* (with 2*n* elements) that contains all the elements from *A* and *B* arranged in numerical order.

16. Write a program that sorts a list of numbers using the merge-sort method. First arrange each pair of numbers in the list in order. Next use the merge technique from Exercise 15 to merge all the pairs of numbers into groups of four. Then merge the groups of four into groups of eight. Keep repeating this process until all the elements have been merged into one sorted list. (Assume that the entire list contains 2^k elements, where k is an integer.)

If necessary, refer to a book on algebra to do Exercises 17 and 18.

*17. Write a program that calculates the matrix product of two 4 by 4 arrays A and B.

*18. Write a program that calculates the inverse of a 4 by 4 matrix A.

19. Write a program that identifies which elements of a list A are turnaround points. [$A(I)$ is a turnaround point if $A(I) > A(I+1)$ and $A(I) > A(I-1)$, or if $A(I) < A(I+1)$ and $A(I) < A(I-1)$.]

20. A and B are two lists. Write a program that calculates how many elements are contained in both array A and array B.

21. Write a program that calculates the total number of elements in either array A or array B. (If an element occurs in both A and B, count it only once.)

CHAPTER 10

Character Variables and User-Defined Types

Character Variables

So far our computer has dealt mostly with numbers. However, there are many
applications of computers that don't involve numbers at all. For example, we might want
our computer to keep track of the names on a mailing list. Before we can do that, we
need to create some new types of data. So far we have discussed the data types REAL,
INTEGER, and BOOLEAN. If you would like the computer to work with letters or other
character data, you need to use variables of type *character* (abbreviated CHAR). The
value of a character variable consists of a single character. Character variables are
declared in the declare section. For example:

```
VAR
    letter, query, digit, blank : CHAR;
```

Now we can use these variables in assignment statements, like this:

```
letter := 'A';
query := 'Y';
digit := '6';
blank := ' ';
```

Note that the value of a character variable can be one of the digits 0 to 9 (but a character variable with the value '6' is quite different from an integer variable with the value 6). Also note that a character variable can have the value ' '—in other words, a blank. Character variables may also take on special values, such as punctuation marks.

Character variables can be used in output statements:

```
WRITELN(letter);
```

will cause the output A in this case.

You cannot tell the computer to perform arithmetic operations on character variables, of course. It makes no sense to try to calculate 'Q' + '?' * '4'. However, you may compare two characters to see if they are equal. For example, the expression letter = 'A' will be TRUE if letter has the value 'A'. Otherwise it will be false. Here is a simple program illustrating the use of the equal sign for characters:

```
PROGRAM stars (INPUT,OUTPUT);
VAR
   query : CHAR;
BEGIN
REPEAT
    WRITELN('*********************');
    WRITELN('Type N to stop. Else type Y.');
    READLN(query);
UNTIL query = 'N'
END.
```

You also may compare two character variables using the > (greater than) or < (less than) signs. If you compare two letters, then the letter that appears earliest in the alphabet is treated as being less than the other letter. For example,

'z' > 'y'   is TRUE

and

'c' > 'd'   is FALSE

If one or both of the characters you are comparing is not a letter, then the computer will make some arbitrary decisions about what order they belong in. For example, does '2' come before 'B'? Does ' ' come before '?' ? The computer will make its decisions according to a predetermined sequence of characters called a *collating sequence*. Different computers have different collating sequences. One of the most common sequences is called the ASCII collating sequence. You will have to check with your computer to see what collating sequence it uses.

As you have probably realized, we cannot use simple character variables to keep track of names (unless your name happens to be only one letter long). In the next chapter we will develop a way to store names. Meanwhile, we will first look at another interesting feature of Pascal. If you're bored with the four data types supplied with Pascal, you may create your very own data types.

Ordinal Types

Up to now we have been using the four data types which are commonly referred to as the scalar types—integer, real, boolean, and character. Before examining how you can define your own data types, it is useful to define a subset of the scalar types. We will refer to the set made up of the integer, boolean, and character types as the ordinal types. The importance of this distinction will become clear in a moment when we discuss four more standard Pascal functions. For now, we will simply say that an ordinal type is a group of values of any given type which are ordered and countable.

In order to perform computations on characters, we have been using the six relational operators available to us. There are, however, four more functions available to perform operations on characters.

PRED('X')   This returns the value of the predecessor of X in a given type.

SUCC('X')   This returns the value of the successor of X in a given type.

ORD('X')   This returns the ordinal position of X in a given type. The first position in a type is the position 0, not 1.

CHR(I)   This will give the character representation of the integer I in a given type.

To illustrate how these functions work, let's look at a data type defined as CHAR and based on the ASCII collating sequence. Examples of the PRED and SUCC functions are:

PRED('C') = 'B'

PRED('Z') = 'Y'

SUCC('A') = 'B'

SUCC('G') = 'H'

Examples of the ORD and CHR functions are:

ORD('A') = 65

ORD('Z') = 90

CHR(67) = 'C'

CHR(80) = 'P'

Keep in mind that these examples are based on the ASCII collating sequence. If the collating sequence on your computer is different, the answers you get may be different.

You may have noticed that the PRED and SUCC functions, as well as the ORD and CHAR functions, are inverse functions—one function will counteract the effects of the other. Because of this fact the following relations hold:

PRED(SUCC('X')) = 'X'

SUCC(PRED('X')) = 'X'

CHR(ORD('X')) = 'X'

ORD(CHR(I)) = I

It is also possible to write equations for the PRED and SUCC functions using ORD and CHR:

PRED('X') = CHR(ORD('X')−1)

SUCC('X') = CHR(ORD('X')+1)

The examples of PRED and SUCC have involved character type data sets. It is also possible to use PRED and SUCC with integer types and boolean types (when using boolean types, keep in mind that TRUE is greater than FALSE). The examples also illustrate why these functions would not work with a data type defined as real. The possible answers for the function PRED(2.1) are infinite. Should the answer be 2.09 or 2.09999? By the same token what would be the value of ORD(1.0)? The ordinal position of 1.0 in the set of numbers from, say, 0.0 to 2.0 would depend on the increments involved in ordering the set. It may be useful if we could define the increments involved using the ORD statement in this way. However, since we cannot do this, there is no point in using the ORD statement with a real data type.

Assume you are writing a program which will keep track of a student's score on a test and the student's grade. Further assume that the score can range from 0 to 100 and that the grade can be in the range of A to F. Using the types we have learned about so far, you would probably do something like this to define the variables:

```
VAR
     score : INTEGER;
     grade : CHAR;
```

What happens if a score of 700 is accidentally typed in? Nothing! The score would be processed with all the other scores. The computer has no way of knowing the highest valid score is 100. Defining grade as we did above poses the same problem—an "M" is just as valid as a grade of "C".

One way to let the computer know what is and isn't valid is to define your own ordinal data types.

User-Defined Types

Before looking specifically at how to write a user-defined ordinal type, let's first look at where the type definitions are placed in the program. Using reserved words to outline a program, we see the following:

```
        PROGRAM heading;

        CONST definitions;

        TYPE definitions;

        VAR declarations;

        PROCEDURE or FUNCTION declarations;

        BEGIN

            statements;

        END.
```

The syntax of the TYPE definitions is as follows:

```
        TYPE

            type-identifier = (constant-identifier, constant-identifier, etc.);
or
            type identifier = lower-limit . . upper-limit;
```

Note that like the constant definition, an equals sign is used without a colon and that a number of type definitions may occur under the single reserved word TYPE.

There are two ways to define an ordinal type: enumeration and subrange definition. Enumeration simply means we list the set of constants which will make up our user-defined ordinal type. Using this method to create a user-defined ordinal type for the valid student grades discussed earlier, we could write:

```
TYPE
   validGrade = (A, B, C, D, E, F);
VAR
   grade : validGrade;
```

We now have an ordinal type which contains the letters A to F and is identified as the type validGrade. We also have the variable grade which belongs to the type validGrade and contains any of the possible letters in the type validGrade. Trying to assign a value to grade which is not in the type validGrade, for example M, will cause a type clash and result in a program error.

There is a shortcut method which will accomplish the same thing without using both TYPE and VAR. By simply writing

```
VAR
   grade :  (A, B, C, D, E, F);
```

we now have the same situation as above—grade can only take on values between A and F. By using this method, however, you have not given a name to the new data type and therefore cannot declare other variables as belonging to that type. Declaring grade in this manner may also not be as meaningful as declaring grade to be of type validGrade.

When using enumeration, it is not legal to have a constant identifier belonging to two data types. For example, the following is illegal since A and E are in two defined types:

```
TYPE
   grade = (A, B, C, D, E, F);
   vowels = (A, E, I, O, U);
```

It is important to keep in mind that when you define a type using enumeration, you not only assign the contents of the type, but you also define the order of the values with respect to each other. In our example of type validGrade, the following relations are true:

$$A < B < C < D < E < F$$

If we define the following type:

```
TYPE
   animals = (lion, frog, dog, eagle)
```

we can use the following functions to get these results:

PRED(dog) = frog

SUCC(lion) = frog.

What is the value of PRED(lion)? The value is undefined since lion is the first value of the type and has no predecessor. Similarly, the value of SUCC(eagle) is undefined since it is the last element in the type and has no successor. Using the ORD function, we have

ORD(lion) = 0

ORD(dog) = 2

Subranges

The second method of defining an ordinal data type is through the use of subranges. For example:

```
TYPE
    midletters = 'J'..'N';
```

The two dots between the lower and upper limits indicate that all values between the two bounds, and including the two bounds, make up that data type.

A subrange data type can be defined using any subsequence of any ordinal types which have been previously defined or are standard Pascal ordinal types. Again using our example of scores and grades, we could define

```
TYPE
    validScore = 1..100;
    validGrade = (A,B,C,D,E,F);
    passingGrade = A..D;
    failingGrade = E..F;
```

The type validScore contains the scores between 1 and 100, and is a subrange of the type integer. It is possible to define a subrange of integer, character, and boolean.

Why is it possible to have types passingGrade and failingGrade when we stated earlier that we could not have the same constant in more than one enumerated type? The reason lies in the way the type is formed. When you use enumeration, you are creating new defined types made up of the constants you include in the type definition. When you use a subrange, however, you are simply giving a type name to a particular segment of a standard type or previously defined type. The types passingGrade and failingGrade are simply named segments of the existing type validGrade.

When using subranges, it is important to make sure that none of the subranges have overlapping elements. The following would be illegal:

```
TYPE
    validGrade = (A,B,C,D,E,F);
    passingGrade = A..D;
    failingGrade = E..F;
    middleGrade = C..E;
```

This is illegal because the type middleGrade overlaps the types passingGrade and failingGrade.

As was the case with enumerated data types, you can use a shortcut method of defining the variable type. The following two methods accomplish the same thing.

```
TYPE
    validGrade = 'A'..'F';
VAR
    grade : validGrade;
```

is the same as;

```
VAR
    grade : 'A'..'F'
```

When setting the limits of the subrange, the lower limit must be less than the upper limit. It is allowable to use constant identifiers to set the limits of the subrange. For example, the following is legal:

```
CONST
    maxValue = 10;
TYPE
    validScores = 1..maxValue;
```

```
VAR
    score : validScores;
```

It is not allowable to use variables, function calls, or expressions to set the limits since this may cause the limits of the subrange to change during the execution of the program.

An important distinction is made in Pascal between types which are identical and types which are compatible. Variables are identical if they are defined by the same type identifiers. For example, the following variables are of identical types:

```
TYPE
    range = 1..10;
VAR
    score : range;
    count : range;
```

The variables score and count are of the identical type.

The next example shows two variables with types which are not identical, but are compatible.

```
TYPE
    alphabet = A..Z;
VAR
    letter : alphabet;
    position : CHAR ;
```

The variables letter and position are compatible. Assigning the value in letter to position will certainly work since the type CHAR contains the letters A to Z. An assignment of the value in position to letter may or may not work depending on the value of position since the CHAR type contains some nonletter values. If position contains a nonletter value and an attempt is made to assign the value to letter, a type clash will result.

This distinction is important since it relates to procedures and functions that you create. A variable-parameter's type must be identical to its argument. If we have procedure printinitial with the following variable-parameter:

```
PROCEDURE printinitial (VAR middleinitial : alphabet);
```

only the variable letter can be passed as an argument since it is of the type alphabet, identical to middleinitial.

A value-parameter's type must be compatible with its argument. In the following example the variable letter and, depending on the value, the variable position may be passed as an argument.

```
PROCEDURE printinitial (middleinitial : alphabet);
```

Earlier we looked at a shortcut method of defining your own ordinal type, and we also mentioned a few reasons for not using the shortcut method. One other reason which relates to procedures and functions is that when you create a variable-parameter, value-parameter, or function, the type must have a name (type identifier). You could not rewrite the procedure printinitial shown above as

```
PROCEDURE printinitial (middleinitial : 'A'..'Z');
```

It is now time to see how a user-defined ordinal type can be used in a program. User-defined ordinal types can be used just as any other ordinal type with one important limitation: The constant values which make up the user-defined ordinal type cannot be used as input or output. You cannot read a constant value with READ or READLN, and you cannot write a constant value with WRITE or WRITELN.

In the following program notice the use of the variable workday which is of type day, a user-defined ordinal type. The user-defined ordinal values Monday through Sunday are used to set the limits of the FOR loop, and also to specify the different cases in the CASE structure.

```
PROGRAM totalhours (INPUT,OUTPUT);
    {This program will keep track of the number of hours worked on
    a particular day.}
TYPE
    day = (Monday, Tuesday, Wednesday, Thursday, Friday, Saturday,
    Sunday);
VAR
    workday : day;
    numberemploy, hoursworked, totalhours, employcount : INTEGER;

PROCEDURE printday (dayvalue : day);
    BEGIN
        CASE workday OF
            Monday : WRITE('Monday');
            Tuesday : WRITE('Tuesday');
            Wednesday : WRITE('Wednesday');
            Thursday : WRITE('Thursday');
            Friday : WRITE('Friday');
            Saturday : WRITE('Saturday');
            Sunday : WRITE('Sunday');
        END
END; {printday procedure}

BEGIN {main program block}
    FOR workday : = Monday TO Sunday
        DO BEGIN
            WRITE('Enter number of employees who worked on ');
            printday (workday);
            WRITELN;
            READLN (numberemploy);
            totalhours : = 0;
            FOR employcount : = 1 TO numberemploy
                DO BEGIN
                    WRITELN('Enter hours by employee ', employcount);
                        READLN (hoursworked);
                        totalhours : = totalhours + hoursworked
                END; {inner loop}
            WRITE('Total hours worked on ');
            printday (workday);
            WRITELN(' ', totalhours)
        END
END.
```

Chapter 10 Exercises

1.   What is the difference between an ORDINAL type and a REAL type?

Given the following type definition, give the value of the following expressions.

```
TYPE
    color = (black, white, orange, red, blue, green, yellow);
```

2.   PRED(white)

3.   SUCC(black)

4.   SUCC(PRED(red))

5. ORD(green)

6. CHR(ORD(blue)+1)

7. What is wrong with the following type definition and declaration?

    ```
    TYPE
       shape = (circle, square, triangle, rectangle);
    VAR
       circle : Boolean;
    ```

8. Which type definitions are illegal?

    ```
    number = 1 .. 10;
    gpa = 0.0 .. 4.0;
    weather = (sun,rain,snow);
    alphabet = 'Z' .. 'A';
    sport = (baseball,basketball,hockey,football);
    ```

9. Is the following legal?

    ```
    VAR
       max,min : INTEGER;
       range : min..max;
    BEGIN
       WRITELN('Enter the minimum value.');
       READLN(min);
       WRITELN('Enter the maximum value.');
       READLN(max);
    ```

10. What is wrong with the following (if anything)?

    ```
    TYPE
       weekday = (Sunday, Monday, Tuesday, Wednesday, Thursday,
                   Friday, Saturday);
    VAR
       day : weekday;
    BEGIN
       WRITELN('Which day of the week do you wish to look at?');
       READLN(day);
    ```

11. Write a program which will print out the days of the week using an array subscripted by a user-defined type. You will need to use another array which will keep track of the user-defined type of days.

CHAPTER 11

Character Strings

Strings

We have discussed how to use character variables. However, single-character variables are seldom of much practical use. So, we need to develop a way to keep track of variables consisting of several characters. A group of characters is called a *string*. For example, 'George Washington', 'Abraham Lincoln', 'abc', 'q' are all character strings. In Pascal, strings are defined as arrays of characters. For example, we can declare *pres1* to be a character string consisting of 17 characters:

```
VAR
    presl : PACKED ARRAY[1..17] OF CHAR;
```

[The term PACKED is included for the benefit of the computer. A packed array is stored in a more compact form than a regular array. The only thing that you need to remember about the word PACKED is that arrays of characters (or booleans) should generally be declared to be PACKED. Other types of arrays generally should not be PACKED.]

After the string *pres1* has been declared, we can use it in an assignment command:

```
presl := 'George Washington';
```

However, note that since pres1 is declared to consist of 17 characters, you must assign to it a string consisting of exactly 17 characters.

Since we will be using strings frequently, it will be useful to declare strings to be a special type. We discussed user-defined types in the previous chapter. Suppose you plan to use strings consisting of 20 characters. Then the type declaration for type string looks like this:

```
TYPE
    string = PACKED ARRAY [1 .. 20] OF CHAR;
```

Or you could define the type like this:

```
CONST
    stringlen = 20;
TYPE
    string = PACKED ARRAY [1 .. stringlen] OF CHAR;
```

The advantage of doing it this way is that you can easily change the constant stringlen if you decide you would like to change the lengths of the strings you use.

We will frequently want to print or display the values of character strings. Fortunately, if *string1* is a string variable, then the command WRITELN(string1); will cause the value of string1 to be displayed. However, here is a procedure that we could write to accomplish the same purpose:

```
PROCEDURE printout (x: STRING);
VAR
    i : INTEGER;
BEGIN
    i := 0;
    REPEAT
        i := i + 1;
        WRITE (x [i]);
    UNTIL i = 20; {Assuming that we are using 20-character strings}
    WRITELN
END;
```

Printing Names

Here is a simple program that assigns some values to some character strings and then prints the values:

```
PROGRAM names (INPUT, OUTPUT);
    {This program illustrates the use of character string arrays.}
TYPE
    string = PACKED ARRAY [1 .. 20] OF CHAR;
VAR
    name1, name2, name3 : STRING;

PROCEDURE printout (x: STRING);
VAR
    i : INTEGER;
BEGIN
    i := 0;
    REPEAT
        i := i + 1;
        WRITE (x [i]);
    UNTIL i = 20;
    WRITELN
END;

BEGIN {Main program block.}
    name1 := 'Kermit              ';
    name2 := 'Miss Piggy          ';
    name3 := 'Statler and Waldorf ';
```

```
      printout(name1);
      printout(name2);
      printout(name3)
   END.
```

The output is:

```
Kermit
Miss Piggy
Statler and Waldorf
```

Arrays of Strings

In most practical computer problems involving names, the computer will need to keep track of many different names. It would be far too cumbersome to assign a string variable name to each different name. What we'll do, of course, is use arrays of strings. Once we have defined the type string, we can create arrays of that type. For example:

```
VAR
   namelist : ARRAY[1..50] OF STRING;
```

In Chapter 9, we wrote a program that read in a number from 1 to 365 and then calculated the month and day corresponding to that year date. However, that program only told us the number of the month. It would be much nicer to see the name of the month printed out. We will create a 20-element string array called mlist. mlist[1] will be 'January ', mlist[2] will be 'February ', and so on. Here is the new version of the program:

```
PROGRAM calendar (INPUT, OUTPUT);
   {This program reads in a number from 1 to 365 and then
    determines what month and day correspond to that year date.}
TYPE
   string = PACKED ARRAY[1..9] OF CHAR;
VAR
   mlist : ARRAY [1..12] OF string;
VAR
   yd, month, day: INTEGER;

PROCEDURE date(yeardate: INTEGER);
VAR
   stop : BOOLEAN;
   m : ARRAY[1..13] OF INTEGER;
BEGIN
   m[1]:=0; m[2]:=31; m[3]:=59; m[4]:=90; m[5]:=120; m[6]:=151;
   m[7]:=181; m[8]:=212; m[9]:=243; m[10]:=273; m[11]:=304;
   m[12]:=334; m[13]:=365;

   month : = 0;
   stop : = FALSE;
   REPEAT
     month : = month + 1;
     IF yeardate < (m[month+1]+1)
          THEN BEGIN
                    day : = yeardate – m[month];
                    stop : = TRUE
               END
   UNTIL stop
END;

BEGIN {Main program block}
   mlist[1]: = 'January '; mlist[2]: = 'February ';
   mlist[3]: = 'March         ';
```

```
        mlist[4]:= 'April    '; mlist[5]:= 'May       '; mlist[6]:= 'June      ';
        mlist[7]:= 'July    '; mlist[8]:= 'August   '; mlist[9]:= 'September ';
        mlist[10]:= 'October '; mlist[11]:= 'November '; mlist[12]:=
          'December ';
        REPEAT
          WRITELIN('Input year date: ');
          READLN(yd);
          date(yd);
          WRITELN(mlist[month],day:3);
        UNTIL yd = 0   {The program stops when you type in 0.}
      END.
```

Here is a sample output:

```
Input year date:
1
January 1
Input year date:
31
January 31
Input year date:
359
December 25
Input year date:
284
October 11
```

We will also need a procedure to read in string variables. We will use the input command READ to read in the string one character at a time. We will keep reading characters until we come to the end of the line—in other words, until the RETURN key is pressed. Pascal comes equipped with a special boolean function called EOLN, which stands for "end of line." Normally, EOLN is FALSE. However, when you reach the end of the line, EOLN suddenly becomes TRUE. Therefore, we will use a REPEAT/UNTIL loop until EOLN becomes true. However, suppose that the computer is looking for a string of length 20, but the user only types in 11 characters before hitting the return key. In cases like that we will add blanks to fill the remaining characters in the string. Here is the readin procedure:

```
      PROCEDURE readin (VAR x: string);
      VAR
        i,j: INTEGER;
        c: CHAR;
      BEGIN
        i := 1;
        REPEAT
          READ(c);
          x[i] := c;
          i := i + 1;
        UNTIL EOLN; {Keep going until the end of the line.}
        FOR j:= i TO stringlen DO x[j] := ' '
      END;
```

Note the form of the procedure heading:

```
      PROCEDURE readin (VAR x : string);
```

The word VAR means that *x* is a variable-parameter, rather than a value-parameter. (See Chapter 8 if you would like to review the difference between these two types of parameters.) This means that the statement readin(q) will cause the procedure readin to be executed. At the end of the procedure, the value of the dummy parameter *x* will be assigned to the string variable *q*.

Here is a program that reads in a list of names and then prints them out:

```
PROGRAM names (INPUT, OUTPUT);
    {This program reads in a list of names and then
    prints them out.}
CONST
    stringlen = 20;
TYPE
    string = PACKED ARRAY[1..stringlen] OF CHAR;
VAR
  n : INTEGER;
  namelist : ARRAY[1..100] OF string;
PROCEDURE readin (VAR x : string);
VAR
  i,j: INTEGER;
  c: CHAR;
BEGIN
  i := 1;
  REPEAT
    READ(c);
    x[i] := c;
    i := i + 1;
  UNTIL EOLN; {Keep going until the end of the line.}
  FOR j:= i TO stringlen DO x[j] := ' '
END;

PROCEDURE namein;
VAR
  j : INTEGER;
  q : string;
BEGIN
  WRITELN('Type in the number of names: ');
  READLN(n);
  FOR j := 1 TO n DO
    BEGIN
      readin(q);
      namelist[j] := q
    END
END;

PROCEDURE printout (x: STRING);
VAR
  i : INTEGER;
BEGIN

  i := 0;
  REPEAT
    i := i + 1;
    WRITE(x[i]);
  UNTIL i = stringlen;
  WRITELN
END;

PROCEDURE nameout;
VAR
  j : INTEGER;
```

```
BEGIN
  FOR j := 1 TO n DO
    printout(namelist[j])
END;

BEGIN  {Main program block.}
  namein;
  WRITELN('******');
  nameout
END.
```

Here is a sample of the output:

```
Type in the number of names:
6
Kermit
Fozzie
Piggy
Statler
Waldorf
Scooter
******
Kermit
Fozzie
Piggy
Statler
Waldorf
Scooter
```

Alphabetizing

In a practical problem, it would help a lot to be able to put the names in alphabetical order. We can write a program that reads in a list of names and then prints them out in alphabetical order. In Chapter 9 we used a bubble sort procedure to sort a group of numbers. We can follow a similar procedure to put the names in order. We will write a function called *inorder* that determines whether or not two strings are in alphabetical order. The result will be a boolean value. If the two strings are in order, then the result will be TRUE; otherwise it will be FALSE. If the result is FALSE, then we know that the bubble sort procedure requires us to swap the two character strings. We can write a procedure swap to perform that function.

Here is the program:

```
PROGRAM alphbet (INPUT, OUTPUT);
    {This program reads in a list of names and then
    alphabetizes them.}
CONST
    stringlen=20;
TYPE
    string = PACKED ARRAY[1..stringlen] OF CHAR;
VAR
    n : INTEGER;
    namelist : ARRAY[1..100] OF string;

PROCEDURE readin (VAR x: string);
VAR
    i,j: INTEGER;
    c: CHAR;
```

```
        BEGIN
          i : = 1;
          REPEAT
            READ(c);
            x[i] : = c;
            i : = i + 1;
          UNTIL EOLN;
          FOR j : = i TO stringlen DO x[j] : = ' '
        END;

        PROCEDURE namein;
        VAR
          j : INTEGER;
          q : string;
        BEGIN
          WRITELN('Type in the number of names: ');
          READLN(n);
          FOR j : = 1 TO n DO
            BEGIN
              readin(q);
              namelist[j] : = q
            END
        END;

        PROCEDURE printout (x: STRING);
        VAR
          i : INTEGER:
        BEGIN
          i : = 0;
          REPEAT
            i : = i + 1;
            WRITE(x[i]);
          UNTIL i = stringlen;
          WRITELN
        END;

        PROCEDURE nameout;
        VAR
          j : INTEGER;

        BEGIN
          FOR j : = 1 TO n DO
            printout(namelist[j])
        END;

        FUNCTION inorder (a,b : string) : BOOLEAN;
            {inorder is a function with two arguments of type string.
            The result is of type boolean. If string a comes before
            string b in alphabetical order, or if the two strings are the
            same, then the result is TRUE; otherwise it is FALSE.}
        VAR
          i : INTEGER;
          result, continue : BOOLEAN;
        BEGIN
          result : = TRUE;
          continue : = TRUE;
          i : = 1;
          WHILE continue DO
```

```
            BEGIN
                IF a[i] > b[i]
                    THEN BEGIN
                            result := FALSE;
                            continue := FALSE
                         END
                    ELSE IF a[i] < b[i]
                            THEN continue := FALSE
                            ELSE i := i + 1;
                IF i = stringlen THEN continue := FALSE
            END;
        inorder := result
    END;

    PROCEDURE swap (i,j: INTEGER);
        {This procedure swaps namelist[i]
        and namelist[j].}
    VAR
        temp : string;
    BEGIN
        temp := namelist[j];
        namelist[j] := namelist[i];
        namelist[i] := temp
    END;

    PROCEDURE bubsort;
    VAR
        i, j: INTEGER;
    BEGIN
        FOR i := 1 TO n DO
            BEGIN
                FOR j :=1 TO (n - i) DO
                    IF NOT inorder(namelist[j],namelist[j+1])
                            THEN swap(j, j+1)
            END
    END;

    BEGIN  {Main program block}
        namein;
        bubsort;
        WRITELN('******');
        nameout
    END.
```

Here is a sample of this program:

```
Washington
Adams
Jefferson
Madison
Monroe
Adams
Jackson
Van Buren
Harrison
Tyler
Polk
Taylor
```

```
Fillmore
Pierce
Buchanan
Lincoln
Johnson
Grant
Hayes
Garfield
Arthur
Cleveland
Harrison
McKinley
Roosevelt
Harding
Coolidge
Hoover
Roosevelt
Truman
Eisenhower
Kennedy
Johnson
Nixon
Ford
Carter
Reagan
******
Adams
Adams
Arthur
Buchanan
Carter
Cleveland
Coolidge
Eisenhower
Fillmore
Ford
Garfield
Grant
Harding
Harrison
Harrison
Hayes
Hoover
Jackson
Jefferson
Johnson
Johnson
Kennedy
Lincoln
Madison
McKinley
Monroe
Nixon
Pierce
Polk
```

```
Reagan
Roosevelt
Roosevelt
Taft
Taylor
Truman
Tyler
Van Buren
Washington
Wilson
```

By now we have covered most of the important features of Pascal. (We have yet to cover sets, records, and files, which we will discuss in Chapter 14.) However, just because we have learned a programming language does not mean that we're finished with the subject of computer programming.

We still have a difficult lesson to learn. All the programs that we have done up to now have been reasonably simple. They have been so simple, in fact, that we have been able to keep track of everything that the computer has done. But we will soon come to programs that are so long that they're too confusing for us to remember how they work or even what they do. If we make the slightest mistake in such a program, it might take hours to find the error.

We have learned the Pascal programming language, but we have yet to learn the essence of programming. We have yet to learn a strategic way to develop an *algorithm* to solve a particular problem.

Note to Chapter 11

■ The readin procedure listed in the chapter will run into problems if someone types in a character string that is longer than 20 characters. You may wish to add an extra test to the program so that it will stop reading characters when it reaches 20.

Chapter II Exercises

1. Write a program that creates a character string variable consisting of 30 stars, without having to type all 30 stars into the program.

2. Write a program that reads in a character string and then prints "YES" if the string contains the character A and prints "NO" otherwise.

3. Write a program that reads in a number and then prints out the number with commas inserted between every three digits. For example, if the program is given 164329186, it will print out 164,329,186.

4. Write a program that reads in a letter and then prints out 1 if the letter is A, 2 if it is B, 3 if it is C, and so on.

5. Write a conversational exam question program. Have one character string array containing questions and another character string array containing the correct answers. The program should display the question and then read in the person's answer. If the answer is not correct, the person should be given one more try. If the second try is incorrect, the computer should print the correct answer along with an appropriate message. After all the questions have been asked, the computer should tell how many were answered correctly on the first try, how many were answered correctly on the second try, and how many were not answered correctly.

6. Write a simple word processing program. The program should store a page of text as a one-dimensional array of strings. (Each string should be one line of the page.) When you start the program, it should ask you to type in a code

indicating which action you'd like to take. The possible actions should be
1. Adding a new line to the page
2. Deleting a line
3. Inserting a new line between two existing lines
4. Retyping an entire line
5. Retyping a specified part of a line
6. Stopping the program
After the computer has finished one command, it should go back to the beginning and ask you what it should do next. (If you actually use a word processor, you will not write your own word processing program. Instead, you will use a program that has already been written and comes with the word processing package.)

7. Write a program that reads in a paragraph of text and then prints a list of all words that occur in the paragraph, with each word followed by a number telling how many times it occurs. (*Hint:* See Chapter 9, Exercise 7.)

8. Write a program that does the same thing as Exercise 7, except that it prints out the words in alphabetical order.

9. Write a Fake Personalized Form Letter program. The program should read in some relevant information, such as the name of the person to whom you are sending the letter, the age, school, or hobbies of the person, and the address of the person. Then have the program print out a letter that sounds as if it is a personal letter because it inserts personal information in the middle of the letter.

CHAPTER 12

Programming Strategy

Examples of Algorithms

"What's an algorithm?" An algorithm is a set of instructions that specify exactly how to solve a particular problem in a finite number of steps. For example, here is an algorithm to determine the denomination of the largest bill you currently have in your wallet.

1. Take the first bill out of your wallet and hold it in your hand.

2. Look at the next bill in your wallet.

3. If the next bill in your wallet is greater than the bill in your hand, put the bill in your hand down and put the next bill in your hand.

4. Otherwise, take the next bill out of your wallet and put it down.

5. If there are any more bills in your wallet, go back to step 2.

6. The denomination of the bill in your hand is now the highest denomination you had in your wallet.

An algorithm can be expressed in many different languages such as English or French. In order for a computer to execute an algorithm, however, it needs to be translated into a computer programming language such as Pascal. Thus there are two distinct jobs involved in writing a computer program: the problem-solving part, which involves developing the algorithm, and the coding part, which involves writing that algorithm in a computer language.

Imagine that we have just been given a very complicated computer programming problem. How do we go about solving it? In this chapter we'll develop some general rules that can be helpful in developing algorithms for computers to solve. The first rule follows:

STRATEGY RULE 1
As far as possible, try to write the program so that people can understand it.

Write Programs People Understand

A computer program needs to be understood by two quite different types of creatures—computers and people. The computer will be able to understand the program just fine if the program is boring, if it contains no comments, and if it has variable names that have no particular meanings. The computer doesn't care whether the variable you use to represent height has the name height or Q7. The computer will be satisfied with any method that works, even if it is very difficult to know why the method works.

However, there are several reasons why an effort should be made to write programs that are understandable by people. The process of writing the program will be much easier if you try to understand what you're doing while you're doing it. It will be much easier to make changes in a program or correct errors in it if the program is written so as to be people-oriented. And other people will be able to adapt your program if you specify very clearly what is going on.

The rest of the rules include suggestions for how to write programs that people understand.

STRATEGY RULE 2
Break a major problem into smaller problems and, if necessary, break the smaller problems into still smaller problems.

Break Problems into Bite-Sized Pieces

If you face a very large unmanageable problem, there is no general way to tackle it. However, if you break the problem down into bite-sized pieces, it becomes much easier to handle. The final program then becomes a group of modules, that is, separate parts with different purposes that fit together. This type of approach to programming is sometimes called the *top-down* approach because you start at the top and look at the whole problem first before you look at the details. While you're working at the top level, you decide exactly what each part is supposed to do, but you don't have to worry about how the subparts work until later. Each subpart is small enough that it is possible for you to understand how it works.

Here is a non–computer programming example of the top-down approach, which illustrates Strategy Rule 2. Suppose you need to plan a driving trip across the country from New York to Los Angeles. The wrong way to plan the trip would be first to pull out the street map of New York and figure out what streets you need to drive on to get out of New York. It would be even worse to pull out a map of Kansas City and plan your route through that city since you won't even know for sure whether you'll go through

Kansas City. What you should do first is look at a map of the entire United States and then figure out what your general course will be without worrying about the specific details. Then you should make a list of all the states you will go through and look at maps of those states. Finally, after you know what road you will be on when you go into a city and what road you will be on when you leave it, you can look at a detailed street map for that city to plot your course through it.

Pascal does have another annoying feature. When writing a program, you should write the most general part (the main program block) first. Then write the more general procedures. Finally, write the most detailed nitty-gritty procedures. However, in a Pascal program, the procedures must be included before the main program block. Even worse, some Pascal compilers require you to put the detailed procedures first, because a procedure must be defined before it can be called by another procedure. However, just because the Pascal compiler wants the program parts to appear in this order does not mean that you should write them in this order.

STRATEGY RULE 3
Whenever possible, a variable name should give some indication of what that variable represents.

Make Variable Names Meaningful

A mnemonic device is a way to help us remember something, so we can say that a variable name should be a mnemonic variable name.

For example, if you need to calculate the height of something, the variable representing height should probably be named height.

STRATEGY RULE 4
Use a comment to explain in English what each important Pascal statement does.

Include Comments

The beginning of a program should contain a comment that explains what the program itself does. (You may also like to include your name and the date that the program was written in a comment.) A comment should contain some useful information and not just repeat what is obvious by looking at the program.

STRATEGY RULE 5
The appearance of the program listing is important.

Make the Program Look Good

A program will be easier to read if it looks neat. Statements should be indented so that BEGINs are aligned with their corresponding ENDs. You will notice that the programs in this book follow a consistent indentation pattern which you may decide to follow for your own programs. It is especially important to make sure that the major sections of a program are clearly separated. This can be done by inserting blank lines. Or you may like to insert rows of asterisks enclosed by { }. Working on the appearance of the program listing can often be a nice break from the rigors of actual programming.

STRATEGY RULE 6
Spend time to make the program output look nice.

Make the Output Look Good

Make sure that everything is labeled with explanatory messages, and arrange lists of numbers in neat rows and columns. Decide on the correct number of decimal places that need to be displayed for each numerical result, and make sure that each number is rounded off by the appropriate amount. The effort spent on maintaining neat program output will be well worth it.

However, it is important not to spend time worrying about how the output will look while you're working on the main problem. The development of the main program algorithm requires a lot of creative thinking, whereas writing the section of the program that directs the computer to print the output is a tedious and often boring task. You shouldn't let the creative algorithm development task be interrupted by worrying about petty details such as whether to use WRITELIN(x:7:3) or WRITELN(x:6:3). Develop the main part of the program first. Then, after you've rested up from the arduous creative task, spend some time to get the output format right.

STRATEGY RULE 7
Whenever possible, be as general as you can.

Be General

This rule means that it is a good idea to use variable names or defined constants instead of numbers as much as possible in the middle of a program. For example, suppose you need to find the average of seven numbers. You can use this program segment:

```
total : = 0;
FOR i : = 1 TO 7 DO
  BEGIN
    READLIN(x);
    total : = total + x
  END;
average : = total/7;
```

Suppose that some other day you want to find the average of eight numbers. It would have been much easier if you had originally written this program segment:

```
num : = 7;
total : = 0;
FOR i : = 1 TO num DO
  BEGIN
    READLN(x);
    total : = total + x
  END;
average : = total/num;
```

Now, to make the program work for eight numbers, all you need to do is change the first line to num := 8. If you expect a lot of variation in the number of items you will need to average, it would be a good idea to change the first line to READLN(num);

For another example, suppose you wrote a program in 1977 to calculate the average per-game statistics for National Football League (NFL) teams. The wrong way to do it would have been to fill your program with statements such as average := total/14. These statements would have worked if the NFL schedule had always stayed 14 games long. But if you wanted to run the program in 1978, you would have found that the NFL schedule now contained 16 games for each team, so you would have had to go through the entire program and change each 14 to a 16. It would have been much better to make the constant definition numgames = 14 at the beginning of the program. Then you would only need to change that one line and the program would work just fine for a 16-game season.

Is It Right?

After you have followed all these procedures, there still remains one nagging problem: How do you know that the program you have written is correct? In other words, how do you know that the program does what you want it to?

With a simple program you should be able to tell just by looking at it whether it is correct. The task is more difficult with complicated programs. The easiest way is to check the output of the program to see whether the program gave the correct answer. Of course, this is often impossible since if you had known the correct answer in advance, you wouldn't have needed to write the program. However, there are some cases where you can tell just by looking whether the output is correct. For example, if you write a program to sort a list of numbers, you can scan through the output list to make sure that the numbers really have been put in the correct order. There will also be cases in which the program answer is obviously wrong, for example, if the program prints a negative result for a variable that you know must be positive. In those cases you know that you have to go back to the program to make changes.

There will be other programs for which you won't know in general what the correct answer will be, but you will know what the answers will be for some values of the input data. Then you can test the program by running those data through the program.

STRATEGY RULE 8
Before a program is used in normal operation, it should be checked using test data, that is, data for which the correct results have already been determined.

Test the Program

It will be necessary to run several tests of a program to see if it really works since it is possible that the program might give the correct answer for some values just by accident. The test data used should be varied enough so that several of the possible conditional paths through the program are followed.

Now we come to an even more difficult problem. What if you test run the program and find that, horror of horrors, it doesn't work? Then what? That means that the program is infested with an error or, as computer people say, it has a bug. (There is a slight possibility that an error might be caused by hardware failure, that is, the computer failing to execute correctly the instructions it has been given. However, such errors are relatively rare on most computers.)

Getting the Bugs Out

The process of correcting a program to remove bugs is called debugging. If you have thought carefully about the program before running it, then it should not take too long to debug. However, sometimes debugging can be one of the longest and most frustrating parts of programming.

There are several different types of bugs for which to be on the lookout. The first type of errors are typographical errors or simple syntax errors. Examples of these include mismatched parentheses or misspelled key words. They can occur because you were careless in translating your program idea into Pascal or because you hit the wrong key on the typewriter. These types of errors are the easiest to correct since the computer will usually print an informative message to tell you what kind of error has occurred. Then you just have to examine the statement with the error carefully and rewrite it. One helpful technique in examining complicated expressions is to draw lines connecting each opening parenthesis with its closing parenthesis. For example:

$$Y: = B*SQRT(1 - (((X + E * A)/A)**2));$$

This procedure allows you to make sure that the parentheses match up correctly and that the operations will be executed in the order that you intend.

Remember that the Pascal program is first sent to a special program called the Pascal compiler. It is the job of the Pascal compiler to translate the Pascal program into a form that the computer can understand. If you make a syntax error, the compiler will notice the error and print a message to you. There are other types of errors that the compiler will catch. For example, the compiler will make sure that each BEGIN statement has a corresponding END statement. Don't panic if you see many error messages because sometimes the computer will print several error messages that result from only one error. For example, if you make an error in a declaration statement, the computer will print an error message whenever it comes to a statement that refers to the variable that was incorrectly declared. You can make all those error messages go away merely by correcting the declaration statement.

Even if the syntax of the program is entirely correct, there are other types of errors that the computer might uncover. For example, suppose the computer is running the program and it comes across the instruction a := 1/b, where b has the value 0. Since the computer cannot divide by 0, it will have to print an error message. This type of error is called an execution time error. An execution time error can also occur if the result of a calculation is a number too big for the computer to handle (this is called an overflow error) or if an array subscript is used that is not permissible for that array.

There are several possible reasons for these types of errors. They could be the result of a simple mistake; for example, you might have typed 1/b when you meant 1/v. Or they could result because the computer is being asked to calculate a special case for which the formula you are using doesn't work. For example, a simple program using the quadratic formula will not work if a = 0, even if the program will work fine in all other cases. When this situation arises, you will need to add some modification to your program to take care of the special case. In the case of an overflow error it is also possible that the problem you are attempting is simply beyond the capability of the computer; for example, the computer cannot calculate 100,000 factorial.

Computer error messages can be very annoying. However, all the preceding types of errors are easier to correct than a program logic error. With the preceding types of errors the computer will give you some clue as to what kind of error has been made and where it occurred. However, suppose the computer generates no error messages at all and happily prints results. You need to check the program using test data, but suppose you do that and find that the program gives the wrong results for the test data?

Here are two possible ways to locate program logic errors. The first is to have the computer display the changes in a particular variable; the second is to execute the program by hand yourself. To display the changes in a variable, insert several auxiliary

WRITELN statements in strategic locations in the middle of the program. For example, if your program has the statement

```
x1 : = x2 * cos (L) + y2 * SIN (L) ;
```

you can insert the statement

```
WRITELN ('x1 = ', x1, ' x2 = ', x2, ' y2 = ', y2, ' L = ', L) ;
```

before and after the statement we are interested in. Then you can check to make sure that the values of the variables change in the way you want them to. This method often allows you to catch errors since you can pinpoint which variables are not taking on the values they're supposed to. After you've corrected all the errors and the program is ready to run, you can remove all the auxiliary WRITELN statements.

You might ask: How do I know what the correct values of the variables are? You will have to do some calculations on your own. It will help to have the description of each variable available, and often the process of writing that description can help with debugging the program.

The first method—checking the values of key variables at strategic points in the program—is the best way to detect the errors if you have a hunch about what variables are ending up with wrong values or if you think you can localize an error to a specific region of the program. But if you have no idea about where the error is, you may have to use the second method: the hand-check method. Take a piece of paper, a small calculator, and a printed listing of your program. Then, starting at the top, pretend that you are the computer and do everything that the program tells you to do. Everytime you come to an assignment statement, calculate the new value for that variable and write it down. Eventually you will find the error. The hand-check method will probably work, but it is very tedious since it requires you to do all the work that you wanted the computer to do for you.

One advantage of the hand-check method is that you will quickly catch an error that arises when a variable is given the wrong initial value. Many program errors result because of a failure to properly initialize variables.

Now we're ready. The next five chapters will contain some examples of long programs. All these programs are much more complicated than the ones we have looked at up to now. Writing complicated programs requires a lot of careful thought. To make things more interesting, we'll discuss some programs that play games as well as those programs that perform applications from several different fields.

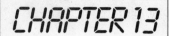

Special Techniques: Recursion and Backtracking

Calculating Roommate Possibilities

Let's suppose that we are on a trip with a group of 12 friends. The 12 people need to be split up into groups of 2 roommates to spend the night. Let's calculate the total number of possible ways of breaking the group into roommates. We will write a Pascal program that solves the general problem: How many ways are there of dividing n people into groups of 2?

If n is not an even number, then it is impossible to divide the group evenly into pairs. If n is 2, then clearly there is only one possibility. If n is 4, then there are three possibilities. If we label the people A, B, C, and D, here are the possibilities:

possibility 1: AB, CD

possibility 2: AC, BD

possibility 3: AD, BC

We'll make up a function called Roommate, such that Roommate(n) is the number of ways of dividing a group of n people into roommates. We have seen that Roommate(2) = 1 and Roommate(4) = 3. Now, let's consider Roommate(n). There are

$n - 1$ choices for the first person's roommate. After the first person's roommate has been chosen, $n - 2$ people are left. They can be divided into roommates in Roommate($n - 2$) ways. Therefore:

$$\text{Roommate}(n) = (n - 1) * \text{Roommate}(n - 2)$$

Recursion

There is something very strange about that definition. Notice that the function Roommate is used in its own definition. This type of function definition is an example of *recursion*. Ordinarily if you use the object you're defining in its own definition, you end up with an infinite circular loop. However, we avoid that problem because we give a straightforward (nonrecursive) definition for Roommate(2).

In Pascal, a recursive function is a function that calls itself. Any use of recursion must include some part that is not recursive to avoid the infinite loop problem. Here is an example of a Pascal program to calculate the number of roommate combinations:

```
PROGRAM rmte (INPUT, OUTPUT);
    {This program reads in the number of people in
    a group and then calculates the number of
    possible ways of dividing that group into
    roommates with two people in each room.
    The program uses recursion.}
VAR
 number : INTEGER;

FUNCTION roommate (n: INTEGER) : INTEGER;
 VAR
  result : INTEGER;
 BEGIN
  IF (n MOD 2) <> 0
    THEN result : = 0

    ELSE IF n = 2 THEN result : = 1
                 ELSE result : = (n-1)*roommate(n-2);
                           {Here is the recursion.}
  roommate : =result
 END;



 BEGIN {Main program block}
 REPEAT
  WRITELN('Type in the number of people.');
  READLN(number);
  WRITELN('There are ',roommate(number),' possible roommate
    combinations.');
 UNTIL(number MOD 2) <> 0
     {The program stops when you type in a number that
     is not divisible by 2.}
 END.
```

If $n = 2$, then the roommate function uses the straightforward statement result := 1. However, if n is greater than 2, then the function uses recursion.

Here is a sample of the output:

```
Type in the number of people.
2
There are 1 possible roommate combinations.
Type in the number of people.
4
There are 3 possible roommate combinations.
Type in the number of people.
6
There are 15 possible roommate combinations.
Type in the number of people.
8
There are 105 possible roommate combinations.
Type in the number of people.
10
There are 945 possible roommate combinations.
Type in the number of people.
12
There are 10395 possible roommate combinations.
```

This particular program will not work if the number is larger than 12 because the integer values become too large for Pascal to handle.

Recursion can be a very powerful programming tool, but it can be difficult to write recursive programs that work correctly. For one thing, you must make sure that all variables affected by a recursive function are local to that function. Recursive programs can take up a lot of memory because the computer needs to keep track of each level of the recursion. Also, make sure that you check with your local compiler. Some versions of Pascal require that a special signal be included if the program uses recursion.

The roommate problem was relatively simple, and it would have been easier to write a program that did not use recursion. In general, recursion is useful when the solution to a problem is expressed in terms of simpler versions of the solution to the same problem. We will discuss a mathematical problem where recursion is very valuable.

A square arrangement of numbers is called a *matrix*. Here are some examples:

$$2 \times 2 \text{ matrix: } \begin{pmatrix} 10 & 11 \\ -6 & 3.5 \end{pmatrix} \qquad 3 \text{ by } 3 \text{ matrix: } \begin{pmatrix} 7.5 & 2.4 & 3 \\ 2 & 0 & 6 \\ 11 & 9 & -4 \end{pmatrix}$$

$$4 \times 4 \text{ matrix: } \begin{pmatrix} 1 & 20 & 30 & 50 \\ -2 & -7 & -8 & 5 \\ 6 & 0 & 11 & 14 \\ 0 & -2 & 1 & 1 \end{pmatrix}$$

Determinants

Each number in a matrix is called an *element* of the matrix.

It is frequently important in math to calculate a quantity called the *determinant* of a matrix. If you have a matrix with 2 rows and 2 columns, then the definition of the determinant is quite simple:

$$\det \begin{pmatrix} a & b \\ c & d \end{pmatrix} = \begin{vmatrix} a & b \\ c & d \end{vmatrix} = ad - bc$$

Note that the determinant of a matrix is symbolized by writing the matrix inside two vertical lines.

Here is how to calculate the determinant of a 3 by 3 matrix (3 rows and 3 columns). The *minor* of the element in row i and column j is the matrix formed by crossing out all the elements in row i and column j. For example, the minor of the element 16 in the 3 by 3 matrix:

$$\begin{pmatrix} 12 & 16 & 18 \\ 23 & 27 & 29 \\ 2 & 7 & 6 \end{pmatrix}$$

is the 2 by 2 matrix:

$$\begin{pmatrix} 23 & 29 \\ 2 & 6 \end{pmatrix}$$

To calculate the determinant of a matrix, start with the first element in the first row. Multiply that element by the determinant of its minor. Then subtract the product of the second element in the first row multiplied by the determinant of its minor. Then, add the product of the third element and its minor. The formula for the determinant of a 3 by 3 matrix looks like this:

$$\begin{vmatrix} a_1 & a_2 & a_3 \\ b_1 & b_2 & b_3 \\ c_1 & c_2 & c_3 \end{vmatrix} = a_1 \begin{vmatrix} b_2 & b_3 \\ c_2 & c_3 \end{vmatrix} - a_2 \begin{vmatrix} b_1 & b_3 \\ c_1 & c_3 \end{vmatrix} + a_3 \begin{vmatrix} b_1 & b_2 \\ c_1 & c_2 \end{vmatrix}$$

$$= a_1(b_2 c_3 - b_3 c_2) - a_2 (b_1 c_3 - b_3 c_1) + a_3 (b_1 c_2 - b_2 c_1)$$

Therefore, to calculate a 3 by 3 determinant, you need to calculate three 2 by 2 determinants. The same method will work for a determinant of any size. Move along the first row and calculate the product of each element and the determinant of its minor. Then alternately add or subtract these results. (See a book on algebra for details.) However, you can see the problem: To calculate a 4 by 4 determinant, you will need to calculate four 3 by 3 determinants. To calculate a 5 by 5 determinant, you will need to calculate five 4 by 4 determinants. This sounds like a job for recursion. Here is a Pascal program that calculates the determinant of a matrix:

```
PROGRAM detm (INPUT, OUTPUT);
    {This program uses recursion to calculate the determinant of a
    matrix.}
TYPE
    table = ARRAY[1..10,1..10] OF REAL;
VAR
    num,query : INTEGER;
    a : table;
PROCEDURE matin;
    {This is the matrix input procedure.}
VAR
    i,j : INTEGER; x : REAL;
BEGIN
    WRITELN('Type in the number of rows in the matrix: ');
    READLN(num);
    FOR i := 1 TO num DO
        BEGIN
            WRITELN('Input elements in row ',i);
            FOR j := 1 TO num DO
                BEGIN
                    WRITELN(j,':');
```

```
                    READ(x);
                    a[i,j] := x
                END
        END
END;

FUNCTION dtm (n: INTEGER; arr: table) : REAL;
    {This is the routine that actually calculates the
    determinant.}
VAR
    m, k: INTEGER;
    total, sign, coeff, determ: REAL;
    b : table;
{********************    nested procedure }

PROCEDURE minor;
VAR
    i, j, j2 : INTEGER;
    {This procedure calculates the minor of a matrix element.}
BEGIN
    FOR i := 1 TO (n−1) DO
        BEGIN
            j2 := 0;
            FOR j := 1 TO n DO
                BEGIN
                    IF j<>k
                        THEN BEGIN
                                j2 := j2 + 1;
                                b[i,j2] := arr[(i+1),j]
                            END
                END
        END
END;
{************* end of nested procedure}

  {Start of main block for procedure ''dtm.''}
  BEGIN
    IF n > 2
        THEN BEGIN
                m := n − 1;
                total := 0;
                sign := 1;
                FOR k := 1 TO n DO
                    BEGIN
                        minor;
                        coeff := arr[1,k];

                        determ := dtm(m,b); {Here is the recursion.}
                        total := total + sign * coeff * determ;
                        sign := 0 − sign
                    END;
                dtm := total
            END
        ELSE dtm := (arr[1,1] * arr[2,2]) − (arr[2,1] * arr[1,2])
END;
```

```
{Here is the main program block}
BEGIN
query : = 1;
REPEAT
   matin; {Input the matrix.}
   WRITELN('Determinant: ', dtm(num, a) : 7: 4);
   WRITELN('Type 1 to repeat. '); READLN(query);
UNTIL query <> 1
END.
```

The function detm calculates the determinant. If you are trying to calculate the determinant of a 2 by 2 matrix, then the function uses the formula:

$$dtm : = arr[1, 1] * arr[2, 2] - arr[2, 1] * arr[1, 2]$$

However, if the size of the determinant is larger than 2 by 2, then the function uses recursion.

Jump Game

Now we will look at another special programming method that can sometimes help with difficult problems. We will play a game. We have placed 32 pegs on a board containing 33 holes, arranged as shown in Figure 13-1.

FIGURE 13-1

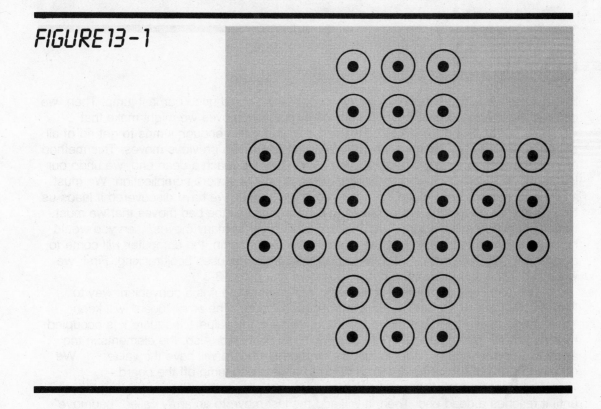

Our goal is to get rid of all the pegs except one. We do this by jumping over pegs. One peg is allowed to jump over another peg provided that the square it is jumping to is open. The peg that has been jumped over is removed from the board. (No diagonal jumps are allowed.)

Suppose we start playing the game for a while. Let's say we end up in a situation where we have four pegs left, but no more possible jumps. (See Figure 13-2.)

FIGURE 13-2

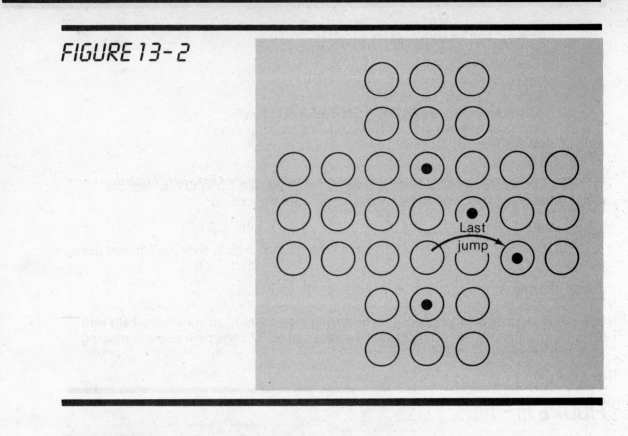

Last jump

Backtracking

In that case we lost the game. However, suppose we could undo our last jump. Then, we could look around to see if there are any other possible moves we might make that would be better. Suppose we still don't find a way to make enough jumps to get rid of all the pegs except one. Then we would have to undo our two previous moves. This method of problem solving is called *backtracking.* Whenever we reach a dead end, we undo our last move and look at other possibilities. There is only one more complication: We must make sure that we don't make the same move again once we have discovered it leads us to a dead end. Therefore, we will need to keep track of all the bad moves that we must remember not to make again. If you have to backtrack for many moves, then you would have trouble keeping track of all the possibilities. Once again, the computer will come to our rescue. We will write a program to play this game that uses backtracking. First, we will number the squares on the board as shown in Figure 13-3.

(This particular numbering scheme is chosen because it is a convenient way to keep track of which squares you might possibly jump to.) The array "board" will keep track of the positions on the board. board[k] will have the value 1 if square k is occupied by a peg. It will have the value 0 if square k is not occupied. Also, the elements in the array that correspond to squares that are outside the board will have the value −1. We do this to prevent the computer from trying to have a peg jump off the board.

The array "movelist" keeps track of moves. The computer will keep making moves until it reaches a dead end. Then, it will add the last move to an array called "badmove" and then backtrack by undoing that move. Eventually it will finally reach the situation where there is only one more peg left.

Here is the program:

```
PROGRAM jumpgame (INPUT, OUTPUT);
VAR
    movelist: ARRAY[1..31,1..2] OF INTEGER;
    badmove: ARRAY[1..31,1..30,1..2] OF INTEGER;
```

```
bmovect: ARRAY[1..31] OF INTEGER;
board: ARRAY[11..99] OF INTEGER;
store: ARRAY[1..33,1..2] OF INTEGER;
index: ARRAY[11..99] OF INTEGER;
adlist: ARRAY[1..4] OF INTEGER;
k,k1,k2,oldk,oldk1,oldk2,movenum,bmove,
           goal : INTEGER;
continue : BOOLEAN;
```

FIGURE 13-3

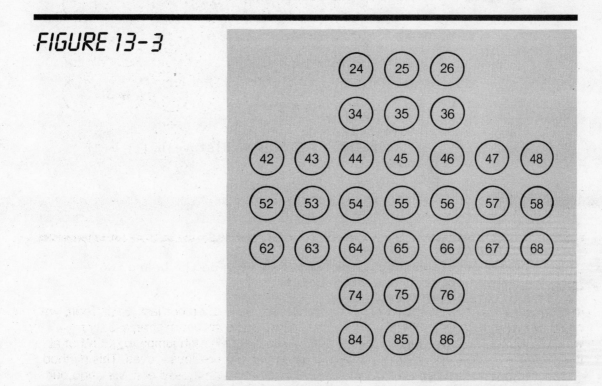

```
PROCEDURE initialize;
   {This procedure sets up the board.}
VAR h,i,j,k: INTEGER;
BEGIN
  FOR i:= 1 TO 9 DO
    BEGIN
      FOR j:=1 TO 9 DO
         BEGIN
            k:= 10*i + j;
            board[k]:= -1
         END
    END;
  FOR i:= 2 TO 8 DO
    BEGIN
      FOR j:= 4 TO 6 DO
         BEGIN
            k:= 10*i + j;
            board[k]:= 1
         END
    END;
```

```
        FOR i: = 4 TO 6 DO
            BEGIN
                FOR j: = 2 TO 8 DO
                    BEGIN
                        k: = 10*i + j;
                        board[k] : = 1
                    END
            END;
        board[55] : = 0; {This is the center square.}

        h : = 0;
        FOR k: = 11 to 99 DO
            BEGIN
                IF board[k] = 1
                    THEN BEGIN
                            h : = h + 1;
                            store[h, 1] : = k;
                            store[h, 2] : = 1;
                                {store[h, 2] is 1 if board[store[h, 1]] is 1}
                            index[k] : = h
                        END
            END;
        FOR i : = 1 TO 31 DO bmovect[i] : = 0
    END;

    FUNCTION count : INTEGER;
        {This function counts the number of pegs on the board. Note
        that it does not use any parameters.}
    VAR h, total : INTEGER;
    BEGIN
        total : = 0;
        FOR h : = 1 TO 33 DO
                total : = total + store[h, 2];
        count : = total
        {store[h, 2] is 1 if there is a peg on the square represented by
        board[store[h, 1]]. Otherwise it is 0.}
    END;

    FUNCTION testmove: BOOLEAN;
        {This function returns the value TRUE if it finds a legal move
            that is not on the badmove list.
        Otherwise it returns the value FALSE.}
    VAR
        a, m, h, square1, square2, i5: INTEGER;
        findmove, nomove: BOOLEAN;
    BEGIN
        h : = 1;
        findmove : = FALSE;
        nomove : = FALSE;
    REPEAT
            IF store[h, 2] = 1
                THEN BEGIN
                        k : = store[h, 1];
                        m : = 1;
                        WHILE ((NOT findmove) AND (m < 5)) DO
                            BEGIN
                                a : = adlist[m];
```

```
                    k1 := k + a;
                    k2 := k + 2*a;
                        {We are testing to see if we can jump from
                        square k to square k2, thereby removing the peg
                        on square k1.}
                IF (board[k1]=1) AND (board[k2] = 0)
                    THEN BEGIN
                            findmove := TRUE;
                            {We have found an allowable move, but we
                                must check to see if this move is listed in
                                the badmove list.}
                            For i5 := 1 TO bmovect[movenum] DO
                            BEGIN
                                square1 := badmove[movenum, i5, 1];
                                square2 := badmove[movenum, i5, 2];
                                IF (k = square1) AND (k2 = square2)
                                    THEN findmove := FALSE
                            END
                        END;
                    m := m + 1
                    END {while loop}
                END;
            h := h + 1;
            IF h > 33 THEN nomove := TRUE;
        UNTIL (nomove OR findmove);
        testmove := findmove
    END;

PROCEDURE jump;
BEGIN
{k is square we're jumping from
k2 is square we're jumping to
k1 is square we're jumping over}

    board[k] := 0;      store[index[k], 2] := 0;
    board[k1] := 0;     store[index[k1], 2] := 0;
    board[k2] := 1;     store[index[k2], 2] := 1
END;

PROCEDURE undo;
BEGIN
    board[oldk]:= 1;    store[index[oldk], 2] := 1;
    board[oldk1]:=1;    store[index[oldk1], 2] := 1;
    board[oldk2]:=0;    store[index[oldk2], 2] := 0
END;

PROCEDURE printout;
VAR i: INTEGER;
BEGIN
    FOR i := 1 TO 31 DO
        WRITELN ('Move: ', i, ': Jump from',
                movelist[i, 1], ' to ', movelist[i, 2])
END;

BEGIN      {Main program block}
    adlist[1] := 10;    adlist[2] := -1;
    adlist[3] := 1;     adlist[4] := -10;
```

```
WRITELN('Goal: ');
READLN(goal);
initialize;
movenum : = 0;
continue : = TRUE;
WHILE continue DO
   BEGIN
      IF testmove
         THEN BEGIN
                 movenum : = movenum + 1;
                 movelist[movenum, 1] : = k;
                 movelist[movenum, 2] : = k2;
                 jump;
                 oldk : = k;
                 oldk1 : = k1;
                 oldk2 : = k2
              END
         ELSE BEGIN
                 IF count <= goal
                    THEN BEGIN
                            WRITELN ('******We won!!!!');
                            printout;
                            continue : = FALSE
                         END
                    ELSE BEGIN
                            undo;
                            bmovect[movenum] : =0;
                            movelist[movenum, 1] : =0;
                            movelist[movenum, 2] : =0;
                            movenum : = movenum - 1;
                            bmove : = bmovect[movenum] +1;
                            bmovect[movenum] : =bmove;
                            badmove[movenum, bmove, 1] : =oldk;
                            badmove[movenum, bmove, 2] : =oldk2;
                            oldk : = movelist[movenum, 1];
                            oldk2 : = movelist[movenum, 2];
                            oldk1 : = (oldk+oldk2) DIV 2
                         END
              END
   END
END.
```

We will not spoil the surprise by including the output here. (Run the program yourself.) It will take a while for the computer to find the winning strategy. The computer will first ask you for your goal. You have your choice as to whether you will be satisfied with five, four, three, or two pegs left. Or you could decide to go all the way and wait for the computer to find the strategy that only leaves one peg left.

Chapter 13 Exercises

1. Write a program that calculates *n*! (*n* factorial) using recursion.

2. Write a program that calculates the nth number in Fibonacci's sequence:

   1 1 2 3 5 8 13 21 34 · · ·

Note that each number is the sum of the preceding two numbers. Use recursion.

3. Write a program using recursion that calculates the sum of n terms in the geometric series $a + ar + ar^2 + ar^3 + ar^4 + \cdots + ar^{n-1}$

*4. Write a program that solves a system of n linear simultaneous equations using Cramer's Rule. See a book on algebra.

*5. Write a program that calculates a way to place eight queens on a chess board in such a position that no queen can capture any other queen. Use backtracking.

CHAPTER 14

Sets and Records

Sets

In the next two chapters we will look at three more structured data types that can be used in Pascal. We have already examined and used the simple data types (the standard Pascal types and user-defined ordinal types) along with one of the structured data types available (arrays). Pascal provides for three more structured data types: sets, records, and files.

Let's go back to Chapter 10 briefly and look at our user-defined ordinal type relating to student grades. In that chapter we defined a set of valid grades (A through F) and a subrange called passing grades (A through D). In order to check whether or not a variable is a passing grade, we could try to assign a value to the variable of type passing grade. As long as the grade is a passing grade, everything is fine. If, however the grade is not a passing grade, a program error caused by a type clash will be the result. If this happens several times, it could become a nuisance. An easier way to do this would be to compare the value we want to check to the allowable values in the type passing grade. If the grade is not valid, we could simply write an error message or perform some other action which does not require rerunning the program. In Pascal we can use *sets* to do this type of thing.

A set is simply a collection of members of the same ordinal type. The type of the members is the *base type*. The general syntax for sets is

TYPE

    identifier = SET OF *base type*;

As usual the shortcut method can be used by using the reserved words SET OF in the variable declaration. The base type may take the form of an identifier of a previously defined ordinal type, a standard Pascal type (subject to a restriction we will discuss shortly), a constant list (enumeration), or a subrange. Types which are structured (arrays, records, files, and sets, for example) are not allowed as base types. The base type may take one of the following forms:

> type identifier
>
> (constant,constant, . . . ,constant)
> constant . . constant

The following are examples of legal set types:

```
TYPE
    fruit = (apple, blueberry, pumpkin, cherry);
    pie = SET OF fruit;
    pet = SET OF (dog, cat, bird, fish);
    letter = SET OF 'A'..'Z';
    symbol = SET OF CHAR;
VAR
    dessert: pie;
    animal: pet;
    firstinit, lastinit: letter;
    byte: symbol;
```

In these examples pie, pet, letter, and symbol are set types. The set variables are dessert, animal, firstinit, lastinit, and byte. The number of members in a set is referred to as the *cardinality* of the set. The maximum cardinality of a set is determined by your local computer. The maximum cardinality will usually be in the range of 64 to 256. This limit will affect your choice of base types for a set. Why could you never use INTEGER as a base type? Because the INTEGER type will always exceed the maximum cardinality. A user-defined type will in most cases be less than the maximum cardinality.

In our previous example the set-structured variables dessert, animal, firstinit, lastinit, and byte do not yet represent any values. They do have the potential of representing any, or all, values of their set types. In order to give values to the variables, we must assign members to the set-structured variables. We do this by assigning a set-valued expression to a set-structured variable. Notice that the assignment is made to the set-structured variable and not to the set type which is defined. We will therefore make assignments to dessert, and not pie, in our previous example. Individual members of a set are enclosed in square brackets [   ] when used in set-valued expressions. The exception to this is when we use an identifier of a set-structured variable (of an identical type) to make the assignment. In this case the square brackets are not used. When the square brackets are used, you may supply a constant list or a subrange to list the members. You may also use an expression to represent the member of a set. If we want our set to initially contain no members, we can assign an empty set to the variable. The empty set is represented by a set of square brackets with nothing in between [   ].

Using our previous example, we could make the following assignments:

```
dessert := [apple..cherry];
animal := [dog];
firstinit := ['C'];
lastinit := firstinit;
byte := [   ];
```

One last point about members of sets: When you assign the members, you simply give values to the variables. You do not give an order to the members. Members of a set are unordered.

Set Operators

We have just seen how you can create a set using square brackets to assign individual members. We can also create sets by performing operations on sets using standard Pascal set operators. The operations we can perform on sets are *union, difference,* and *intersection.* To see how these work, let's first make the following definitions:

```
TYPE
   letter = 'A'..'Z';
   symbol = SET OF letter;
VAR
   firstset,secondset,newset: symbol;
```

The union of two sets will create a set using the members of both sets. If there is a member in both sets, it will be used only once. To show a union of two sets, we use the addition sign (+). If we define the following sets:

```
firstset := ['A','G','M','V'];
secondset := ['B','G','N'];
newset := [ ]; {Notice how we define this since it
              is initially undefined.}
```

we can create a new set by finding the union of firstset and secondset. We would write the expression as

```
newset := firstset + secondset;
```

The contents of newset will now be 'A','B','G','M','N','V'.

The difference of two sets creates a set which contains members of the first set which are not in the second set. To take the difference of two sets, we use the subtraction sign (−). Looking at our previously defined sets, if we use the expression

```
newset := firstset − secondset
```

the contents of newset will be 'A','M','V'. Using the expression

```
newset := secondset − firstset;
```

the members of newset will now be 'B','N'.

Creating a set which is the intersection of two sets will yield a set containing the members which are common to both of the original sets. A multiplication sign (∗) is used to show an intersection operation. Again using our previously defined sets, the set resulting from the operation:

```
newset := firstset ∗ secondset;
```

will contain the member 'G'.

Up to now we have used identifiers of set-structured variables in our set expressions. We could have just as easily used the bracket notation to show individual members. The following examples would have been perfectly legal:

newset := ['D','F'] + firstset;

   (newset will contain 'A','D','F','G','M','V')

newset := ['H','Y'] − secondset;

   (newset will contain 'H','Y')

newset := ['K','U','W'] ∗ secondset;

   (newset will be the empty set since there are no
   common members)

We can form boolean set expressions by using the standard relational operators, plus an additional Pascal set operator (IN).

To test for set equality, we simply use the equal sign, for example,

firstset = secondset is false.

However,

secondset = ['N','B','G'] is true.

(Remember sets are unordered.)

To test for set inequality, we use the <> sign. Examples are:

firstset <> secondset is true.

['A','C'] <> ['C','A'] is false.

To see whether or not a set contains another set, we use the sign >=. To find out if set A contains set B, we would write

set A >= set B;

This expression is true if set A contains set B.

We can use the <= sign to find out if a set is contained in another set. The expression

set A <= set B

would be true if set A is contained in set B.

Pascal provides a special function. IN, which will test the set membership of a particular value. The syntax is

expression IN *identifier of set variable;*

where the expression is any expression that returns a value. If the value is in the set, the function is true. If we assign the value 'D' to a new variable called letter, we can use any of the following expressions to see if it is contained in firstset:

```
'D' IN firstset;
'D' IN['A','G','M','V'];
letter IN firstset;
letter IN['A','G','M','V'];
```

Records

Pascal allows another structured data type called a *record.* You may think of a record as being analogous to the information contained in a business file. Looking at a school's filing system, the information relating to a particular student makes up that student's record. When creating a file of student records, there is going to be information which would have to be known for each student (for example, name, birthdate, student number, address). One way of handling this would be to declare a separate variable for each student name, each student's student number, etc. Doing this, we would end up with something like:

```
VAR
    studentname1: string;
    studentname2: string;
    studentnum1: INTEGER;
    studentnum2: INTEGER;
```

As you can see, this is a very cumbersome method. Not only does this require a lot of storage, but whenever we add a new student we need to declare more variables.

A more efficient, and certainly easier, way to handle this would be to define a general format for the record made up of name, birthdate, number, and address, which can be used for all students. Whenever a new student is added, you just need to make assignments to the related variables for each student.

This is the idea behind records. You can define a general format of the variables involved, which are called the *fields* of the record, and then use the general format (the record) when needed. The general syntax for defining a record is as follows:

TYPE

   identifer=

   RECORD

      field identifier : type;

      field identifier, field identifier : type

   END;

As with other structured types you may use the shortcut method of defining the record when you declare the variables. The list of field identifiers is referred to as the *field list*. The types used for each field can be any standard Pascal type, any user-defined ordinal type previously defined, or any subrange. You can not give a list of constants (enumeration) for the field type. The types may also be simple or structured; therefore it is possible for a record to be used as a field type. The following are examples of legal fields:

```
passed : Boolean
grade : 'A'..'F' {subrange of char}
studentnum : INTEGER;
studentyear : status; {status is an identifier of a user-
                       defined type}
studentschedule : classrecord; {a previously defined
                                record}
gpa : REAL;
```
The following would be illegal:

```
passinggrade : (A,B,C,D)
```

Note that the END statement is used to end the field list. Leaving this off will provide you with several unwelcome results.

Looking at our student record, we could now define the following:

```
TYPE
   string = PACKED ARRAY[1..20] OF CHAR;
   name =
      RECORD
         firstname, lastname : string;
         middleintl : 'A'..'Z'
      END;
   studentinfo =
   RECORD
      studentname : name;
      address : string;
      studentnum : INTEGER;
      gpa : REAL
   END;
VAR
   studentrec : studentinfo;
```

We now have the record studentrec which is of type studentinfo. The student's name is of record type name which is made up of the student's first name, last name, and middle initial. The student's address is of type string, the student number is of type INTEGER, and the student's grade point average is of type REAL.

The scope of each field in a record is restricted to that record. Looking at our example the variable firstname is restricted to the record type name. What this means is that if we create another record, we can assign the identifier firstname to one of its fields. Any assignments made to the field firstname in our new record will not affect the value of firstname in our original name record. We can do this because each record is given its own name list; so an identifier needs to be unique only within its record. To avoid confusion, however, it is a good idea to use a field identifier only once in a program.

Each field in a record can be thought of as a variable. The operations that can be done on a field are those that are compatible with the field type. When you use a variable of record type in a function or procedure, it can be passed as either a value-parameter or a variable-parameter.

The only operation that can be done on the record as a whole is an assignment. You can assign the values of one record variable to another record variable if they are of identical types. If we had defined the following record variables:

```
VAR
    freshman, soph, junior, senior : studentinfo
```

we could transfer the contents of a freshman's record to a sophomore record at the end of the year with the simple assignment

```
soph : = freshman
```

There are two methods of accessing individual fields of a record. The first method is very simple—you simply list the record name and field you wish to access separated by a period. For example, if we wish to access the student's grade point average, we would refer to it as:

```
studentrec. gpa : = 3. 2
```

which means get the field gpa from studrec and assign it the value 3.2. If we wanted to get a student's last name, we would have to write:

```
studentrec. studentname. lastname
```

We now have two records: studentrec and studentname. The field lastname is in the record studentname which itself is in the record studentrec. Why didn't we use name instead of studentname? The reason is because studentname is the record variable identifier; name is the identifier of the record type. This is also why studentrec and not studentinfo is used.

The WITH Statement

If we have several records or access the fields often, we can see how this type of notation can become quite tedious. For this reason Pascal provides a second access method: the WITH statement. The syntax of the WITH statement is:

WITH *record identifier*

DO *statements*

Like the period notation we use the record variable identifier and not the identifier of the record type. Unlike the period notation we need to specify the record variable identifier only once. Any field identifiers used in the statements following the WITH will be associated with the record specified. Looking again at our student record, we could use the WITH to make the following assignments to studentrec:

```
WITH studentrec
DO BEGIN
   gpa := 3.2;
   studentnum := 83246;
   studentname.firstname = 'CHRISTOPHER
END;
```

Notice that we can use the period notation within the WITH. Here we use it to assign CHRISTOPHER to the firstname field of the record studentname. If we had to make several assignments to a record contained with the original record, we could use the tedious period notation again or we could nest a series of WITH statements. To make the assignments to firstname and lastname, we could use:

```
WITH studentrec
   DO WITH studentname
      DO BEGIN
         firstname:='CHRISTOPHER
         lastname:='SMITH
      END
   END;
```

A shortcut method of writing this is:

```
WITH studentrec, studentname
   DO BEGIN
      firstname:='CHRISTOPHER
      lastname:='SMITH
   END
```

The last record named acts as the innermost record when we nest WITH statements as we did above. How do we know where to find firstname? The fields listed are local to the last record named that it is contained in. firstname and lastname will be interpreted as being local to studentname, and studentname will be interpreted as being local to studentrec. To make assignments to studentrec using nested WITH statements, we could write:

```
WITH studentrec, studentname
   DO BEGIN
      gpa := 3.2;
      studentnum := 64215;
      firstname := 'CHRISTOPHER
      lastname := 'SMITH
   END
```

What happens to gpa and studentnum since they are not fields in studentname? They will be assigned to studentrec as we wanted since that is the last named record to which they belong.

Nested WITH statements are not restricted to two records. We can use several records if we wish although it may become confusing. To keep things clear, simply remember that when looking at the scope of nested records, the innermost record variable's field identifiers take precedence. If we have the following nested WITH:

```
WITH record1, record2, record3
   DO
      field1 := some value
```

in which field1 is contained in all three records, the assignment will be made to record3.field1 since record3 is the last record named.

Record Variants

So far we have seen records with field lists that were fixed—each record had the same field. Since there may be times when you want the fields to change, Pascal allows *record variants*. This means that a record may have a varying field list with varying types.

Let's look again at a student record. This time, however, we want to keep the following information for each student: student year (senior,junior,sophomore,freshman) and grade point average for all students. For seniors we will also want to know what quarter the student is expected to graduate (fall,winter,spring,summer) and if the student is expected to graduate with honors. For juniors we will want to know if the student has applied for graduation. Using records with fixed fields, we would have the following record:

```
TYPE
    quarter=(fall,winter,spring,summer);
    status=(senior,junior,sophomore,freshman);
        RECORD
          studentinfo =
              studentyr:status;
              gpa: REAL;
              gradqtr:quarter;
              honors,gradapp:BOOLEAN
        END;
    VAR
        studentrec:studentinfo;
```

The problem in defining the record like this is that not all fields are needed for each student. If the student is a sophomore or freshman, we have three unnecessary fields. By using record variants, we can solve this problem. The general syntax of record variants is:

```
TYPE

    identifier =

      RECORD

        CASE tagfield: type OF

            tagvalue: (variant field : type);

            tagvalue: (variant field : type);

            tagvalue,tagvalue : (variant field, variant field : type);

      END;
```

Notice that the record variant structure uses the reserved word CASE. Unlike the CASE structure we're familiar with, the END does not end the record variant part. The END which ends the record structure also ends the record variant part. The tag values of the tagfield determine the variant fields associated with that record variant. If we have a tag value with no associated variant fields, we can show this with a set of parentheses with no field list (). To separate the variant fields and the associated type, we use a semicolon. Using record variants to rewrite our student record, we have the following:

```
TYPE
    quarter = (fall,winter,spring,summer);
    status = (senior,junior,sophomore,freshman);
    studentinfo =
```

```
RECORD
    CASE studentyr: status OF
        senior: (gpa1:REAL; gradqtr:quarter; honors:BOOLEAN);
        junior: (gpa2:REAL; gradapp:BOOLEAN);
        sophomore,freshman: (gpa3:REAL)
    END;
VAR
    studentrec:studentinfo;
```

We now have a record which will take on different variant fields depending on the value of studentyr. In order to avoid confusion, a variant identifier can be used only once within a record variant. This is why we have to use gpa1, gpa2, and gpa3 for the gpa fields.

Until we define the value of studentyr (the tag field), the remainder of the record variant structure is undefined. Before we make an assignment to any of the variant fields, we must first make the assignment to the tagfield. Looking at our student record, if we make the following assignment:

```
studentrec.studentyr := senior
```

we have now created the variant fields gpa1, gradqtr, honors. If we try to make an assignment to a variant field not associated with senior, we will get an error since the other variant fields don't exist. If we change the value of studentyr, we create a new set of variant fields. Notice that when making the assignment to the tagfield, we must use the period notation since the tagfield is still a part of the record.

To make the record structure more flexible, Pascal allows us to create a record which contains a fixed part and a record variant part. The fixed part of the record *must* come before the record variant part, and we are limited to *one* record variant structure in a record. We can, however, nest record variants. Creating a record with a fixed part and a record variant now gives us the following syntax:

TYPE

  identifier =

  RECORD

Fixed   ⎰ *field identifier*: *type*;
field list   ⎱ *field identifier*, *field identifier*: *type*;

Tag field   CASE *tag field*: *type* OF

             ⎧ *tag value*:(*variant field*: *type*; *variant field*: *type*);
Variant   ⎪ *tag value*, *tag value*:(*variant field*: *type*);
field list   ⎨ *tag value*:(*variant field*: *type*);
             ⎩ *tag value*:()

  END;

A student record with a fixed and variant part may look like this:

```
TYPE
    quarter=(fall,winter,spring,summer);
    status=(senior,junior,sophomore,freshman);
    string=PACKED ARRAY[1..20] OF CHAR;
    name=
    RECORD
        firstname,lastname: string;
        middleinit:'A'..'Z'
    END;
```

```
studentinfo=
  RECORD
    studentname: name;
    address: string;
    studentnum: INTEGER;
    CASE studentyr: status OF
        senior: (gpal:REAL; gradqtr:quarter;
         honors:BOOLEAN) ;
        junior: (gpa2:REAL; gradapp:BOOLEAN);
        sophomore,freshman: (gpa3:REAL)
    END;
VAR
   studentrec:studentinfo;
```

In Chapter 17 we will see how records may be used in data processing programs.

Chapter 14 Exercises

Given the following definitions, evaluate the set expressions in Exercises 1 to 10.

```
vowels : SET OF (A, E, I, O, U) ;
first : SET OF (A, B, C, D, E, F, G) ;
last : SET OF (V, W, X, Y, Z) ;
letters : SET OF (A, C, F)
```

1. vowels + first

2. first − vowels

3. vowels * last

4. vowels * first

5. last − first

6. letters + vowels

7. letters >= first

8. first >= letters

9. vowels <= letters

10. (vowels * letters) IN first

11. Given the following definitions, list all the possible sets that alpha can represent.

    ```
    TYPE
       letter = SET OF (A, C, F)
    VAR
       alpha : letter
    ```

12. What is wrong with the following?

    ```
    TYPE
       range = SET OF 1..10;
    VAR
       legalnum : range;
    BEGIN
       WRITELN('Enter a number from 1 to 10. ');
       READLN(number) ;
       IF number NOT IN legalnum THEN
       WRITELN('Incorrect entry') ;
    ```

13. Use sets to write a program which will convert army time to civilian time. In army time the hours following 12:00 noon do not start out at 1:00 but instead go from 13:00 to 24:00 (1:00 P.M. is 13:00).

14. Write a record format for *A* which will keep track of the following information for each book in a bookstore:

    ISBN NUMBER (INTEGER)

    TITLE

    AUTHOR

    PRICE

    PUBLISHER

15. Modify the above record format to allow for variant fields according to the following guidelines. For all books the title, author, and price are needed. For hardback books the ISBN number and publisher are needed. For paperback books the publisher and publication date are needed.

16. What is wrong with the following portion of this program?

```
TYPE
   string = PACKED ARRAY [1..20] OF CHAR;
   name =
      RECORD
         firstname, lastname : string;
         middleinit : CHAR;
VAR
   studentname : name;
BEGIN
```

17. Given the following record definitions:

```
TYPE
   date =
      RECORD
         month, day, year : INTEGER
      END;
   bookinfo =
      RECORD
         isbn : INTEGER;
         pubndate : date;
         price : REAL
      END;
VAR
   bookrec : bookinfo;
```

    make the following assignments first using the period notation and then the WITH statement.

    month = 03

    day = 10

    year = 84

    isbn = 0140378963

    price = 15.95

CHAPTER 15

Files

Files

The file is the basic module of information in Pascal. In fact we have been using two standard Pascal files throughout this book: INPUT and OUTPUT. In an interactive environment the program will take the input from the standard INPUT file, usually the keyboard. The output goes to the standard OUTPUT file, usually the screen or a printer.

A file is made up of elements which are of the same type or structure. In general, computers can access elements of a file in two different ways. The first way is by random, or direct, access. Using this method, we can access elements in any order we choose. The second method of access is sequential access. Using this method to get to a particular element, we must first access all preceding elements. We can think of disk as a random access storage medium and tape as a sequential access medium. Pascal uses sequential access when processing a file. The Pascal file is also dynamic, meaning that the length of the file may change during the program.

The syntax for declaring a file is:

TYPE

    identifier = FILE OF *element type identifiers*

VAR

    filename : *identifier*

or

VAR

filename : FILE OF *element type identifiers*

The element-type identifiers may be of any type, standard or user-defined. However, it is generally illegal to declare a file of type file.

An important distinction is made between external files and internal files. An external file (or permanent file) is a file that is external to the program, while an internal file is one which is created and used within the program but not stored once the program is finished. External and internal files are identical except for the requirement that external files must be passed as a file parameter in the program heading. For example, if we had a file of student names, called names, stored on disk that we wished to use in our program, we might write something like this:

```
PROGRAM students (OUTPUT, names);
```

Before using a file in a program, every file variable, whether it is external or internal, must be declared. The only exceptions to this are the standard INPUT and OUTPUT files. Once the file is declared, the only legal operation on the file is writing to or reading from the file. When using a file variable in a procedure or function it must *always* be passed as a variable parameter. Just as we have not used type identifiers on operations, we do not use the type identifiers of the file when reading or writing to file. We use instead the filename variable which is declared as a variable. We will refer to this simply as the filename.

Because most of the files we will want to deal with will involve characters, Pascal provides a standard file type for this. If we wanted to define a character file on our own, we might write:

```
TYPE
    text = FILE OF CHAR
VAR
    names : text;
```

TEXT Files

The type TEXT is a predefined Pascal type. We therefore would not need to define the type text in the example above before using it with our variable declaration. A file of this type is called a *textfile*. Textfiles have a special set of commands which we will discuss shortly.

RESET and REWRITE

Before reading from any file or writing to any file, that file must be opened for processing using RESET or REWRITE. The RESET statement will put us at the beginning of a file so we will be able to read the first element of the file. Before reading from the file called names, we need to include the statement

```
RESET (names);
```

This will position us at the first element in the filenames.

The REWRITE statement essentially creates an empty file. If we use an identifier which already exists, the REWRITE statement would erase the contents of the file with that identifier. If we wanted to create a file called students, we would use the following statement:

```
REWRITE (students);
```

This will create the empty file students.

Once a file has been opened, it can either be written to or read from, but not both at the same time. You cannot read from a file and then immediately write to the same file (unless you precede the write statement with REWRITE which would have the effect of destroying anything that is currently in the file).

The File Window

An important concept when examining files is the concept of the *file window*. A Pascal file is made up of elements which are ordered sequentially and which can only be read one at a time. The file window marks the current file position, acting as a buffer between the computer and the file. The file window stores the current file element. The file window is also called the buffer variable. The file window identifier of a particular file is the name of the file followed by an arrow ↑ or caret ˆ. For example, the file window for the file name is name↑ or nameˆ. (From here on we will use the ˆ in our discussions.) When we read an element from a file, we are actually reading the current element in the file window since the file window is positioned on the current element. When we write to a file, we actually write to the file window which is then written to the file. The concept of the file window will become important as we learn about the several file access commands.

The EOF Marker

We will start our examination of file operations with a closer look at text files. The text file as mentioned earlier is a predefined Pascal type which is of type CHAR. When we read the contents of a file, text or nontext, how will we know when to stop? *Every* Pascal file is marked by an end-of-file character which indicates the end of the file. To test for this condition, Pascal provides the EOF (filename) function. This is a boolean function which will return the value TRUE when the file window is positioned on the end-of-file marker. When EOF is true, the content of the file window is undefined and trying to read it will result in an error. The filename used can be of any type, text or nontext. If we want to read a file, we might start out with something like this:

```
WHILE NOT EOF (filename)
    DO BEGIN
```

It is a good idea to check for an end-of-file condition before performing any operations on the file because trying to read past the end of file will result in an error. To test for the end of file, we will normally use the statements above. If we use the following statements:

```
RESET (filename)
    REPEAT
       read in from file
    UNTIL EOF (filename);
```

we will get a serious error if the file was originally empty (remember the actions in a REPEAT UNTIL loop are carried out at least once).

In addition to an end-of-file marker a textfile contains end-of-line markers. A textfile is divided into lines with each line ending with a special end-of-line marker. To test for the end of a line, Pascal provides the EOLN(textfile) function. This function is true if the file window is positioned on the end-of-line marker. Trying to read this marker from the file window will result in a blank regardless of how the end of line is represented internally. If we want to read a line in a textfile, we might write:

```
WHILE NOT EOLN (textfile)
    DO BEGIN
```

To read from a textfile, Pascal provides two methods which are generally associated with textfiles: READ and READLN. We have been using these two commands throughout the book, and the effect of each is essentially the same as we have already learned. When using a READ or READLN with a textfile, the syntax is

```
READ (sometextfile, element)
READLN (sometextfile, element)
```

Before using either of these commands, the function EOF(filename) must be false. Trying to read when EOF(filename) is true results in a program error. Each of these commands will read the element in the file window. The difference is in where the file window is positioned after reading from the file window. After a READ the file window is positioned on the next character on the current line in the textfile. After a READLN the file window is positioned on the first character in the next line in the textfile. This is exactly what we have learned so far, and in fact you can see why from the following comparisons:

```
READ (number)
```

is the same as

```
READ (INPUT, NUMBER)
```

and

```
READLN (anothernumber)
```

is the same as

```
READLN (INPUT, anothernumber)
```

What can we read from a textfile? We can read any standard Pascal type (not just CHAR) from a textfile since they are stored as simply a sequence of CHAR values.

To write to a textfile, we can use the standard Pascal statements:

```
WRITE (filename, element)
WRITELN (filename, element)
```

After performing a WRITE or WRITELN, the file window will be positioned on the EOF marker and therefore will be undefined. When writing to a file, the element will be appended to the end of the file. Using a WRITE will append the element to the current line in the textfile. WRITELN will write a complete line of text, which is what we are familiar with. If we do not include an element with the WRITELN, the current line in the specified file is terminated. Any standard Pascal type can be written to a textfile. However, user-defined types cannot be written to a textfile.

Let's use these commands to put together a program block which will read the contents of one textfile into another textfile. We will read from textfile original, and we will read into textfile copy. The EOLN markers will be transferred.

```
RESET (original) ;
REWRITE (copy) ;
WHILE NOT EOF (original)
    DO BEGIN
        WHILE NOT EOLN (original) DO
            BEGIN
                READ (original, onecharacter) ;
                WRITE (copy, onecharacter)
            END;
        READLN (original) ;
        WRITELN (copy)
END;
```

We first open the textfile original to read from using the RESET command. We then open the textfile copy to write to using the REWRITE command. The first WHILE loop will be performed when we reach the end of the file. The inner loop will be done when we reach the end of each line. Inside the loop we will read a character from the current line in textfile original. We will then write the character to the current line in textfile copy. Once we reach the EOLN marker, we exit the loop. The next command is a READLN. This command is needed here to copy the file correctly. Remember that when EOLN(original) is true, the EOLN character is in the file window waiting to be read. We need the READLN to position the file window on the next line. If we leave the READLN out of the program, the EOLN character, represented as a space in the file window, will appear as the first character of the next line in the textfile. The space will appear on the next line because the effect of the WRITELN with no variable is to terminate the current line in the textfile and the EOLN character has not been written to the file—it is the *next* character that will be READ.

The fact that Pascal will automatically do the conversions necessary to read and write integer and real types to textfiles may pose a few problems when we try to check for the EOF condition. In the next section we will see how we can correct this problem by checking for blank spaces or for a true EOF condition.

Here is a program that will use these ideas to merge two textfiles into one file:

```
PROGRAM testcopy (INPUT, OUTPUT);
CONST
  filemax = 5;
  stringmax = 20;
TYPE
  strin = PACKED ARRAY [1..stringmax] OF CHAR;
VAR
  original, addition, temporary: TEXT;
  word; strin;
PROCEDURE readin (VAR word: strin);
VAR
  c: CHAR;
  count1, count2: INTEGER;
BEGIN
    count1 := 1;
    REPEAT
      READ(c);
      IF NOT EOLN THEN word[count1] := c;
      count1 := count1 + 1
    UNTIL EOLN;
    FOR count2 := (count1-1) TO stringmax DO
      word[count2] := ' '
END;
PROCEDURE createfile (VAR newfile: TEXT; word: strin);
VAR
  c: CHAR;
  count1, count2: INTEGER;
BEGIN
  FOR count1 := 1 TO filemax DO
    BEGIN
      WRITELN('Enter element ', count1, ' to file.');
      readin (word);
      FOR count2 := 1 TO stringmax DO
        BEGIN
          c := word[count2];
          WRITE (newfile, c)
        END;
```

```
                    WRITELN (newfile);
                    WRITELN;
            END
    END;
    PROCEDURE copyfile (VAR oldfile, newfile : TEXT);
    VAR
        currentchar : CHAR;
        BEGIN
            RESET (oldfile);
            WHILE NOT EOF (oldfile) DO
                BEGIN
                    WHILE NOT EOLN (oldfile) DO
                        BEGIN
                            READ (oldfile, currentchar);
                            WRITE (newfile, currentchar)
                        END;
                    READLN (oldfile);
                    WRITELN (newfile)
                END
    END; {procedure copyfile}
    PROCEDURE displayfile (VAR printfile: TEXT);
    VAR
        c: CHAR;
    BEGIN
        RESET (printfile);
        WHILE NOT EOF (printfile) DO
            BEGIN
                WHILE NOT EOLN (printfile) DO
                    BEGIN
                        READ (printfile, c);
                        WRITE (c)
                    END;
                    READLN (printfile);
                    WRITELN
            END
    END;

    BEGIN
        REWRITE (original);
        createfile (original, word);
        displayfile (original);
        REWRITE (addition);
        createfile (addition, word);
        displayfile (addition);
        REWRITE (temporary);
        copyfile (original, temporary);
        copyfile (addition, temporary);
        REWRITE (original);
        copyfile (temporary, original);
        displayfile (original)
    END.
```

Before moving on to nontextfiles, two points need to be made about the file access commands. First, it is generally possible to use the READ and WRITE command with a nontextfile. When Pascal was first developed, the READ and WRITE were meant to be used only with textfiles. However, most installations now allow the use of READ and

WRITE with nontextfiles. The second point to make is that the commands can be used with multiple variable-parameters. For example, we could write:

```
READ (textfile, A);
READ (textfile, B);
READ (textfile, C);
```

as

```
READ (textfile, A, B, C);
```

We can use multiple variable-parameters with READ, READLN, WRITE, or WRITELN. If, however, we use the READ or WRITE with a nontextfile, we can only use a single variable-parameter.

Up to now we have looked at textfiles which are of the general format:

VAR

filename : *text*;

There may be times when we wish our file to contain elements which are not of type CHAR. The following are examples of legal nontextfiles:

```
TYPE
    day = (sunday, monday, tuesday, wednesday, thursday,
        friday, saturday);
    week = FILE OF days;
    studentinfo =
        RECORD
        {field list would go here}
        END;
        studentfile = FILE OF studentinfo;
            range = 1..9999;
        numfile = FILE OF range;
        gpafile = FILE OF REAL;
    VAR
        days: week;
        studentrecs: studentfile;
        studentnums: numfile;
        studentgpas: gpafile;
```

We have created four files: days, studentrecs, studentnums, and studentgpas. The elements of file days are of the ordinal type day. The elements of file studentrecs are of the record type studentinfo. The elements of file studentnums are of type range, and the elements of file studentgpas are of type REAL.

When we deal with nontextfiles, an understanding of the file window concept becomes important because we will explicitly make assignments to or from the file window and then move the file window in the file. Even though the commands we are about to discuss are associated with nontextfiles, there will be occasions when we will want to use them with textfiles. This is perfectly legal.

GET and PUT

When we read from a file, we are actually doing two things. We first read the contents of the file window into some variable, and then we move the file window to the next element that is to be read. We can carry out these two steps with the following commands:

```
V := f^;
GET (f);
```

The first command will assign the element in the file window of file f (denoted as f^) to the variable V. The next command uses the reserved word GET to assign the next element of file f to the file window. These statements are equivalent to the statement READ(f,V) which was discussed earlier. The equivalent of READLN(f), where f is a textfile, using this new notation is:

```
WHILE NOT EOLN (f)
      DO GET (f) ;
GET (f) ;
```

We discard the current line and position the file window at the first element on the next line or the EOF character if there is no next line. Trying to GET the EOF character will cause a program crash.

When we write to a file, we follow a similar two-step operation. We first assign to the file window and append the contents of the file window to the end of the file. The equivalent of WRITE(f,x) is then:

```
f^ : = x;
PUT (f) ;
```

The first command assigns the values contained in the variable x to the file window. We then use the reserved word PUT to write the contents of the file window at the end of the file.

One advantage of using these methods of accessing a Pascal file is their flexibility. If we have an element which is of a structured type, we can access any part of the structured type. For example, if we have a file called studentrecs made up of elements which are of record type studentinfo, we can access a particular field using the period notation. If we need to assign the field studentname to the variable name, we can use the notation:

```
name : = studentrecs^. studentname
```

This will assign the studentname field of the particular record in the file window to the variable name. We can access an element of an array type using the following notation:

`filename^arrayname`	This will access an entire array.
`filename^arrayname[10]`	This will access the 10th element of the array.

We mentioned earlier that reading integers or real numbers stored in a textfile may cause problems when checking for the end of file. If we read a variable which is an integer or real type from a textfile, a statement of READ(textfilename,number) is equivalent to:

```
WHILE textfilename^=' '
  DO GET (textfilename) ;
```

(After this is executed, the value in the file window is assigned to the variable number.)

These statements will cause blank spaces and new lines to be skipped before the numerical value is read into the variable number. (New lines will be skipped because the file window will contain a blank space at the end of a line, the end-of-line representation in the file window, and we are skipping blanks in the file window.) After the assignment to number, this window contains the next character. If the textfile contains blanks at the end of the file, the loop will cause the blanks to be skipped. Immediately before getting to the end of the file the file window will contain a blank. The loop will cause the program to skip the blank and try to GET the next character which is the EOF character, which is undefined, and will cause a program crash.

Because of this we cannot use the block shown below to read and process integer data from a textfile:

```
WHILE NOT EOF (textfile)
      DO BEGIN
         READ (textfile, number);
         [statements which process the data]
      END;
```

In performing the read statement, we may cause a program crash as we try to get the EOF marker. We cannot correct the situation by using the following test:

```
WHILE NOT EOF (textfile) AND (textfile^=' ')
```

because when EOF(textfile) is true, textfile^ is undefined and textfile^ will be evaluated in order to test the condition of the loop.

A procedure which will correctly check for blanks is shown below. It should be included in any program which reads integer or real values from a textfile. If we look at our earlier version of the block for processing data, we would place the procedure call in two spots: one call before entering the WHILE loop and one call after we have processed the data. The second call has the effect of checking for EOF before the next READ, thus avoiding the possibility of trying to get the EOF marker.

```
PROCEDURE checkfile (VAR filename: text)
   VAR
      finished: BOOLEAN;
   BEGIN
      finished: =false;
   REPEAT
      IF EOF (filename)
         THEN finished : = true
         ELSE IF filename^ =' '
            THEN GET (filename)
            ELSE finished: =true;
   UNTIL finished
END;
```

This procedure will return to the file window a value that is not blank and not the EOF character. The portion of the READ statement that checks for blanks (using the WHILE loop) is essentially ignored since the file window will never be a blank. All that needs to be done in the READ is to assign the value we have just placed in the file window to our integer or real variable.

Now suppose that we have two files that are in alphabetical order. We would like to merge these two files into one new file that is still in order. Here is a program that will accomplish this task.

```
PROGRAM testmerge (INPUT, OUTPUT);
CONST
   filemax = 5;
   stringmax = 20;
TYPE
   strin = PACKED ARRAY [1.. stringmax] OF CHAR;
   student =
      RECORD
         name: strin;
         num : INTEGER
      END;
   stufile = FILE OF student;
VAR
   first: stufile;
   second: stufile;
```

```
            new: stufile;
            word: strin;
    PROCEDURE getname (VAR word: strin);
    VAR
        c: CHAR;
        count 1, count2: INTEGER;
    BEGIN
        count1 : = 1;
        REPEAT
            READ (c);
            IF NOT EOLN THEN word[count1] : = c;
            count1 : = count1 + 1
        UNTIL EOLN;
        FOR count2 : = (count1−1) TO stringmax DO
            word[count2] : = ' '
    END;

    PROCEDURE createfile (VAR newfile: stufile);
    VAR
        word: strin;
        number, count1: INTEGER;
    BEGIN
        REWRITE (newfile);
        FOR count1 : = 1 TO filemax DO
            BEGIN
                WRITELN ('Enter last name of student # ', count1);
                getname (word);
                newfile^. name : = word;
                WRITELN ('Enter the student i. d. number. ');
                READLN (number);
                newfile^. num : = number;
                PUT (newfile)
            END
    END;

    PROCEDURE mergefiles (VAR first, second, new: stufile);
        {This procedure will merge two files which are
        made up of records containing a name field. The
        file new is created and will be ordered alphabetically
        by the name. The two files to be merged must be in
        alphabetical order to begin with.}
    VAR
        firstcount, secondcount, newcount: INTEGER;
    BEGIN
        firstcount : = 0;
        secondcount : = 0;
        newcount : = 0;
        WHILE (NOT EOF (first)) AND (NOT EOF (second)) DO
            BEGIN
                IF (first^. name <= second^. name)
                    THEN BEGIN
                    new^ : = first^.
                    firstcount : = firstcount + 1;
                    IF NOT EOF (first)
                        THEN GET (first)
                END {then structure}
```

```
            ELSE BEGIN
                IF (second^. name < first^. name)
                  THEN BEGIN
                      new^ : = second^;
                      secondcount : = secondcount + 1;
                      IF NOT EOF (second)
                          THEN GET (second)
                  END {then structure}
                END; {else structure}
      PUT (new) ;
      newcount : = newcount + 1;
  END; {while loop}
IF EOF (first)
  THEN BEGIN
      WHILE NOT EOF (second) DO
          BEGIN
              new^ : = second^;
              PUT (new) ;
              newcount : = newcount + 1;
              secondcount : = secondcount + 1;
              IF NOT EOF (second)
                  THEN GET (second)
          END {while}
  END {then};
IF EOF (second)
  THEN BEGIN
      WHILE NOT EOF (first) DO
          BEGIN
              new^ : = first^;
              PUT (new) ;
              newcount : = newcount + 1;
              firstcount : = firstcount + 1;
              IF NOT EOF (first)
                  THEN GET (first)
          END
  END:
  WRITELN ('Records written from first file: ', firstcount: 1);
  WRITELN ('Records written from second file: ', secondcount: 1);

  WRITELN ('Total records written to new file: ', newcount: 1)
END; {procedure mergefiles}

PROCEDURE displayfile (VAR printfile: stufile);
VAR
   studentrec : student;
BEGIN
   RESET (printfile) ;
   WHILE NOT EOF (printfile) DO
       BEGIN
           studentrec : = printfile^;
           WITH studentrec DO
               BEGIN
                   WRITE (name) ;
                   WRITELN (num)
               END;
           IF NOT EOF (printfile)
```

```
                    THEN GET (printfile)
          END
     END;

     BEGIN {main program block}
        REWRITE (first);
        createfile (first);
        displayfile (first);
        REWRITE (second);
        createfile (second);
        displayfile (second);
        RESET (first);
        RESET (second);
        REWRITE (new);
        mergefiles (first, second, new);
        WRITELN ('**********   *******');
        displayfile (new)
     END.
```

Before plunging into the task of writing programs which deal with files, it would be a good idea to check your own computer for nonstandard file commands and processing methods. For example, the Pascal version used to run the programs in this book allows random access to files and has a special set of commands for this purpose. This particular version also has a special command to define external files, it is not a standard Pascal command. It is also advisable to look at the processing of textfiles for your installation. Some nonstandard Pascal versions will remove trailing blanks at the end of text lines, while other versions will add trailing blanks. It is also possible on some versions for the EOLN function to be undefined before the start of input.

In Chapter 17 we will use files in a program to keep track of a school's student records.

Note to Chapter 15

■   One feature to note about the READ and WRITE operations on textfiles: They work on one character at a time, in contrast to the way READ and WRITE work on INPUT and OUTPUT.

Chapter 15 Exercises

1.   Explain the difference between random and sequential access. Which is associated with Pascal files?

2.   What are the standard (predefined) file parameters?

3.   Rewrite the following using the GET and PUT commands:
     (a) READLN(somefile,value)
     (b) WRITELN(somefile,value)

4.   What statement would you use to access:
     (a) The seventh element of the array *scores* which defines the type for the file *students*
     (b) The *firstname* field of the record *studentrec* which defines the type for the file *studentmstr*

5.   Write the portion of a program that will count the number of blank lines in a textfile.

6.   Write a program that will keep track of the books coming into a bookstore and store the information in the file *BOOKMSTR*. For each book the following information is kept:

title, author, price, publisher, date received

7. Do you always need to include the nonstandard file names of the files used in the program in the program header?

8. What is wrong with the following program which creates the file *grades*?

```
TYPE
   value : INTEGER;
   scores : FILE OF INTEGER;
VAR
   grades : scores;
BEGIN
   WRITELN('Enter students score. ');
   READLN(value);
   WRITELN(grades,value);
```

9. When reading a textfile, why should a WHILE loop be used rather than a REPEAT loop?

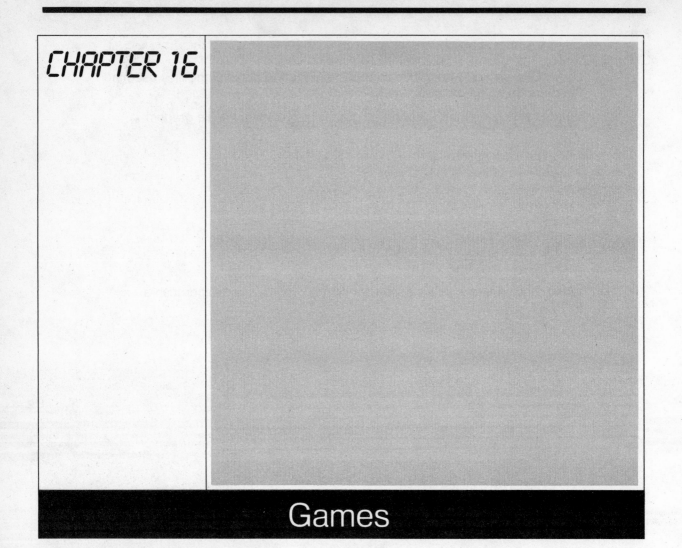

CHAPTER 16

Games

Computer Ticktacktoe

We have discussed many serious applications of computers, but we also should realize that computers can play games. We will write a Pascal program that teaches our computer to play ticktacktoe. The program itself will be quite complicated, but it will consist of several different procedures. Each procedure will be simple enough that you will be able to understand what it does. We will have a procedure called makemove that determines the computer's next move, a procedure called playermove that reads in the player's move from the keyboard, a procedure called update that calculates the new position of the board after each move is made, and a procedure called printboard that displays the new status of the board after each computer move. We will also need several procedures to initialize the various arrays and a procedure to control the program at the end of the game.

We will represent the position of the markers on the board as a two-dimensional array called board. The array board will have three rows and three columns. The array element board[i,j] will be 0 if there is no marker on the square in row i and column j; it will be 1 if the computer has placed an "O" on that square, and it will be −1 if the opponent has placed an "X" on that square. For purposes of reading in the moves, we will number the squares on the board as shown in Figure 16-1.

Now we need to decide on a ticktacktoe strategy. The program we will write will only play games in which the computer makes the first move. If you like, you may write a program in which the computer responds when the first move is made by the player. We

FIGURE 16-1

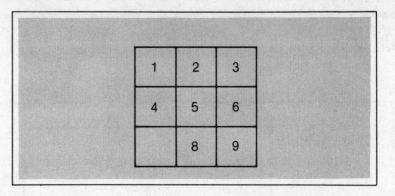

have already developed a strategy to use. We will start by having the computer move to square 3 (the upper right-hand corner). If the opponent moves to 2, then the computer will move to 9; if the opponent moves to 1, the computer will move to 7; if the opponent moves to 4, we will move to 9; if the opponent moves to 5, we will move to 1; and if the opponent moves to 8, we will move to 1. We can illustrate these possibilities in a diagram. See Figure 16-2.

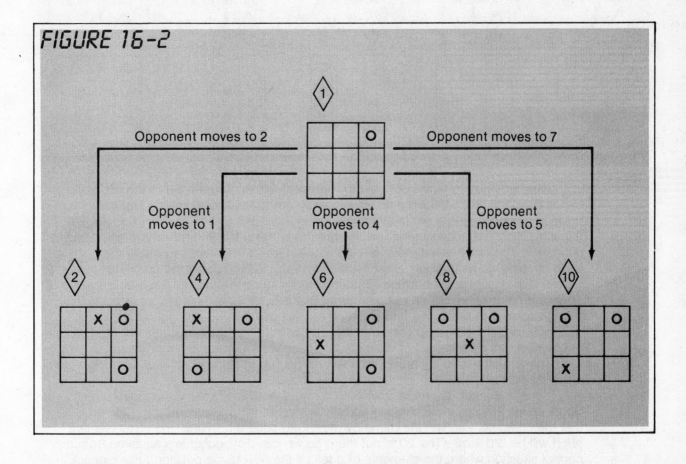

FIGURE 16-2

Now we have to figure out a response to the opponent's second move. In each situation shown above, the computer has two in a row. So, our move is obvious if the opponent does not move to block us. We simply place our "O" to complete the row of 3. If the opponent does move to block us, then the computer's move requires more thought. Figure 16-3 shows the move we will have the computer make in response to each of these possibilities.

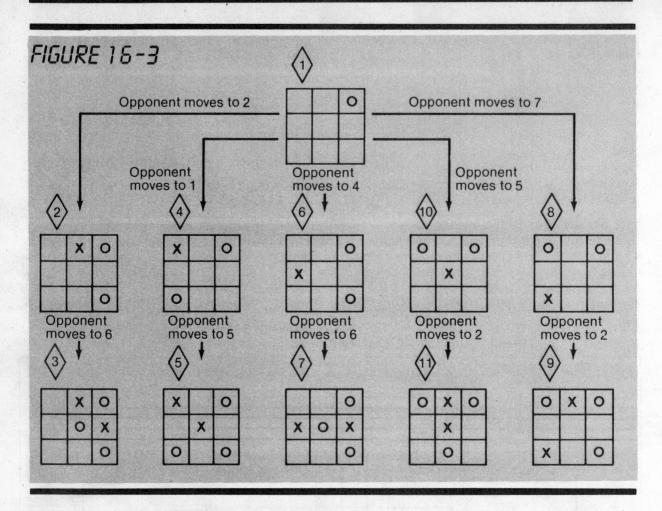

FIGURE 16-3

Now we need to figure out how to represent this strategy in terms the computer can understand. We will give a number to each possible game position. The game position numbers are shown in diamonds in Figures 16-2 and 16-3. For example, the game position immediately after the computer has made the first move is game position number 1. The array called move will tell us what move the computer made that lead to each possible game position. For example, move[2] is 9 because the computer moved to square 9 to create game position 2. Each time the opponent makes a move, we move to a new game position. So we need an array that tells us what the new game position will be. The array that fulfills this task is called a. Suppose that we are initially in game position j, and then the opponent moves to square i. Then the array element $a[i,j]$ will tell us the new game position. For example, suppose we are currently in game position 8. If the opponent moves to square 2, then we will end up in game position 9. Therefore, the array element $a[2,8]$ is 9.

If the computer can make a winning move, then we will use a shortcut method. Suppose we are in game position j and the opponent moves to square k. Now suppose that the computer can win the game by moving to square m. Then, the array element $a[k,j]$ will be $(20 + m)$. (The 20 is put there so we can distinguish this situation from the normal situation where the elements of a tell us the new game position.) For example, suppose we are in game position 2 and the opponent moves to square 5. Then the computer can win the game by moving to square 6; so the array element $a[5,2]$ is 26.

It is also possible that the game may end up in a tie. (This situation is sometimes called a cat's game.) If the computer can move to square m and thereby tie the game, then the element in the array a will be equal to $-m$.

You may notice that the diagram in Figure 16-3 does not take into account the possibility that the opponent might initially move to square 6, 8, or 9. Since a ticktacktoe board is symmetric, the strategy is fundamentally the same when the opponent moves to 6 as it is when the opponent moves to 2, Likewise, an opening move to 9 is fundamentally the same as an opening move to 1; and an opening move to 8 is fundamentally the same as an opening move to 4. Therefore, we will use a reflection routine in order to save space in the strategy array. We will have a boolean variable called reflection. If the opponent's opening move is not 6, 8, or 9, then the variable called reflection will be set to FALSE and we will ignore the reflection routine for the rest of the game. Otherwise it will be set to TRUE. When reflection is TRUE, then we must put the player's move through the reflection routine before we look in the strategy array. After we have calculated the computer's move, we must then put that move through the reflection routine in order to calculate the actual move that we want the computer to make.

The program is complicated, but if you look at it a piece at a time you can understand what it does.

```
PROGRAM ticktacktoe (INPUT,OUTPUT);
TYPE
   boardtype = ARRAY[1..3,1..3] OF INTEGER;
   reflecttype = ARRAY[1..9] OF INTEGER;
   movetype = ARRAY[1..15] OF INTEGER;
   strattype = ARRAY[1..9,1..15] OF INTEGER;
   outchartype = ARRAY[1..3] OF CHAR;
CONST
   starrow = '*************';
VAR
   fflag : CHAR;
   board : boardtype
   reflectpos : reflectype;
   move : movetype;
   a : strattype;
   outchar: outchartype;
   gamepos, player, row, column, initsquare,
   finalsquare: INTEGER;
   openmove, reflection, gameover, finished : BOOLEAN;
   result: INTEGER;

PROCEDURE initl;
VAR i,j: INTEGER;
BEGIN
FOR i:=1 TO 9 DO FOR j := 1 TO 15 DO a[i,j]:=0;
a[1,1]:=4;a[1,2]:=26;a[1,3]:=27;a[1,6]:=26;a[1,7]:=27;
a[2,1]:=2;a[2,4]:=25;a[2,5]:=28;a[2,6]:=26;=a[2,7]:=21;
   a[2,8]:=9;a[2,10]:=11;
a[4,1]:=6;a[4,2]:=26;a[4,3]:=21;a[4,4]:=25;a[4,5]:=28;
   a[4,8]:=22;a[4,9]:=26;a[4,10]:=22;a[4,11]:=12;
   a[4,14]:=29;
a[5,1]:=10;a[5,2]:=26;a[5,4]:=5;a[5,6]:=26;a[5,8]:=22;
   a[5,9]:=26
END;

PROCEDURE init2;
BEGIN
a[6,1]:=2;a[6,2]:3;a[6,4]:=25;a[6,5]:=28;a[6,6]:=7;
   a[6,8]:=22;a[6,9]:=25;a[6,10]:=22;a[6,11]:=13;
   a[6,15]:=27;
a[7,1]:=8;a[7,2]:=26;a[7,3]:=21;a[7,6]:=26;a[7,7]:=21;
   a[7,10]:=22;a[7,11]:=14;a[7,12]:=29;a[7,13]:=-9;
```

```
              a[7,15] :=-6;
      a[8,1] :=6; a[8,2] :=26; a[8,3] :=21; a[8,4] :=25; a[8,5] :=26;
        a[8,6] :=26; a[8,7] :=21; a[8,8] :=22; a[8,9] :=26; a[8,10] :=22;
      a[9,1] :=4; a[9,4] :=25; a[9,8] :=22; a[9,10] :=22; a[9,11] :=15;
        a[9,12] :=-7; a[9,13] :=27; a[9,14] :=-4
      END;

    PROCEDURE initreflect (VAR reflectpos : reflecttype);
    BEGIN
        reflectpos[1] : = 9;
        reflectpos[2] : = 6;
        reflectpos[3] : = 3;
        reflectpos[4] : = 8;
        reflectpos[5] : = 5;
        reflectpos[6] : = 2;
        reflectpos[7] : = 7;
        reflectpos[8] : = 4;
        reflectpos[9] : = 1
    END;

    PROCEDURE initmove (VAR move: movetype);
    BEGIN
      move[1]  : = 3; move[2]  : = 9; move[3]  : = 5; move[4]  : = 7;
      move[5]  : = 9; move[6]  : = 9; move[7]  : = 5; move[8]  : = 1;
      move[9]  : = 9; move[10] : = 1; move[11] : = 8; move[12] : = 6;
      move[13] : = 4; move[14] : = 6; move[15]  : = 4
    END;

    PROCEDURE initout (VAR outchar : outchartype);

    BEGIN
      outchar[1] : = 'X';
      outchar[2] : = '  ';
      outchar[3] : = 'O'
    END;

    PROCEDURE initboard (VAR board: boardtype);
    VAR count1, count2 : INTEGER;
    BEGIN
     FOR count1 : = 1 TO 3 DO
       BEGIN
         FOR count2 : = 1 TO 3 DO board[count1,count2] : = 0
       END
    END;

    PROCEDURE update (VAR board: boardtype;
                      VAR row,column: INTEGER;
                      player, square : INTEGER);
    BEGIN
      row : = TRUNC((square + 2)/3);
      column : = square - (3*row) + 3;
      board[row,column] : = player
    END;

    PROCEDURE printboard (outchar: outchartype;
                                board : boardtype);
    VAR
      count1, count2 : INTEGER;
    BEGIN
```

```
        WRITELN (starrow);
      FOR count1 : = 1 TO 3 DO
           BEGIN
               WRITE ('*');
               FOR count2 : = 1 TO 3 DO
                       WRITE (' ', outchar [2 + board [count1, count2]], ' *');
               WRITELN; {prints a row}
               WRITELN (starrow)
           END
   END;

   PROCEDURE makemove (VAR finalsquare : INTEGER;
                            VAR move: movetype;
                            VAR reflectpos : reflecttype;
                            gamepos : INTEGER; reflection : BOOLEAN);
   VAR
      initsquare: INTEGER;
   BEGIN
      initsquare : = move [gamepos];
      IF reflection
           THEN finalsquare : = reflectpos [initsquare]
           ELSE finalsquare : = initsquare;
      WRITELN ('Computer move to ', finalsquare)
   END;

   PROCEDURE playermove (VAR gamepos, initsquare : INTEGER;
                            VAR openmove, reflection : BOOLEAN;
                            a: strattype ;
                            reflectpos: reflecttype);
   VAR
      finalsquare : INTEGER;
   BEGIN
      WRITELN;
      WRITELN ('Your move: ');
      READLN (initsquare);
      IF openmove
           THEN BEGIN
                   IF (initsquare = 6) OR (initsquare = 8) OR
                       (initsquare = 9)
                   THEN reflection : = TRUE
                   ELSE reflection : = FALSE;
                   openmove : = FALSE
           END;
   IF reflection
           THEN finalsquare : = reflectpos [initsquare]
           ELSE finalsquare : = initsquare;
   gamepos : = a [finalsquare, gamepos];
   IF gamepos = 0
           THEN BEGIN
                   WRITELN ('Illegal move');
                   playermove (gamepos, initsquare, openmove,
                   reflection,
                           a, reflectpos)
               END
   END;

   PROCEDURE endgame (VAR finished : BOOLEAN);
```

```
            VAR
               response : CHAR;
            BEGIN
            WRITELN;
            WRITELN('Do you wish to play another game? Y or N. ');
            READLN(response);
            IF response = 'N' THEN finished : = TRUE
         END;

      BEGIN    {Main Program block}
         finished : = FALSE;
         init1; init2;
         initreflect(reflectpos);
         initmove(move);
         initout(outchar);
         WHILE NOT finished DO
            BEGIN
               initboard(board);
               gamepos : = 1;
               player : = 1;
               openmove : = TRUE;
               reflection : = FALSE;
               gameover : = FALSE;
               WHILE NOT gameover DO
                  BEGIN
                     makemove(finalsquare, move, reflectpos, gamepos,
                          reflection);
                     update(board, row, column, player, finalsquare);
                     printboard(outchar, board);
                     player : = − player;
                     playermove(gamepos, initsquare, openmove,
                          reflection, a, reflectpos);
                     update(board, row, column, player, initsquare);
                     player : = −player;
                     IF gamepos < 0
                        THEN BEGIN
                                finalsquare : = −gamepos;
                                update(board, row, column, player,
                                   finalsquare);
                                WRITELN('Cats game');
                                printboard(outchar, board);
                                gameover : = TRUE;
                                endgame (finished)
                              END;
                     IF gamepos > 20
                        THEN BEGIN
                                initsquare : = gamepos − 20;
                                IF reflection
                                   THEN finalsquare : =
                                         reflectpos[initsquare]
                                   ELSE finalsquare : = initsquare;
                                update(board, row, column, player,
                                   finalsquare);
                                WRITELN('Computer wins');
                                printboard(outchar, board);
                                gameover : = TRUE;
```

```
                    endgame (finished)
                  END {then}
              END {inner while loop}
          END {outer while loop}
      END.
```

Here is a sample of the output of this program:

```
Computer move to 3
* * * * * * * * * * * *
*     *     *  O  *
* * * * * * * * * * * *
*     *     *     *
* * * * * * * * * * * *
*     *     *     *
* * * * * * * * * * * *
Your move:
7
Computer move to 1
* * * * * * * * * * * *
*  O  *     *  O  *
* * * * * * * * * * * *
*     *     *     *
* * * * * * * * * * * *
*  X  *     *     *

Your move:
2
Computer move to 9
* * * * * * * * * * * *
*  O  *  X  *  O  *
* * * * * * * * * * * *
*     *     *     *
* * * * * * * * * * * *
*  X  *     *  O  *
* * * * * * * * * * * *

Your move:
6
Computer wins
* * * * * * * * * * * *
*  O  *  X  *  O  *
* * * * * * * * * * * *
*     *  O  *  X  *
* * * * * * * * * * * *
*  X  *     *  O  *
* * * * * * * * * * * *

Do you wish to play another game? Y or N.
Y
Computer move to 3
* * * * * * * * * * * *
*     *     *  O  *
* * * * * * * * * * * *
*     *     *     *
* * * * * * * * * * * *
*     *     *     *
* * * * * * * * * * * *
```

Your move:
5
Computer move to 1
```
* * * * * * * * * * * *
*  O  *     *  O  *
* * * * * * * * * * * *
*     *  X  *     *
* * * * * * * * * * * *
*     *     *     *
* * * * * * * * * * * *
```

Your move:
2
Computer move to 8
```
* * * * * * * * * * * *
*  O  *  X  *  O  *
* * * * * * * * * * * *
*     *  X  *     *
* * * * * * * * * * * *
*     *  O  *     *
* * * * * * * * * * * *
```

Your move:
7
Computer move to 6
```
* * * * * * * * * * * *
*  O  *  X  *  O  *
* * * * * * * * * * * *
*     *  X  *  O  *
* * * * * * * * * * * *
*  X  *  O  *     *
* * * * * * * * * * * *
```

Your move:
9
Cats game
```
* * * * * * * * * * * *
*  O  *  X  *  O  *
* * * * * * * * * * * *
*  O  *  X  *  O  *
* * * * * * * * * * * *
*  X  *  O  *  X  *
* * * * * * * * * * * *
```

Do you wish to play another game? Y or N.
Y
Computer move to 3
```
* * * * * * * * * * * *
*     *     *  O  *
* * * * * * * * * * * *
*     *     *     *
* * * * * * * * * * * *
*     *     *     *
* * * * * * * * * * * *
```

Your move:
4
Computer move to 9
```
* * * * * * * * * * *
*   *   * O *
* * * * * * * * * * *
* X *   *   *
* * * * * * * * * * *
*   *   * O *
* * * * * * * * * * *
```

Your move:
6
Computer move to 5
```
* * * * * * * * * * *
*   *   * O *
* * * * * * * * * * *
* X * O * X *
* * * * * * * * * * *
*   *   * O *
* * * * * * * * * * *
```

Your move:
1
Computer wins
```
* * * * * * * * * * *
* X *   * O *
* * * * * * * * * * *
* X * O * X *
* * * * * * * * * * *
* O *   * O *
* * * * * * * * * * *
```

Do you wish to play another game Y or N.
N

Printouts 16-1A,B,C

The game of ticktacktoe is simple enough that we can have the computer examine all possible game outcomes. That way we can make sure that the computer will either win or tie. However, this procedure cannot be followed for more complicated games, such as chess. If you want to write a program that plays chess, you will only be able to have the computer evaluate the consequences of its actions for only a few moves into the future. There is no algorithm to play chess. In other words, there is no method guaranteed to find a winning chess strategy. Therefore, computer chess programs follow a problem-solving method known as a *heuristic* approach. Heuristic basically means to follow an approach of educated guessing. The best computer chess programs are good players, but they have yet to establish that they are clearly superior to the best human masters.

Computer Football

Let's work on another game. Here's an example of a football strategy game program. This time, instead of playing against the computer, we will use the computer to referee a game between two people. We'll set up the game so that the offensive player has a choice of 12 plays and the defensive player has a choice of 7 defensive strategies. Each player will type in a strategy number without letting the other person see it. Then the computer will calculate the results of the play. If, for example, the offensive player chooses play 1 (run over center) and the defensive player chooses defense 1 (crowd the center), the play will not gain many yards. However, if the offensive player chooses play 10 (throw a long pass) and the defensive player is using defense 1, the play will probably go for a long gain. The game is therefore basically a game of psychology: The idea is to guess what strategy your opponent will use while making sure that your own strategy is a surprise.

To keep the game from becoming predictable, we'll add a random element. We will write a function called rnd that generates a pseudorandom number between 0 and 1. The number is not a true random number, because it is generated according to a fixed rule. However, the number generated by the rnd function is sufficiently unpredictable that it will serve our purpose. We will use the rnd function to add or subtract from the result of the play before it is displayed. We'll also use the rnd function to determine whether a fumble occurs, whether a pass is complete, whether an interception occurs, how long a punt will be, and whether or not a field goal or extra point attempt will be good.

Here is the program:

```
PROGRAM football (INPUT, OUTPUT);
    {This program conducts a football game between two players—
    the visiting team player and the home team player. For each
    play, both the offense player and the defense player input
    their play number. Then the computer calculates the result of
    the play.
        Offensive strategies are:
            1: run over center
            2: run off tackle -- strong side
            3: run off tackle -- weak side
            4: run end sweep -- strong side
            5: run end sweep -- weak side
            6: draw
            7: screen pass
            8: pass to tight end
            9: short pass pattern
           10: deep pass pattern
           12: punt
           13: field goal attempt   14: stop the game
        Defensive strategies are:
            1: crowd center
            2: crowd strong side
            3: crowd weak side
            4: standard 4-3
            5: blitz
            6: pass coverage emphasis
            7: prevent}
TYPE
    offset = SET OF 1..13;
    defset = SET OF 1..7;
    runset = SET OF 1..6;
    passset = SET OF 7..10;
    kickset = SET OF 11..12;
    resultarray = ARRAY[1..8,1..10] OF INTEGER;
    completion = ARRAY[1..8,1..4] OF REAL;
```

```
                intarray = ARRAY [1. . 8, 1. . 4] OF REAL;
VAR
   home, visitor, ballposs, distance, down, yds, yline,
   offplay, defplay, gain, whichpass : INTEGER;
   territory : CHAR;
   q: REAL;
   run : runset;
   passes : passset;
   kick : kickset;
   r : resultarray;
   pc : completion;  {pc is the array of pass completion
                       probabilities}
   pi : intarray;     {pi is the array of pass interception
                       prob. s}
   offenses : offset;
   defenses : defset;
   sameteam, finished : BOOLEAN;
FUNCTION rnd : REAL;
   {This function calculates a pseudorandom number between 0 and
   1.}
VAR c : REAL;
BEGIN
q: = (1+q) *987654;
c : = TRUNC (q/1000) ;
q : = c/1000000;
c : = ABS (q − TRUNC (q) ) ;
q : = c*1000000;
rnd : = c
END;

PROCEDURE init1;
BEGIN
  r [1, 1] : =−5 ; r [1, 2] : =0 ; r [1, 3] : =0 ; r [1, 4] : = 6;
  r [1, 5] : =5   ; r [1, 6] : =0; r [1, 7] : =0  ; r [1, 8] : = 6;
  r [1, 9] : =8   ; r [1, 10] : =100;

  r [2, 1] : = 2 ; r [2, 2] : =−4; r [2, 3] : =6 ; r [2, 4] : =−6;
  r [2, 5] : = 8 ; r [2, 6] : = 2; r [2, 7] : = 6; r [2, 8] : = 0;
  r [2, 9] : = 6 ; r [2, 10] : =20;

  r [3, 1] : = 2 ; r [3, 2] : =6 ; r [3, 3] : =−4; r [3, 4] : =8 ;
  r [3, 5] : =−6 ; r [3, 6] : =2 ; r [3, 7] : = 6; r [3, 8] : =21;
  r [3, 9] : =6 ; r [3, 10] : =20;

  r [4, 1] : =1  ; r [4, 2] : = 2; r [4, 3] : = 1; r [4, 4] : = 2;
  r [4, 5] : = 1 ; r [4, 6] : =2 ; r [4, 7] : = 6; r [4, 8] : = 6;
  r [4, 9] : = 6 ; r [4, 10] : =12;

END;
PROCEDURE init2;
BEGIN
  r [5, 1] : = 2 ; r [5, 2] : =3 ; r [5, 3] : = 3; r [5, 4] : =3 ;
  r [5, 5] : = 3 ; r [5, 6] : =30; r [5, 7] : =32; r [5, 8] : =0 ;
  r [5, 9] : =0  ; r [5, 10] : =0 ;

  r [6, 1] : =3  ; r [6, 2] : =6 ; r [6, 3] : = 6; r [6, 4] : =4 ;
  r [6, 5] : =4  ; r [6, 6] : = 0; r [6, 7] : = 0; r [6, 8] : =5 ;
  r [6, 9] : =4 ; r [6, 10] : =12;
```

```
   r[7,1]:=9 ;r[7,2]:=11;r[7,3]:=11;r[7,4]:=7 ;
   r[7,5]:=7 ;r[7,6]:= 5;r[7,7]:= 0;r[7,8]:=0 ;
   r[7,9]:=0 ;r[7,10]:=0 ;

   r[8,1]:= 1 ;r[8,2]:= 0;r[8,3]:= 4;r[8,4]:= 0;
   r[8,5]:= 2 ;r[8,6]:= 1;r[8,7]:=0 ;r[8,8]:= 8;
   r[8,9]:= 9 ;r[8,10]:=20;
END;
PROCEDURE init3;
BEGIN
   pc[1,1]:=0 ;pc[1,2]:=0.4;pc[1,3]:=0.4;pc[1,4]:=0.7;
   pc[2,1]:=0.5;pc[2,2]:=0 ;pc[2,3]:=0.6;pc[2,4]:=0.4;
   pc[3,1]:=0.5;pc[3,2]:=0.6;pc[3,3]:=0.6;pc[3,4]:=0.4;
   pc[4,1]:=0.3;pc[4,2]:=0.5;pc[4,3]:=0.6;pc[4,4]:=0.3;
   pc[5,1]:=0.8;pc[5,2]:= 0;pc[5,3]:= 0;pc[5,4]:= 0;
   pc[6,1]:=0 ;pc[6,2]:=0.2;pc[6,3]:=0.2;pc[6,4]:=0.3;
   pc[7,1]:=0 ;pc[7,2]:= 0;pc[7,3]:= 0;pc[7,4]:=0;
   pc[8,1]:=0 ;pc[8,2]:=0.8;pc[8,3]:=0.8;pc[8,4]:=0.5;
END;
PROCEDURE init4;
BEGIN
   pi[1,1]:=0.2;pi[1,2]:=0.2;pi[1,3]:=0.2;pi[1,4]:= 0;
   pi[2,1]:=0.1;pi[2,2]:=0.8;pi[2,3]:=0.1;pi[2,4]:=0 ;
   pi[3,1]:=0.1;pi[3,2]:= 0;pi[3,3]:=0.1;pi[3,4]:= 0;
   pi[4,1]:=0.1;pi[4,2]:=0.1;pi[4,3]:=0.1;pi[4,4]:=0.1;
   pi[5,1]:=0 ;pi[5,2]:=0.3;pi[5,3]:=0.3;pi[5,4]:=0.3;
   pi[6,1]:=0.5;pi[6,2]:=0.3;pi[6,3]:=0.3;pi[6,4]:=0.3;
   pi[7,1]:=0.7;pi[7,2]:=0.7;pi[7,3]:=0.7;pi[7,4]:=0.7;
   pi[8,1]:=0.1;pi[8,2]:=0 ;pi[8,3]:=0 ;pi[8,4]:=0.1
END;

FUNCTION ydline(VAR territory: CHAR;
                    distance: INTEGER): INTEGER;
BEGIN
   IF distance < 50
        THEN BEGIN
                ydline := distance;
                territory := 'H'
             END
        ELSE BEGIN
                ydline := 100 - distance;
                territory := 'V'
             END
END;

PROCEDURE reset (VAR down, yds, ballposs : INTEGER;
                 home, visitor, distance : INTEGER;
                 territory : CHAR);
BEGIN
   sameteam := TRUE;
   down := 1;
   yds := 10;
   WRITELN;
   WRITELN ('Visitor ',visitor:1,' Home ',home:1);
   IF ballposs = -1
        THEN
           WRITELN('Visiting team ball')
```

```
             ELSE
                 WRITELN ('Home team ball') ;
        WRITELN (down, ' Down ', yds, ' yds to go for First Down') ;
        yline : = ydline (territory, distance) ;
        IF territory = 'H'
             THEN
                 WRITELN ('Home ', yline:1, ' yard line')
             ELSE
                 WRITELN ('Visitor ', yline:1' yard line')
    END;

    PROCEDURE getoffense (VAR offplay: INTEGER;
                          VAR finished: BOOLEAN;
                          offenses : offset) ;
    VAR
       error : BOOLEAN;
    BEGIN
       REPEAT
          WRITELN ('Enter offensive play: ') ;
          READLN (offplay) ;
          IF offplay IN offenses
             THEN error : = FALSE
             ELSE BEGIN

                    IF offplay = 14
                       THEN BEGIN
                               error : = FALSE;
                               finished : = TRUE;
                               sameteam : = FALSE
                            END {Then}
                       ELSE BEGIN
                               WRITELN ('illegal offensive call. ') ;
                               error : = TRUE
                            END {else}
                    END; {else}
       UNTIL NOT error

    END;

    PROCEDURE getdefense (VAR defplay : INTEGER;
                          defenses : defset) ;
    VAR
       error : BOOLEAN;
    BEGIN
       REPEAT
          WRITELN ('Enter defensive play: ') ;
          READLN (defplay) ;
          IF defplay IN defenses
             THEN error : = FALSE
             ELSE BEGIN
                     WRITELN ('Illegal defensive call. ') ;
                     error : = TRUE
                  END; {else}
       UNTIL NOT error
    END;

    PROCEDURE runplay (VAR ballposs, yds, gain: INTEGER;
                       VAR sameteam : BOOLEAN;
```

```
                                    r : resultarray;
                                    offplay, defplay : INTEGER);
        BEGIN
           IF rnd > 0.95
               THEN BEGIN
                         WRITELN('Fumble');
                         gain := 0;
                         ballposs := -ballposs;
                         yds := -100;
                         sameteam := FALSE
                      END  {then}
                  ELSE BEGIN
                         gain := TRUNC(r[defplay,offplay]+2*
                            (rnd-0.5));
                         WRITELN('Yards gained: ',gain:1)
                      END {else}
        END;

        PROCEDURE passplay (VAR gain, ballposs,yds : INTEGER;
                            VAR sameteam : BOOLEAN;
                            pc: completion; pi: intarray;
                            offplay, defplay : INTEGER;
                            r : resultarray);
        VAR
           passresult: (completed, intercepted, incomplete, sack);
           whichpass: INTEGER;
           intprob, comprob, sackprob : REAL;
        BEGIN
           IF defplay = 5
               THEN sackprob := 0.75
               ELSE sackprob := 0.2;
           whichpass := offplay - 6;
           intprob := pi[defplay, whichpass];
           IF rnd < intprob
               THEN passresult := interception
               ELSE BEGIN
                         comprob := pc[defplay,whichpass];
                         IF rnd < (intprob + comprob)
                           THEN passresult := completed
                           ELSE BEGIN
                                    IF rnd < sackprob
                                         THEN passresult := sack
                                         ELSE passresult := incomplete
                                END
                      END;
           CASE passresult OF
             completed : BEGIN
                             gain := r[defplay, offplay];
                             WRITELN('Yards gained: ',gain:1)
                         END;
             interception : BEGIN
                             WRITELN('Interception');
                             gain := 10;
                             ballposs := -ballposs;
                             yds := -100;
                             sameteam := FALSE
```

```
                          END;
            incomplete : BEGIN
                              WRITELN('Incomplete');
                              gain := 0;
                              WRITELN('Yards gained: ',gain:1)
                          END;
                  sack : BEGIN
                              WRITELN('Sack');
                              gain := -8;
                              WRITELN('Yards gained: ',gain:1)
                          END
          END   {case}

END;      {procedure passing play}
PROCEDURE kickplay (VAR sameteam : BOOLEAN;
                    VAR home, visitor, distance,
                      ballposs : INTEGER;
                    offplay : INTEGER;
                    territory : CHAR);
VAR
  puntprob, fgprob : REAL;
  attempt : INTEGER;
  play : (punt, fieldgoal);
BEGIN
  IF offplay = 12
      THEN play := punt
      ELSE play := fieldgoal;
  CASE play OF
      punt : BEGIN
                  puntprob := 35 + 8 * rnd;
                  WRITELN('Punt: ',TRUNC(puntprob),' yards');
                  distance := distance + ballposs * TRUNC(puntprob);
                  IF distance > 99
                      THEN distance := 80;
                  IF distance < 1
                      THEN distance := 20;
                  ballposs := -ballposs;
                  sameteam := FALSE
              END;
  fieldgoal : BEGIN
                  IF ballposs = -1
                      THEN attempt := distance
                      ELSE attempt := 100 - distance;
                  WRITELN(attempt + 17,' yard attempt');
                  fgprob := 10 + 35 * rnd;
                  IF fgprob < attempt
                      THEN BEGIN
                              WRITELN('Kick is no good');
                              IF ballposs = 1
                                  THEN BEGIN
                                          ballposs := -1;
                                          distance := 80
                                      END
                              ELSE BEGIN
                                      ballposs := 1;
```

```
                                          distance : = 20
                                        END {else}
                  END {then}
               ELSE BEGIN
                    WRITELN ('Kick is good');
                    IF ballposs = 1
                        THEN BEGIN
                                 home : = home + 3;
                                 ballposs : = −1;
                                 distance : = 70
                             END
                        ELSE BEGIN
                                 visitor : = visitor + 3;
                                 ballposs : = 1;
                                 distance : = 30
                             END {else}
                    END {else}
             END  {fieldgoal}
        END; {case}
    sameteam : = FALSE
END;

PROCEDURE update (VAR home, visitor, ballposs,
                      down, yds, distance : INTEGER;
                 VAR sameteam : BOOLEAN;
                 gain : INTEGER;
                 territory : CHAR);
VAR
    touchdown : BOOLEAN;
BEGIN
    touchdown : = FALSE;
    distance : = distance + ballposs * gain;
    IF (distance > 99) OR (distance < 1)
          THEN touchdown : = TRUE;
    IF touchdown
        THEN BEGIN
                IF distance > 99
                    THEN BEGIN
                            IF ballposs=-1 THEN BEGIN
                                WRITELN ('Fumble') ;ballposs: =1
                                END;
                            WRITELN ('Home touchdown');
                            home : = home + 6;
                            extrapnt (home, visitor, ballposs);
                            sameteam : = FALSE;
                            distance : = 70

                        END
                    ELSE BEGIN
                            IF ballposs=1 THEN BEGIN
                                WRITELN ('Fumble') ;ballposs: =-1
                                END;
                            WRITELN ('Visitor touchdown');
                            visitor : = visitor + 6;
                            extrapnt (home, visitor, ballposs);
                            sameteam : = FALSE;
```

```
                                distance : = 30
                            END
                        END {touchdown}
                ELSE BEGIN
                        yds : = yds - gain;
                        IF yds < 1
                            THEN reset (down, yds, ballposs, home,
                                        visitor, distance, territory)
                            ELSE BEGIN
                                    down : = down + 1;
                                    IF down > 4
                                        THEN BEGIN
                                                ballposs : = -ballposs;
                                                sameteam : = FALSE
                                            END
                                        ELSE BEGIN
                                                WRITELN (down, ' down, ',
                                                        yds, ' yds to go');
                                                yline : =ydline (territory,
                                                    distance);
                                                IF territory = 'H'
                                                    THEN
                                                        WRITELN ('Home
                                                        ', yline: 1,
                                                        'yard line')
                                                    ELSE
                                                        WRITELN ('Visitor',
                                                        yline: 1, ' yard line')
                                            END
                                END {else-not touchdown}
                    END
END;

PROCEDURE extrapnt (VAR home, visitor, ballposs : INTEGER);
BEGIN
    IF rnd < 0.95
        THEN BEGIN
                WRITELN ('Extra point attempt is good');
                IF ballposs = 1
                    THEN home : = home + 1
                    ELSE visitor : = visitor + 1
            END
        ELSE WRITELN ('Extra point attempt is no good. ');
    ballposs : = - ballposs
END;

BEGIN {Main program block}
    WRITELN ('Enter a 6-digit random number: '); READLN (q);
    init1; init2; init3; init4;
    offenses : = [1..13]; defenses : = [1..7]; run: = [1..6];
    passes : = [7..10];    kick : = [12..13];

    home : = 0;   visitor : = 0;    {set the score to 0}
    ballposs : = -1;   {ballposs is -1 when the visitors have
                        the ball; it is +1 when the home team
                        has the ball.}
    distance : = 70;   {distance is the distance from the ball
```

```
                        to the goal line being defended by the
                        home team.
                             At the start of the game, the visiting
                        team has the ball at its own 30-yard line.}
          finished : = FALSE;
          sameteam : = TRUE;
          WHILE NOT finished DO
               BEGIN
                    reset (down, yds, ballposs, home, visitor, distance,
                        territory);
                    WHILE sameteam DO
                         BEGIN
                              getoffense (offplay, finished, offenses);
                              IF NOT finished
                                   THEN BEGIN
                                        IF NOT (offplay IN kick) THEN
                                             getdefense (defplay, defenses);
                                        IF offplay IN run
                                             THEN runplay (ballposs, yds, gain, sameteam,
                                                       r, offplay, defplay);

                                        IF offplay IN passes
                                             THEN passplay (gain, ballposs, yds,
                                                       sameteam, pc, pi,
                                                       offplay, defplay, r);

                                        IF offplay IN kick
                                             THEN kickplay (sameteam, home, visitor,
                                                       distance, ballposs,
                                                       offplay, territory);

                                        IF sameteam
                                             THEN update (home, visitor, ballposs,
                                                       down, yds, distance, sameteam,
                                                       gain, territory);

                                   END {IF}
                         END {WHILE}
               END; {WHILE}
          WRITELN ('Final score: ');
          WRITELN ('Home: ', home, ' Visitor: ', visitor)
     END.

          Here is a sample game:
     Enter a 6-digit random number:
     167601

     Visitor 0 Home 0
     Visiting team ball
     1 Down 10 yds to go for First Down
     Visitor 30 yard line
     Enter offensive play:
     7
     Enter defensive play:
     4
     Yards gained: 6
     2 down, 4 yds to go
     Visitor 36 yard line
```

Enter offensive play:
9
Enter defensive play:
1
Incomplete
Yards gained: 0
3 down, 4 yds to go
Visitor 36 yard line
Enter offensive play:
10
Enter defensive play:
4
Incomplete
Yards gained: 0
4 down, 4 yds to go
Visitor 36 yard line
Enter offensive play:
12
Punt: 35 yards

Visitor 0 Home 0
Home team ball
1 Down 10 yds to go for First Down
Home 29 yard line
Enter offensive play:
9
Enter defensive play:
3
Yards gained: 6
2 down, 4 yds to go
Home 35 yard line
Enter offensive play:
6
Enter defensive play:
5
Yards gained: 29

Visitor 0 Home 0
Home team ball
1 Down 10 yds to go for First Down
Visitor 36 yard line
Enter offensive play:
10
Enter defensive play:
4
Yards gained: 12

Visitor 0 Home 0
Home team ball
1 Down 10 yds to go for First Down
Visitor 24 yard line
Enter offensive play:
3
Enter defensive play:
3
Yards gained: -3
2 down, 13 yds to go

Visitor 27 yard line
Enter offensive play:
3
Enter defensive play:
2
Yards gained: 6
3 down, 7 yds to go
Visitor 21 yard line
Enter offensive play:
7
Enter defensive play:
5
Yards gained: 32
Home touchdown
Extra point attempt is no good.

Visitor 0 Home 6
Visiting team ball
1 Down 10 yds to go for First Down
Visitor 30 yard line
Enter offensive play:
10
Enter defensive play:
1
Yards gained: 100
Visitor touchdown
Extra point attempt is good

Visitor 7 Home 6
Home team ball
1 Down 10 yds to go for First Down
Home 30 yard line
Enter offensive play:
1
Enter defensive play:
7
Yards gained: 9
2 down, 1 yds to go
Home 39 yard line
Enter offensive play:
8
Enter defensive play:
3
Incomplete
Yards gained: 0
3 down, 1 yds to go
Home 39 yard line
Enter offensive play:
8
Enter defensive play:
3
Yards gained: 21

Visitor 7 Home 6
Home team ball
1 Down 10 yds to go for First Down
Visitor 40 yard line

Enter offensive play:
5
Enter defensive play:
2
Yards gained: 7
2 down, 3 yds to go
Visitor 33 yard line
Enter offensive play:
3
Enter defensive play:
4
Yards gained: 1
3 down, 2 yds to go
Visitor 32 yard line
Enter offensive play:
4
Enter defensive play:
4
Yards gained: 2

Visitor 7 Home 6
Home team ball
1 Down 10 yds to go for First Down
Visitor 30 yard line
Enter offensive play:
2
Enter defensive play:
6
Yards gained: 5
2 down, 5 yds to go
Visitor 25 yard line

Enter offensive play:
2
Enter defensive play:
4
Yards gained: 1
3 down, 4 yds to go
Visitor 24 yard line
Enter offensive play:
1
Enter defensive play:
4
Yards gained: 0
4 down, 4 yds to go
Visitor 24 yard line
Enter offensive play:
13
41 yard attempt
Kick is good

Visitor 7 Home 9
Visiting team ball
1 Down 10 yds to go for First Down
Visitor 30 yard line
Enter offensive play:
14

```
Final score:
Home: 9 Visitor: 7
```

The program does not have any kickoffs. Instead, the receiving team always starts with the ball on its own 30-yard line.

There are many commercially available game programs. However, once you learn to program you can be creative and write your own programs to play your own games.

Chapter 16 Exercises

1. Write a new ticktacktoe program to cover the case in which the opponent makes the first move.

2. Here are some extra modifications you may like to add to the football program.
   (a) Include occasional penalties and the choice of whether or not to accept them.
   (b) Include kickoffs and the possibility of an onside kick.
   (c) Have a way to keep track of the time left in each quarter, subtracting a certain amount for each play depending on whether it was a passing play or a running play.
   (d) Include a coin toss at the beginning of the game to determine who will have possession of the ball.
   (e) Allow for safeties to be scored.
   (f) If you make a first down inside your opponent's 10-yard line, have the computer print first and goal rather than first and 10.
   (g) The program has room for you to add an option play (offensive play 11) in which the offensive player could select the option for the play after seeing what the defense is; however, this play is risky and has a much higher chance of resulting in a fumble.

3. Write a computer program that deals out the cards in a blackjack (21) game.

4. Write a "Clue" strategy program. As you play the game Clue, you slowly gather more information about the identity of the killer. Have the program read in each piece of evidence and then tell you when it has narrowed down the choices so that it knows who the killer is.

5. Write a program that referees a "Monopoly" game. For example, the program will have to keep track of the position of each player's marker on the board, the properties that each player owns, and the amount of money each player has.

6. Write a program to play "hangman."

7. Write a program that stores the positions of all the pieces on a checkerboard and then prints out a display of the board.

8. Write a program that reads in the move made by a checkers player and then prints the new position of the board. (Use the program from Exercise 7.)

9. (This will be very hard.) Try to write your own checkers strategy program. Use the programs from Exercises 7 and 8 to keep track of the position of the checkers on the board. Your program will not be able to consider every single possible checkers game. Instead, it will have to have some rule that allows it to evaluate alternative game positions and then make the move that leads to the best game position. This type of problem is important in artificial intelligence. Don't attempt it unless you are serious about learning quite a bit about this field.

10. Write your own "StarShip" program. Have the program keep track of the position of your starship in the galaxy, the position of the other obstacles, and the amount of power your ship has left. You will have to think of an objective for the game to make it interesting. Be as creative as you can!

11. Write a program that tries to predict the results of major league baseball games by reading in the batting averages and pitching averages for two real teams, and then conducts a simulated game between them.

12. Write a program that keeps track of the scores during a bowling game.

13. Write a program that keeps track of the cards that have already been turned up in a blackjack game and then tells you whether you should ask for another card in a given situation.

CHAPTER 17

Data Processing Applications

If you ask what most big computers do most of the time, the answer is that they spend their time on various data processing applications. Data processing operations are the kinds of tasks for which computers are ideally suited: They require many repetitious operations on large masses of data.

The word datum refers to a single piece of information, that is, a single fact. The word data is the plural of "datum" and means a collection of factual information. The act of data processing consists of manipulating that information in useful ways. Data can be classified according to the following hierarchy. The smallest unit of information is a single character, such as a letter. One character usually occupies 1 computer byte, which is 8 binary digits (bits). A group of characters is called a field, or data item. An example of a field is a person's name. A group of fields is called a record. For example, in the census bureau's monthly survey, all the information on a particular individual is stored as a single record. A group of records is called a file, and a group of files is called a data base.

Examples of Data Processing

People come in contact with data processing applications of computers all the time, and most of the complaints lodged against computers come from their use in this area. Examples of data processing applications of computers include the following:

1. Maintaining an organization's payroll and printing its paychecks (most people like this particular application the best)

2. Keeping track of the balances of the customers at a bank

3. Keeping track of airline reservations and seat assignments

4. Maintaining the records (such as grades) for the students in a school district

5. Sending out bills to customers with credit cards

6. Calculating statistics for major league baseball teams.

7. Maintaining a magazine subscription list

8. Keeping track of the books checked out and returned at a library

A complicated task will require a great deal of memory, and so large organizations usually need large computers to meet their data processing needs. However, there are many data processing tasks you can perform in PASCAL with a small computer. For example, keeping track of your personal finances is a task well suited for small computers.

Mortgages

Here is an example of an important financial application program that you can write for a small computer, especially if you are considering buying a home. Many houses are sold with mortgages, which means that the buyer pays a fixed monthly payment for a period of 20 to 30 years. Each month part of the payment goes to pay the interest charge the buyer owes on the remaining principal balance of the loan. The rest of the payment reduces the principal balance. At the end of the loan period the balance is reduced to zero. At first, most of the buyer's monthly payment goes for interest. That means that the principal amount declines slowly, and the buyer's equity (the portion of the home that he or she actually owns) rises slowly. Near the end of the loan period most of the payment goes to pay off the principal.

This program tells you as a prospective buyer, for every month, how much of your payment will go for interest and how much the remaining principal balance will be. (This type of table is called an amortization table.) You're not likely to need results for every single month during the whole loan period; so the program allows you to select the years for which you would like to have the results printed. Note that this particular program does not require much data storage, but it is the kind of program that would be important to have available at a bank or a loan institution. This program is a good data processing program in that it is written with many execution-time explanatory messages so that the person using the program does not need to know how to program in PASCAL.

```
PROGRAM amorttable (INPUT, OUTPUT);
TYPE
    yeararray = ARRAY [1..100] OF INTEGER;
VAR
    loan, annrate, monrate : REAL;
    years : INTEGER;
    outyear : yeararray;
    finished : BOOLEAN;
    response : CHAR;
FUNCTION power (a, b : REAL) : REAL;
  BEGIN
    power := EXP(b * LN(a));
END; {function power}
```

```
              FUNCTION monpay (VAR monrate : REAL; loan, annrate : REAL;
                              years : INTEGER) : REAL;
              VAR
                denom : REAL;
                months : INTEGER;
              BEGIN
                monrate := power(annrate + 1, 1/12) - 1;
                months := years * 12;
                denom := power(1 + monrate, months) - 1;
                monpay := (loan * monrate * power(1 + monrate, months))/denom
              END; {function monpay}
              PROCEDURE initialize (VAR years : INTEGER;
                                    VAR loan, annrate : REAL;
                                    VAR outyear : yeararray);
              VAR
                yrprint, eachyear, count : INTEGER;
                response : CHAR;
              BEGIN
                WRITELN('Enter principal loan amount.');
                WRITELN(' (Example : 25000 for $25,000)');
                READLN(loan);
                WRITELN('Enter annual interest rate.');
                WRITELN(' (Example : .065 for 6.5%)');
                READLN(annrate);
                WRITELN('Enter the number of years to repay loan.');
                READLN(years);
                WRITELN('Do you wish to print out each year');
                WRITELN('of the loan period? Y or N.');
                READLN(response);
                IF response = 'Y'
                  THEN BEGIN
                    FOR count := 1 TO years DO
                      outyear[count] := count
                      END
                  ELSE BEGIN
                    WRITELN('How many years do you wish to print out');
                    READLN(yrprint);
                    WRITELN('Which years do you wish to print out');
                    WRITELN('Separate each year by a blank.');
                    WRITELN(' (Example : 1 4 15 for the first, fourth and');
                    WRITELN('fifteenth years.)');
                  FOR count := 1 TO yrprint DO
                    BEGIN
                        READ(eachyear);
                        outyear[count] := eachyear
                    END {for loop}
                  END {else portion}
              END; {procedure initialize}
              PROCEDURE printable (loan, annrate, monrate : REAL;
                                   years : INTEGER;
                                   outyear : yeararray);
              CONST
                blanks = '    ';
              VAR
                countyr, countmon, sub : INTEGER;
```

```pascal
            ratepay, monthly, loanred : REAL;
      BEGIN
            monthly : = monpay (monrate, loan, annrate, years);
            sub : = 1;
            FOR countyr : = 1 TO years DO
                  BEGIN
                        FOR countmon : = 1 TO 12 DO
                              BEGIN
                                    ratepay : = monrate * loan;
                                    loanred : = monthly − ratepay;
                                    loan : = loan − loanred;

                                    IF countyr = outyear [sub]
                                          THEN BEGIN
                                                WRITE (blanks, countyr: 3);
                                                WRITE ('      ', countmon: 2);
                                                WRITE (blanks, monthly: 6: 2);
                                                WRITE ('   ', blanks, ratepay: 7: 2);
                                                WRITE ('   ', blanks, loanred: 8: 2);
                                                WRITE ('   ', blanks, loan: 9: 2);
                                                WRITELN;
                                                      END {then portion}
                              END; {inner for loop}
                              IF countyr = outyear [sub]
                                    THEN sub : = sub + 1
                  END {outer for loop}
      END; {procedure printable}
      PROCEDURE headings (loan : REAL);
        CONST
            blanks = '      ';
        VAR
            count : INTEGER;
        BEGIN
            WRITELN;
            FOR count : = 1 TO 6 DO
                  WRITE (blanks);
            WRITELN ('AMORTIZATION TABLE');
            WRITELN;
            WRITE (blanks, blanks, blanks, '     ');
            WRITE ('Monthly', blanks);
            WRITE ('Interest', blanks);
            WRITE ('Principal', blanks);
            WRITE ('Principal');
            WRITELN;
            WRITE (blanks, 'Year Month');
            WRITE (blanks, 'Payment');
            WRITE (blanks, 'Payment ');
            WRITE (blanks, 'Reduction');
            WRITE (blanks, ' Balance');
            WRITELN;
            WRITELN; {blank line}
            FOR count : = 1 TO 10 DO
                  WRITE (blanks);
                  WRITE ('      ');
                  WRITELN (loan: 9: 2)
      END; {procedure headings}
```

```
BEGIN {Main body}
    finished : = FALSE;
    WRITELN('This program creates an amortization table.');
    WRITELN('You will be asked to provide the following:');
    WRITELN('1. the principal loan amount,');
    WRITELN('2. the annual interest rate,');
    WRITELN('3. the repayment period,');
    WRITELN('4. the years to be printed.');
    WRITELN('Do you wish to continue? Y or N.');
    READLN(response);
    IF response = 'N'
        THEN finished : = TRUE;
    WHILE NOT finished DO
        BEGIN
            initialize (years, loan, annrate, outyear);
            headings (loan);
            printable (loan, annrate, monrate, years, outyear);
            WRITELN('Do you wish to continued this program? Y or N');
        IF response = 'N'
            THEN finished : = TRUE
        END; {while loop}
    WRITELN('This concludes the program.')
END. {Program amorttable}
```

Here is a sample of the output of this program:

```
This program creates an amortization table.
You will be asked to provide the following:
1. the principal loan amount,
2. the annual interest rate,
3. the repayment period,
4. the years to be printed.
Do you wish to continue? Y or N.
Y
Enter principal loan amount.
 (Example : 25000 for $25,000)
600
Enter annual interest rate.
 (Example : .065 for 6.5%
.05
Enter the number of years to repay loan.
3
Do you wish to print out each year
of the loan period? Y or N.
Y
```

AMORTIZATION TABLE

Year	Month	Monthly Payment	Interest Payment	Principal Reduction	Principal Balance
					600.00
1	1	17.95	2.44	15.51	584.49
1	2	17.95	2.38	15.57	568.92
1	3	17.95	2.32	15.63	553.29
1	4	17.95	2.25	15.70	537.59

1	5	17.95	2.19	15.76	521.82
1	6	17.95	2.13	15.83	506.00
1	7	17.95	2.06	15.89	490.11
1	8	17.95	2.00	15.96	474.15
1	9	17.95	1.93	16.02	458.13
1	10	17.95	1.87	16.09	442.04
1	11	17.95	1.80	16.15	425.89
1	12	17.95	1.74	16.22	409.67
2	1	17.95	1.67	16.28	393.39
2	2	17.95	1.60	16.35	377.04
2	3	17.95	1.54	16.42	360.62
2	4	17.95	1.47	16.48	344.14
2	5	17.95	1.40	16.55	327.59
2	6	17.95	1.33	16.62	310.97
2	7	17.95	1.27	16.69	294.29
2	8	17.95	1.20	16.75	277.53
2	9	17.95	1.13	16.82	260.71
2	10	17.95	1.06	16.89	243.82
2	11	17.95	0.99	16.96	226.86
2	12	17.95	0.92	17.03	209.83
3	1	17.95	0.85	17.10	192.73
3	2	17.95	0.79	17.17	175.57
3	3	17.95	0.72	17.24	158.33
3	4	17.95	0.65	17.31	141.02
3	5	17.95	0.57	17.38	123.64
3	6	17.95	0.50	17.45	106.19
3	7	17.95	0.43	17.52	88.67
3	8	17.95	0.36	17.59	71.08
3	9	17.95	0.29	17.66	53.42
3	10	17.95	0.22	17.74	35.68
3	11	17.95	0.15	17.81	17.88
3	12	17.95	0.07	17.88	-0.00

Do you wish to continue this program? Y or N.
Y
Enter principal loan amount.
(Example : 25000 for $25,000)
70000
Enter annual interest rate.
(Example : .065 for 6.5%)
.12
Enter the number of years to repay loan.
20
Do you wish to print out each year
of the loan period? Y or N.
N

How many years do you wish to print out
3
Which years do you wish to print out
Separate each year by a blank.
(Example : 1 4 15 for the first, fourth and
fifteenth years.)
1 10 20

AMORTIZATION TABLE

Year	Month	Monthly Payment	Interest Payment	Principal Reduction	Principal Balance
					70000.00
1	1	741.03	664.21	76.82	69923.17
1	2	741.03	663.48	77.55	69845.61
1	3	741.03	662.74	78.29	69767.32
1	4	741.03	662.00	79.03	69688.29
1	5	741.03	661.25	79.78	69608.51
1	6	741.03	660.49	80.54	69527.97
1	7	741.03	659.73	81.30	69446.67
1	8	741.03	658.96	82.07	69364.59
1	9	741.03	658.18	82.85	69281.73
1	10	741.03	657.39	83.64	69198.09
1	11	741.03	656.60	84.43	69113.65
1	12	741.03	655.80	85.23	69028.42
10	1	741.03	527.99	213.04	55431.33
10	2	741.03	525.97	215.06	55216.27
10	3	741.03	523.93	217.10	54999.17
10	4	741.03	521.87	219.16	54780.00
10	5	741.03	519.79	221.24	54558.76
10	6	741.03	517.69	223.34	54335.42
10	7	741.03	515.57	225.46	54109.96
10	8	741.03	513.43	227.60	53882.35
10	9	741.03	511.27	229.76	53652.59
10	10	741.03	509.09	231.94	53420.65
10	11	741.03	506.89	234.14	53186.51
10	12	741.03	504.67	236.36	52950.15
20.	1	741.03	79.37	661.66	7702.91
20	2	741.03	73.09	667.94	7034.97
20	3	741.03	66.75	674.28	6360.69
20	4	741.03	60.35	680.68	5680.02
20	5	741.03	53.90	687.14	4992.88
20	6	741.03	47.38	693.66	4299.22
20	7	741.03	40.79	700.24	3598.99
20	8	741.03	34.15	706.88	2892.10

20	9	741.03	27.44	713.59	2178.51
20	10	741.03	20.67	720.36	1458.15
20	11	741.03	13.84	727.20	730.96
20	12	741.03	6.94	734.10	-3.14

Do you wish to continue this program? Y or N.
N

Managing School Records

Now we'll write a program to keep track of student course selections in a high school. We will develop a simplified program in which there are only 12 classes to choose from and each student takes 6 classes. Our program will need to perform three different tasks:

1 Read in a student's course selection.

2 Print a student's schedule.

3 Print a list of the students in a course.

The information is stored in the files studentfile and classfile. The student file is a field made up of records. Note the structure of the classfile. It is of type array of records. A file window for this file will contain the entire array of class records. Within a class record the field class list is also of type array, and so we indirectly have an array within an array. We also use a master file which is used to cross-reference student names and numbers.

The program uses codes to keep track of the classes offered. The codes are simply the subscripts in the classcode array. Notice how the user-defined ordinal type class is used to print out a class. We define an array of string which will contain the classes offered and uses the ordinal type classes as a subscript. This allows us to output the class name and also makes it easy to reference an element in the file classfile.

The program will print out a class list given a class code, or a student's record given the student name or number. The program will also add a student record to the file, making appropriate changes to the student, class, and master files. When additions are made, we must merge the addition with the existing file into a temporary file and then copy the temporary file back into the original file.

The program listed here does not check for invalid entries by the user. These checks are left as exercises for you to add. Remember that the person actually using the program should not need to know anything about Pascal or how the program works.

Here is the program:

```
PROGRAM schoolrecord (INPUT, OUTPUT);
   {This program keeps track of student records and class lists.
    The program as it is does not use external files.}
CONST
   stringlen = 20;
   classmax = 30;
   periods = 6;
   classchoices = 12;
TYPE
   string = PACKED ARRAY[1..stringlen] of CHAR;
   classes = (ALGEBRA, BIOLOGY, CALCULUS, CHEMISTRY, DRAMA,
             ENGLISH, FRENCH, GERMAN, HISTORY, PE, PHYSICS,
             SPANISH);
   schedule = ARRAY[1..periods] OF INTEGER;
```

```
                studentlist = ARRAY[1..classmax] of INTEGER;
                name =
                  RECORD
                    firstname, middlename, lastname : string;
                  END;
                studentinfo =
                  RECORD
                    studentclass: schedule;
                    studentnum: INTEGER
                  END;
                classinfo =
                  RECORD
                    classcount: INTEGER;
                    classlist: studentlist
                  END;
                masterinfo =
                  RECORD
                    mastername: name;
                    masternum: INTEGER
                  END;
                periodarray = ARRAY[ALGEBRA..SPANISH] OF classinfo;
                periodcodes = ARRAY[1..classchoices] OF classes;
                periodtable = ARRAY[classes] OF string;
                studenttype = FILE OF studentinfo;
                classtype = FILE OF periodarray;
                mastertype = FILE OF masterinfo;
            VAR
                studentfile: studenttype;
                classfile: classtype;
                masterfile: mastertype;
                classarray: periodarray;
                classcodes: periodcodes;
                classtable: periodtable;
                option, response : CHAR;
                finished: BOOLEAN;
            PROCEDURE initialize ;
                {This is used to initialize the classtable and classcode
                arrays.}
            BEGIN
                classcodes[1] := ALBEGRA; classtable[ALGEBRA] := 'Algebra   ';
                classcodes[2] := BIOLOGY; classtable[BIOLOGY] := 'Biology   ';
                classcodes[3] := CALCULUS; classtable[CALCULUS] := 'Calculus   ';
                classcodes[4] := CHEMISTRY; classtable[CHEMISTRY] := 'Chemistry   ';
                classcodes[5] := DRAMA ; classtable[DRAMA] := 'Drama   ';
                classcodes[6] := ENGLISH; classtable[ENGLISH] := 'English   ';
                classcodes[7] := FRENCH ; classtable[FRENCH] := 'French   ';
                classcodes[8] := GERMAN ; classtable[GERMAN] := 'German   ';
                classcodes[9] := HISTORY; classtable[HISTORY] := 'History   ';
                classcodes[10] := PE ; classtable[PE] := 'PE   ';
                classcodes[11] := PHYSICS; classtable[PHYSICS] := 'Physics   ';
                classcodes[12] := SPANISH; classtable[SPANISH] := 'Spanish   ';
            END;

            PROCEDURE firsttime (VAR studentfile: studenttype;
                                 VAR classfile: classtype;
                                 VAR masterfile: mastertype);
```

```
              {This is used when the program is first run to create
              the student, class, master files. The class counts are
              initially set to zero. This procedure becomes
              important when external files are used.}
VAR
   count1: INTEGER;
   tempclass: classes;
   temparray: periodarray;
BEGIN
   REWRITE (studentfile) ;
   REWRITE (masterfile) ;
   REWRITE (classfile) ;
   FOR count1 : = 1 TO classchoices DO
     BEGIN
        tempclass : = classcodes [count1] ;
        temparray [tempclass] . classcount : = 0
     END;
   classfile^ : = temparray;
   PUT (classfile)
END; {firsttime}

PROCEDURE listcodes;
    {This procedure lists the classes and associated codes.}
VAR
   count1: INTEGER;
   tempclass: classes;
BEGIN
   FOR count1 : = 1 TO classchoices DO
     BEGIN
        WRITE (count1, ' = ') ;
        tempclass : = classcodes [count1] ;
        WRITELN (classtable [tempclass])
     END
END; {listcodes}

PROCEDURE copymaster (VAR oldfile, newfile : mastertype) ;
    {This procedure copies the temporary master file into the
    master file which is used in the other procedures.}
   BEGIN
      RESET (oldfile) ;
      REWRITE (newfile) ;
      WHILE NOT EOF (oldfile) DO
         BEGIN
            newfile^ : = oldfile^;
            PUT (newfile) ;
            IF NOT EOF (oldfile)
               THEN GET (oldfile)
         END
END; {procedure copymaster}

PROCEDURE copystudent (VAR oldfile, newfile : studenttype) ;
    {This procedure copies the temporary student file into the
    student file used in the other procedures.}
BEGIN
   RESET (oldfile) ;
   REWRITE (newfile) ;
   WHILE NOT EOF (oldfile) DO
```

```
                BEGIN
                  newfile^ : = oldfile^;
                  PUT (newfile);
                  IF NOT EOF (oldfile)
                    THEN GET (oldfile)
                END
        END; {procedure copystudent}

        PROCEDURE copyclass (VAR oldfile, newfile : classtype);
                    {This procedure copies the temporary class file into
                     the class file used in the other procedures.}
        BEGIN
            RESET (oldfile);
            REWRITE (newfile);
            WHILE NOT EOF (oldfile) DO
                BEGIN
                  newfile^ : = oldfile^;
                  PUT (newfile);
                  IF NOT EOF (oldfile)
                    THEN GET (oldfile)
                END
        END; {procedure copyclass}

        PROCEDURE getname (VAR word: string);
            {This procedure gets the student's first, last and middle
             name.}
        VAR
          c: CHAR;
          count1, count2: INTEGER;
        BEGIN
            count1 : = 1;
            REPEAT
              READ (c);
              IF NOT EOLN THEN word[count1] : = c;
              count1 : = count1 + 1
            UNTIL EOLN;
            FOR count2 : = (count1-1) TO stringlen DO
              word[count2] : = ' '
        END;

        PROCEDURE checkclass (VAR classfile: classtype;
                              VAR tempcode: INTEGER);
            {This procedure checks to see if the class is full. Note that
            we never get another element out of the classfile since the
            entire array will be in the file window after the reset.}
        VAR
          tempclass: classes;
          classfull: BOOLEAN;
          checkcount: INTEGER;
        BEGIN
          RESET (classfile); {the file window now contains an array}
          classfull : = FALSE;
          REPEAT
            IF NOT EOF (classfile)
              THEN BEGIN
                      tempclass : = classcodes [tempcode];
                      checkcount : = classfile^[tempclass].classcount;
```

```
                    IF checkcount > classmax
                        THEN BEGIN
                                WRITELN ('Class is full - enter another
                                    class code. ');
                                READLN (tempcode);
                                classfull : = TRUE
                            END
                        ELSE classfull : = FALSE
                END; {then}
        UNTIL NOT classfull
END;
PROCEDURE mergeclass (VAR classfile: classtype; classin:
    schedule; numberin: INTEGER);
    {This procedure updates the class file by first writing
    the additions to the temporary file and then copying
    file back into the class file. The same type of
    logic is used in the other two merge procedures.}
VAR
    tempfile: classtype;
    temparray: periodarray;
    tempcount, count1: INTEGER;
    tempclass: classes;
BEGIN
    RESET (classfile);
    REWRITE (tempfile);
    temparray : = classfile^;
    FOR count1 : = 1 TO periods DO
     BEGIN
        tempclass : = classcodes [classin [count1]];
        tempcount : = temparray [tempclass]. classcount;
        temparray [tempclass]. classlist [tempcount+1] : = numberin;
        temparray [tempclass]. classcount : = tempcount + 1
     END; {for loop}
    tempfile^ : = temparray;
    PUT (tempfile);
    copyclass (tempfile, classfile)
END;

PROCEDURE mergemaster (VAR masterfile: mastertype;
                            namein: name; numberin: INTEGER);
    {This procedure updates the master file.}
VAR
    merged: BOOLEAN;
    tempmaster: mastertype;
    mastrec: masterinfo;
BEGIN
    REWRITE (tempmaster);
    RESET (masterfile);
    merged : = FALSE;
    IF EOF (masterfile)
    THEN merged : = TRUE;
WHILE (NOT merged) AND (NOT EOF (masterfile)) DO
    BEGIN
        IF mastrec. masternum < numberin
            THEN BEGIN
                    mastrec : = masterfile^;
```

```
                        tempmaster^ : = mastrec;
                        PUT (tempmaster) ;
                        IF NOT EOF (masterfile)
                            THEN GET (masterfile)
                  END

            ELSE BEGIN
                        tempmaster^. masternum : = numberin;
                        tempmaster^. mastername : = namein;
                        PUT (tempmaster) ;
                        WITH namein DO
                            WRITELN (lastname, ', ', firstname, middlename) ;
                        merged : = TRUE
                  END
      END; {while}
    IF NOT merged
      THEN BEGIN
                        tempmaster^. masternum : = numberin;
                        tempmaster^. mastername : = namein;
                        PUT (tempmaster)
            END;
      WHILE NOT EOF (masterfile) DO
        BEGIN
          mastrec : = masterfile^;
          tempmaster^ : = mastrec;
          PUT (tempmaster) ;
          IF NOT EOF (masterfile)
              THEN GET (masterfile)
        END;
      copymaster (tempmaster, masterfile)
END;

PROCEDURE mergestudent (VAR studentfile: studenttype;
                            classin: schedule; numberin: INTEGER) ;
    {This procedure updates the student file.}
VAR
  merged: BOOLEAN;
  tempstudent: studenttype;
  studentrec: studentinfo;
BEGIN
  REWRITE (tempstudent) ;
  RESET (studentfile) ;
  merged : = FALSE;
  IF EOF (studentfile)
      THEN merged : = TRUE;
    WHILE (NOT merged) AND (NOT EOF (studentfile) ) DO
      BEGIN
        studentrec : = studentfile^;
        IF studentrec. studentnum < numberin
          THEN BEGIN
                    tempstudent^ : = studentrec;
                    PUT (tempstudent) ;
                    IF NOT EOF (studentfile)
                        THEN GET (studentfile)
                  END
                ELSE BEGIN
```

```
                tempstudent^. studentnum : = numberin;
                tempstudent^. studentclass : = classin;
                PUT (tempstudent);
                WRITELN ('Student number = ', numberin);
                WRITELN ('period 1 = ', classin[1]);
                WRITELN ('period 2 = ', classin[2]);
                WRITELN ('period 3 = ', classin[3]);
                WRITELN ('period 4 = ', classin[4]);
                WRITELN ('period 5 = ', classin[5]);
                WRITELN ('period 6 = ', classin[6]);
                merged : = TRUE
              END
        END; {while}
    IF NOT merged
      THEN BEGIN
              tempstudent^. studentnum : = numberin;
              tempstudent^. studentclass : = classin;
              PUT (tempstudent)
            END;
    WHILE NOT EOF (studentfile) DO
      BEGIN
        studentrec : = studentfile^;
        tempstudent^ : = studentrec;
        PUT (tempstudent);
        IF NOT EOF (studentfile)
          THEN GET (studentfile)
      END;
      copystudent (tempstudent, studentfile)
    END;

PROCEDURE printstudent (VAR masterfile: mastertype;
                        VAR studentfile: studenttype);
    {This procedure will print out a student record given
    a student number or a student name.}
VAR
    nameout: name;
    response: CHAR;
    count1, codeout, numberout, tempcode: INTEGER;
    tempclass: classes;
    classout: classes;
    match: BOOLEAN;
BEGIN
    WRITELN ('Do you wish to enter the student number? Y or N. ');
    READLN (response);
    match : = FALSE;
    IF response = 'N'
      THEN BEGIN
              WRITELN ('Enter the student last name. ');
              getname (nameout. lastname);
              WRITELN ('Enter the student first name. ');
              getname (nameout. firstname);
              WRITELN ('Enter the student middle name. ');
              getname (nameout. middlename);
              RESET (masterfile);
              WHILE (NOT EOF (masterfile)) AND (NOT match) DO
                BEGIN
```

```
                        IF nameout = masterfile^.mastername
                           THEN BEGIN
                                    numberout := masterfile^.masternum;
                                    match := TRUE
                                END
                           ELSE BEGIN
                                    IF NOT EOF(masterfile)
                                       THEN GET(masterfile);
                                END {else}
                    END {while}
                 END {outer then}

         ELSE BEGIN
                 WRITELN('Enter the student number.');
                 READLN(numberout);
                 RESET(masterfile);
                 WHILE (NOT EOF(masterfile)) AND (NOT match) DO
                    BEGIN
                       IF numberout = masterfile^.masternum
                          THEN BEGIN
                                   nameout := masterfile^.mastername;
                                   match := TRUE
                               END
                          ELSE IF NOT EOF(masterfile)
                                  THEN GET(masterfile)
                    END {while}
                 END; {else}
         WRITE ('Student name: ');
         WITH nameout DO
      BEGIN
         WRITE(lastname,',');
         WRITE(firstname);
         WRITE(middlename)
      END;
   WRITELN;
   WRITELN('Student number: ', numberout);
   RESET(studentfile);
   match := FALSE;
      WHILE (NOT EOF(studentfile)) AND (NOT match) DO
         BEGIN
            IF numberout = studentfile^.studentnum
               THEN BEGIN
                       match := TRUE;
                       FOR count1 := 1 TO periods DO
                          BEGIN
                             tempcode :=
                             studentfile^.studentclass[count1];
                             tempclass := classcodes[tempcode];
                             WRITELN ('Period ',count1,': ',classtable
                                [tempclass])
                          END {for loop}
                    END {then}
               ELSE IF NOT EOF(studentfile)
                  THEN GET(studentfile)
         END {while}
   END;
```

```
PROCEDURE printclass (VAR classfile: classtype;
                      VAR masterfile: mastertype);
     {This procedure will print out a class list given
     the class code.}
VAR
   codeout, count1, studentout, tempcount: INTEGER;
   temparray: periodarray;
   tempclass: classes;
   match : BOOLEAN;
BEGIN
   WRITELN ('Enter class code. ');
   READLN (codeout) ;
   match : = FALSE;
   RESET (classfile) ;
   temparray : = classfileˆ;
   tempclass : = classcodes [codeout];
   WRITELN (classtable [tempclass]);
   tempcount : = temparray [tempclass]. classcount;
   WRITELN ('Number of students = ', tempcount);
   FOR count1 : = 1 TO tempcount DO
      BEGIN
         studentout : = temparray [tempclass]. classlist [count1];
         RESET (masterfile) ;
         match : = FALSE;
         WHILE (NOT EOF (masterfile)) AND (NOT match) DO
            BEGIN
               IF studentout = masterfileˆ. masternum
               THEN BEGIN
                       match : = TRUE;
                       WITH masterfileˆ. mastername DO
                          BEGIN
                             WRITE ('Student name: ', lastname, ', ');
                             WRITE (firstname, ' ');
                             WRITELN (middlename)
                          END {with}
                    END {then}
                    ELSE IF NOT EOF (masterfile)
                       THEN GET (masterfile);
            END {while}
      END {for loop}
END;

PROCEDURE modifyfile (VAR studentfile: studenttype;
                      VAR classfile: classtype;
                      VAR masterfile: mastertype);
     {This procedure accepts new student data from the user
     and calls the proper update procedures.}
VAR
   namein: name;
   count1, numberin: INTEGER;
   classin: schedule;
BEGIN
   WRITELN ('Enter student last name. ');
   getname (namein. lastname);
   WRITELN ('Enter student first name. ');
   getname (namein. firstname);
```

```
            WRITELN ('Enter student middle name. ') ;
            getname (namein. middlename) ;
            WRITELN ('Enter student number. ') ;
            READLN (numberin) ;
            FOR count1 : = 1 TO periods DO
               BEGIN
                  WRITELN ('Enter class code for student class # ', count1) ;
                  READLN (classin [count1]) ;
                  checkclass (classfile, classin [count1])
               END;
            mergemaster (masterfile, namein, numberin) ;
            mergestudent (studentfile, classin, numberin) ;
            mergeclass (classfile, classin, numberin)
         END;

         PROCEDURE displaylist (VAR studentfile: studenttype;
                                VAR classfile: classtype;
                                VAR masterfile: mastertype) ;
                  {This procedure calls the proper print procedure
                  given the user's preference. }
         VAR
            response: CHAR;
         BEGIN
            WRITELN ('Do you wish to print out a student record (S) ') ;
            WRITELN ('or a class list (C)?') ;
            READLN (response) ;
            IF response = 'S'
               THEN printstudent (masterfile, studentfile)
               ELSE printclass (classfile, masterfile)
         END; {displaylist procedure}

         BEGIN {main program block}
            WRITELN ('This program will update a student record or print ') ;
            WRITELN ('a classlist or student record. Do you wish to
               continue?') ;
            WRITELN ('Y or N. ') ;
            READLN (response) ;
            IF response = 'N'
            THEN finished : = TRUE
            ELSE finished : = FALSE;
         IF NOT finished
            THEN BEGIN
               initialize;
               WRITELN ('Have you run this program before? Y or N. ') ;
               READLN (response) ;
               IF response = 'N'
                  THEN firsttime (studentfile, classfile, masterfile)
            END;
         WHILE NOT finished DO
          BEGIN
            WRITELN ('Do you wish to: ') ;
            WRITELN ('1. List the class codes - Type L') ;
            WRITELN ('2. Print a class list or a student record - Type P') ;
            WRITELN ('3. Update a student record - Type U') ;
            READLN (option) ;
            CASE option OF
```

```
          'L': listcodes;
          'P': displaylist(studentfile, classfile, masterfile);
          'U': modifyfile(studentfile, classfile, masterfile)
     END;
         WRITELN('Do you wish to continue? Y or N. ');
         READLN(response);
         IF response = 'N'
           THEN finished := TRUE
           ELSE finished := FALSE
     END {while}
  END.
```

Chapter 17 Exercises

1. Write a program that keeps track of your personal finances. (See some of the suggestions in Chapter 9.) Divide your expenditures and income into broad categories, and then enter the record of each expenditure item into the computer. Have the computer print out a report at the end of the month telling how much you spent in each category that month. Also have the computer keep track of cumulative totals for the year. Some refinements you may like to add are: (1) Have the computer sort the expenditures in order by category so you can see at a glance where you have been spending the most money; and (2) have the computer compare your expenditures for the current month with those for the same month last year. If you have a computer with graphics capabilities, you might like to have the computer make pie charts showing your expenditure categories.

2. Write a program that calculates your personal price index. Estimate what fraction of your income goes for different items, and read in the prices of those items each month. (Obviously you will not be able to do this for everything you buy.) Find out how much it would cost you now to buy the same goods that you bought in the first month you started the program. Compare your own personal inflation rate with the national inflation rate.

3. Suppose you are considering an investment project. Let's say that P is the array that lists how much you will get from the project each year. (If $P[I]$ is negative, as it probably is for $I = 1$, that means that you have to pay out money that year.) The present value of the project is defined to be

    $$P[1] + \frac{P[2]}{1 + r} + \frac{P[3]}{(1 + r)^2} + \frac{P[4]}{(1 + r)^3} + \frac{P[5]}{(1 + r)^4} + \cdots$$

    Write a program that reads in a value for the interest rate r and calculates the present value of the project. If the present value is positive, the program should print "This project is a good idea." If the present value is negative, the program should print "This project is not a good idea."

4. Write a program to keep track of your store discount coupons. Whenever you get a new coupon, give it a number and store it in a box by its number. Type into the computer the number of the coupon, what it is good for, and the expiration date. Before you go to the store, type in the names of the items that you intend to buy and the computer will tell you if you have coupons for any of those items and, if you do, what their numbers are.

5. Write a program that allows you to type in all your recipes on the computer and then displays the recipe you need when you type in its name.

6. Write a program to keep track of the balance in your checkbook.

7. A coliseum has tickets at five different prices. Write a program that reads in the five prices, then reads in the number of tickets sold at each price, and finally calculates the total revenue from the ticket sales each day.

8. Suppose you are directing a table tennis tournament for 20 players. Write a program that designs a 19-day schedule. Each player plays one game each day, and at the end of the tournament each player will have played every other player exactly once.

9. Write a program to keep track of the standings for the tournament in Exercise 8. The program should read in the winners and losers of all the games each day. Every day, it should print a listing of all the players in the order of their win-loss records.

10. Write a program to keep track of reservations and seat assignments for an airline.

11. Write a program to keep track of the inventory in a clothing store.

12. Write a program to keep track of the attendance records of the members of a club.

13. Write a program to read in the test scores from a class of students who take 10 tests during the year and to calculate their average scores and their ranks relative to the rest of the class.

14. Write a payroll program to handle a company where different employees have different hourly rates.

15. Write a program to keep track of your current Christmas or Hanukkah card mailing list.

16. Write a program to keep track of statistics for your local basketball, football, or baseball team. Read the statistics into the computer after each game, and then print out the cumulative season statistics.

17. Write a program to keep track of the charges you owe on a credit card. When the credit card bill arrives, your computer can tell you whether the bill is correct.

18. Write a program to keep track of the books checked out from a library. Have the program perform these functions:

    1: check out books
    2: return books
    3: keep track of reserve requests
    4: keep track of overdue books and fines

CHAPTER 18

Scientific Applications

Computers play an important role in scientific research. Scientists use computers to construct models that allow them to investigate the implications and predictions of their theories. Then they can conduct experiments and perform observations to test whether the theoretical predictions are correct in the real world. And, of course, students encounter many interesting scientific problems that can be solved with computers.

Computer Models

For example, computer models have been essential tools for understanding the way that the sun works. Astronomers make some assumptions about what the center of the sun might be like. For example, they guess what the temperature and pressure at the center of the sun might be and they guess what the composition might be, that is, how much hydrogen, helium, and so on, the sun contains. Then astronomers need to answer the following question: "If the center of the sun really were like this, what would it look like to observers on Earth?" The computer performs the necessary calculations to tell the astronomers how bright the theoretical sun would be and what its spectrum would look like. These theoretical predictions can be compared with the actual results for the real sun. If the theoretical predictions agree with what the real sun looks like, then the theory is a promising model and deserves to be investigated further. However, if the theoretical predictions are not correct, then the model is no good. For example, if the model predicts that the sun will look purple, we know that it's back to the drawing board to develop another model.

Computers can also play an important part in medicine. A doctor diagnoses a patient's illness by observing the patient's symptoms. Most doctors have memorized the symptoms for most common diseases. However, when a patient has an obscure disease with unusual symptoms, the doctor will need to consult a reference manual. A computer program has been developed that acts like a medical reference manual. The doctor types in the patient's symptoms, and the computer responds by telling the doctor what further symptoms to test for. Finally, the computer tells the doctor what possible diseases could be causing these symptoms.

Computers are essential research tools for social sciences such as economics and psychology. Theoretical models in economics are usually written for computers.

Here is an example of an important economics problem: Suppose we change the money supply by x percent, we change the amount of government spending by y percent, and we change the tax rates by z percent. What will happen to the inflation rate? To the unemployment rate? To the interest rate? Ideally, we would like to know the answers to these questions for many different values of x, y, and z so that we could pick the best policy. However, we can't very easily experiment on the real world by varying the level of actual government spending and actual taxes just to see what happens. It would help greatly if a theoretical model capable of being solved by a computer could be developed that could answer this kind of question. However, that is very difficult to do because nobody understands economics well enough.

All scientists must do statistical calculations. When they perform an experiment many times or when they collect many observations, they need to estimate the uncertainty in the results. Computers are essential to perform the long calculations involved.

To write a scientific application program, you need to know a lot about the subject you are investigating. (Sometimes, however, a scientist will describe his or her model to a computer programmer, and the programmer will be left to write the program.) Often you need to know a lot of math. For example, computers are needed to solve many problems involving special types of equations known as differential equations. Problems involving motion usually require differential equations. Most differential equations don't have simple solutions that a mathematician can derive, and so the only way to solve them is with the computer.

Another interesting type of model is a simulation model, or Monte Carlo model. Sometimes a scientist will not be able to predict for certain whether an event will happen, but it is possible to predict the probability that the event will happen. When the program is being run, the random number function will be used to determine whether the event occurs. This method is called the Monte Carlo method because it is like a game of chance. An example is the football game program in Chapter 16. We know what the probability of a fumble occurring is; so the program uses a random number to determine whether a fumble actually occurs on a particular play.

Computers can be even more valuable for scientific purposes when they don't have to wait for users to type in data. In many scientific applications, the computers themselves automatically read the data from the measuring devices. And instead of merely printing results, the computers can be designed to control the movements of machines. For example, the Voyager probes were controlled by computers.

In this chapter we will write three scientific programs. Be warned that these programs use trigonometry and some other mathematical methods.

How Far Is It from Here to There?

Here is an example of a scientific problem with important practical applications. If you are planning to fly on an airplane between two cities, you would like to know the shortest possible distance between them. Because Earth is a sphere, the shortest distance between two cities is not always obvious. For example, the shortest route between cities in the United States and cities in Europe sometimes involves flying over the North Pole.

First, our program will read in the latitudes and longitudes of the two cities. Then it will convert these figures from degrees into radians. Next it will calculate the rectangular coordinates for the two cities, with the origin at the center of Earth, the z axis pointing to the North Pole, and the x axis pointing to 0 degrees longitude (which is the longitude of the observatory at Greenwich, England). Once we know the rectangular coordinates of the two points, we can calculate the straight-line distance d between the two cities. The straight-line distance doesn't help us too much, since we can't travel in a straight line through the middle of Earth. However, we can use the straight-line distance to calculate the surface distance s from the formula:

$$s = 2r \arcsin \frac{d}{2r}$$

(r is the radius of Earth; although it is not a true sphere, we will assume in this chapter that it is.)

Here is the program. Note that, if one city is west of Greenwich and the other is east of Greenwich, we need to convert the east longitude into a west longitude using the formula

West longitude = 360 − east longitude

```
PROGRAM distance (INPUT, OUTPUT);
    {This program reads in the latitude and the longitude of two
    cities and calculates the distance between them following the
    great circle course that connects the cities.}
CONST
    radius = 3960.0;      {radius of Earth in miles}
    pi = 3.14159;
VAR
    lon1, lat1, lon2, lat2, x1, y1, z1, x2, y2, z2, d, d2, s, angle : REAL;
    query : CHAR;
BEGIN
 REPEAT
    WRITELN('Enter longitude of first city. ');
    READLN(lon1);
    WRITELN('Enter latitude of first city. ');
    READLN(lat1);
    WRITELN('Enter longitude of second city. ');
    READLN(lon2);
    WRITELN('Enter latitude of second city. ');
    READLN(lat2);
        {Convert all of these measures into radian measure:}
    lon1 := lon1 * pi/180;
    lat1 := lat1 * pi/180;
    lon2 := lon2 * pi/180;
    lat2 := lat2 * pi/180;
        {Calculate rectangular coordinates for each city.}
    x1 := radius * COS(lat1) * COS(lon1);
    y1 := radius * COS(lat1) * SIN(lon1);
    z1 := radius * SIN(lat1);
    x2 := radius * COS(lat2) * COS(lon2);
    y2 := radius * COS(lat2) * SIN(lon2);
    z2 := radius * SIN(lat2);
```

```
        d : = SQRT ( SQR (x1 − x2) + SQR (y1 − y2) + SQR (z1 − z2) ) ;
                {d is the straight-line distance between the two cities
                assuming that we could travel right through the earth.}
        d2 : = d/2;
        angle : = ARCTAN ( d2 / SQRT ( SQR (radius) − SQR (d2) ) ) ;
                {angle is equal to one-half the angular distance between
                the two cities, in radians.}
        s : = 2 * radius * angle;
            WRITELN ('The great circle distance is: ', s : 7 : 2) ;
            WRITELN ('Type R to repeat the program. Else type S. ') ;
            READLN (query) ;
        UNTIL query <> 'R'
    END.
```

Here is a sample run:

```
    Enter longitude of first city.
    118.23
    Enter latitude of first city.
    34.05
    Enter longitude of second city.
    220.25
    Enter latitude of second city.
    35.75
    The distance is: 5475.06
```

This example shows the distance from Los Angeles to Tokyo.

Calculating Star Positions

Our next program will tell us where in the sky stars and planets will appear. To us the sky appears to be a giant sphere with Earth at the center. This imaginary sphere is called the *celestial sphere*. The position of a star or planet on this sphere is measured by two numbers called *right ascension* and *declination*. Right ascension is similar to the longitude of an object as seen from Earth, and declination is similar to the latitude. If a star is in the plane of Earth's equator, it has a declination of 0°. The declination of other objects is the angular distance between the object and the plane of the equator. Positive declinations mean that the object is north of the equator, and negative declinations mean that the object is south of the equator. For example, the North Star (Polaris) has a declination of almost +90°. The right ascension of an object is the angle between the object and a special point in the constellation Pisces (this special point is actually the point where the sun is on the first day of spring).

Instead of being measured in degrees, right ascension is usually measured in hours, where 1 hour = 15 degrees and 24 hours = 360 degrees. Don't confuse this type of hour with the hours we use to measure time. If we need to measure very small intervals of declination, we can use *minutes*, where 1 minute = 1/60 degree. To measure small intervals of right ascension, we also use a unit called a minute, where 1 minute = 1/60 hour. Note that these two type of minutes are quite different, and neither is the same as the minutes we use to measure time.

Suppose that we know the right ascension and declination of a star, and we would like to know its position in the sky as seen from our location at a particular time. To identify the location of a point in the sky seen from a particular location, we use two coordinates called *altitude* and *azimuth*. The altitude of an object is its angle above the horizon. For example, a star that is right on the horizon has an altitude of 0°. A star that is at the *zenith* (the point directly overhead) has an altitude of 90°. If a star has negative altitude, then the star is below the horizon at this time and therefore cannot be seen. The azimuth of the star tells us in what direction we need to look in order to see it. A star that is due north has an azimuth of 0° or 360°. The direction due east has an azimuth of 90°; due south is at azimuth 180°; and due west is at azimuth 270°. We also need to know about the *meridian*. The meridian is the great circle in the sky that passes from the point due north through the zenith to the point due south.

We have one more thing we need to know. We need to know about *sidereal time*. Sidereal time measures the rotation of the celestial sphere. At sidereal time zero, the stars with right ascension zero are on the meridian. At sidereal time 1 hour, the entire celestial sphere has rotated 15 degrees from its position at sidereal time zero. Figure 18-1 tells how to calculate the approximate sidereal time for a given date at a particular time.

Read across from the left-hand scale for the appropriate date. Read down from the top scale for the appropriate time. Then you may read the approximate sidereal time from the diagonal lines.

Here is our task. We will enter our latitude, the right ascension and declination of the star we are interested in, and the sidereal times we are interested in. Then the computer will calculate the altitude and azimuth of the object. To do this, we will first convert the right ascension and declination into rectangular coordinates. Then we have to perform two coordinate rotations. (See a book on trigonometry to learn about coordinate rotations.) Then we convert the rectangular coordinates into the two angles altitude and azimuth.

Here is the program.

```
PROGRAM sky (INPUT, OUTPUT);
    {This program reads in the right ascension and declination of
    a celestial object, the latitude of the observer, and the
    sidereal time. It then calculates the current altitude and
    azimuth of the object from your location.}
CONST
  pi = 3.14159;

VAR
 ra, dec, time, start, stop, interval, lat, colat, hours: REAL;
 query1, query2 : CHAR;

FUNCTION atn (y, x: REAL) : REAL;
    {This function calculates the arctangent of y/x and places
    the result in the correct quadrant.}
CONST pi = 3.14159;
VAR z: REAL;
BEGIN
  IF x = 0
      THEN IF y > 0 THEN atn := pi/2
                    ELSE atn := 3*pi/2
      ELSE BEGIN
              z := ARCTAN(y/x);
              IF x < 0 THEN z: = z + pi;
              IF z < 0 THEN z := z + 2 * pi;
              atn := z
           END
END;

FUNCTION asn (x : REAL) : REAL;
    {This function calculates the arcsin of x.}
BEGIN
    asn := ARCTAN ( x/ SQRT (1 - SQR (X) ))
END;
```

FIGURE 18-1

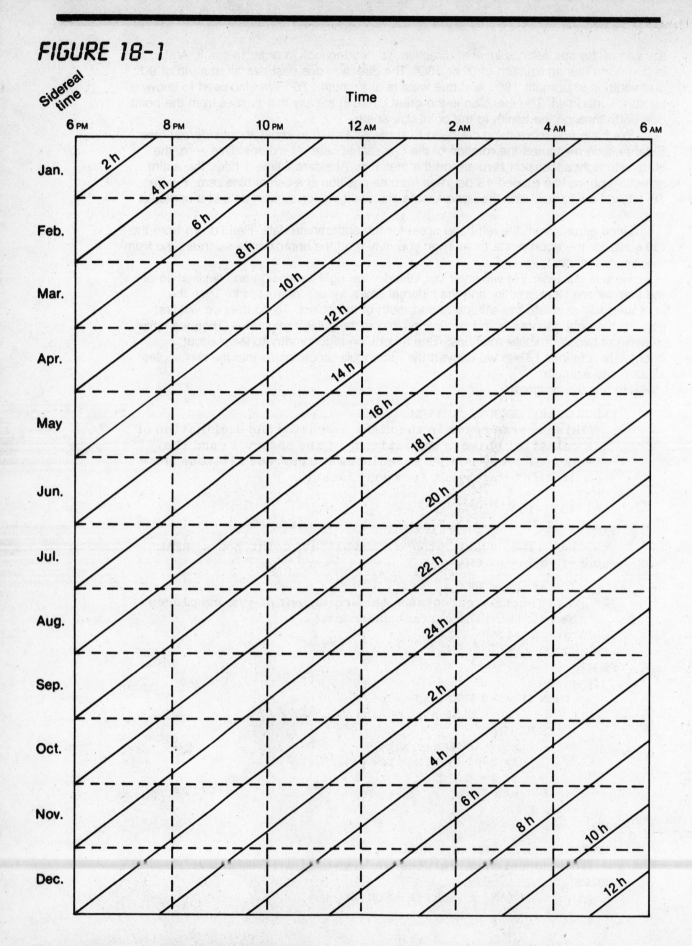

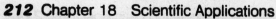

```
PROCEDURE calculate;
VAR
    x1,y1,z1,x2,y2,z2,x3,y3,z3,alt,azi : REAL;
BEGIN
    x1 := COS(dec) * COS(ra);
    y1 := COS(dec) * SIN(ra);
    z1 := SIN(dec);
            {coordinates with x axis pointing at 0 degrees right
            ascension and z axis pointing at north pole}
    x2 := x1 * COS(time) + y1 * SIN(time);
    y2 := y1 * COS(time) - x1 * SIN(time);
    z2 := z1;
            {coordinates with x axis pointing at meridian and z
            axis pointing at north pole}
    x3 := x2 * COS(colat) + z2 * SIN(colat);
    y3 := y2;
    z3 := z2 * COS(colat) - x2 * SIN(colat);
            {coordinates with x axis pointing due south and z axis
            pointing to zenith}

    alt := asn(z3);
    azi := pi - atn(y3,x3);
    IF azi < 0 THEN azi := 2 * pi + azi;

        {Convert to degrees:}
    alt := 180 * alt/pi;
    azi := 180 * azi/pi;
        {Convert to hours:}
     hours := time * 12/pi;
     IF hours > 24 THEN hours := hours - 24;

    WRITELN('Sidereal time: ',hours:5:1,
            ' Altitude: ',alt:8:2,' Azimuth: ',azi:8:2)
END;

BEGIN {Main program block}
    WRITELN('Enter latitude (in degrees): ');
    READLN(lat);
    colat := lat - 90;  {negative of complement of latitude}
    colat := colat * pi/180;  {convert to radians}
    REPEAT
        WRITELN('Enter starting sidereal time (in hours). ');
        READLN(start);
        WRITELN('enter stopping sidereal time. ');
        READLN(stop);
            IF stop < start THEN stop := stop + 24;
            {Convert to radians:}
            start := start * pi/12;
            stop := stop * pi/12;
        WRITELN('Enter sidereal time interval. ');
        READLN(interval); interval := interval * pi/12;
        REPEAT
            WRITELN('Enter right ascension (in hours): ');
            READLN(ra);   ra := ra * pi/12; {convert to radians}
            WRITELN('Enter declination (in degrees): ');
            READLN(dec);   dec := dec * pi/180;
            time := start;
            WHILE time < stop DO
```

```
          BEGIN
            calculate;
            time : = time + interval
          END;

            WRITELN ('Type R to see a new object. Else type S. ');
            READLN (query1);
          UNTIL query1 <> 'R';
          WRITELN ('Type R to reset sidereal time. Else type S. ');
          READLN (query2);
      UNTIL query2 <> 'R'
    END.
```

Now, we will try some sample runs of this program. Let's suppose we are at latitude 40 degrees (which is the latitude of New York, Chicago, and northern California). Let's say we are observing in mid-June. The sidereal time at midnight is 18, the sidereal time in the early evening is 12, and the sidereal time in the early morning is 24. So, we will look at the sky for 1-hour intervals from sidereal time (S.T.) 12 to S.T. 24. We will look at three constellations: Sagitarius, (which is in the direction of the center of the Milky Way galaxy) at right ascension 18.5 and declination −30; the Big Dipper (in Ursa Major), at right ascention 7 and declination 55; and Orion, at right ascension 5.5 and declination 0.
Here is the output for some selected hours:

```
                    Sagitarius
Sidereal time:  12.0  Altitude:  −24.08  Azimuth:  109.87
Sidereal time:  15.0  Altitude:    4.73  Azimuth:  136.42
Sidereal time:  18.0  Altitude:   19.65  Azimuth:  173.11
Sidereal time:  22.0  Altitude:    4.73  Azimuth:  223.58
```

These results mean that Sagitarius is below the horizon at S.T. 12. It has just risen at S.T. 15 and is just about to set at S.T. 22. The highest altitude it reaches during the night occurs near S.T. 18, when it is almost due south.

```
                    Big Dipper
Sidereal time:  12.0  Altitude:  75.00  Azimuth:    0.00
Sidereal time:  15.0  Altitude:  56.85  Azimuth:  312.13
Sidereal time:  19.0  Altitude:  24.38  Azimuth:  322.53
Sidereal time:  24.0  Altitude:   5.00  Azimuth:  360.00
```

The Big Dipper is special because it is visible all night from this latitude. Its lowest point during the night occurs at S.T. 24, when it has an altitude of 5 degrees and an azimuth of 360 degrees (due north).

```
                      Orion
Sidereal time:  16.0  Altitude:  −45.05  Azimuth:  327.20
Sidereal time:  20.0  Altitude:  −37.43  Azimuth:   50.00
Sidereal time:  24.0  Altitude:    5.74  Azimuth:   94.84
```

These results show that Orion cannot be seen at all in June. It rises just before S.T. 24 when it is almost due east, but the sun will have already risen by this time.
An especially interesting result occurs if we look at the point at declination 90 degrees. This point is called the north celestial pole. It is very close to the position of the North Star, Polaris. This point is at altitude 40 degrees and azimuth 0 all night. In fact, this point appears to remain in the same position all of the time. All the stars seem to move in circles around this point.

Calculating Planetary Motion

Here is a more complicated example of a scientific application. We'll write a program that predicts the motion of a planet as seen from Earth. As in any scientific program, this one requires a great deal of specialized knowledge. However, we can use the same general strategy that we used for the other programs we've written. The planetary motion program is very complicated, but it will help if we divide the problem into smaller parts. Some physics ideas will be introduced as we go along.

We need to know that the planets move along orbits, shaped like ellipses, with the sun at one focus. Our first task will be to figure out where along its ellipse a planet will be at a particular time. Since we need to know where the planet will be as seen from Earth, we'll calculate its right ascension and declination. Here is our strategy at the most general level.

1. Determine initial values.

2. Calculate position of planet in its orbit

3. Convert orbital position into position as seen from Earth.

4. Print position.

Now we'll begin work on a procedure to trace the motion of a planet in its own orbit. To figure out the shape of the ellipse (see Figure 18-2), we need to know the semimajor axis a and the eccentricity e. From these values we can determine the semiminor axis b:

$$b = a\sqrt{1 - e^2}$$

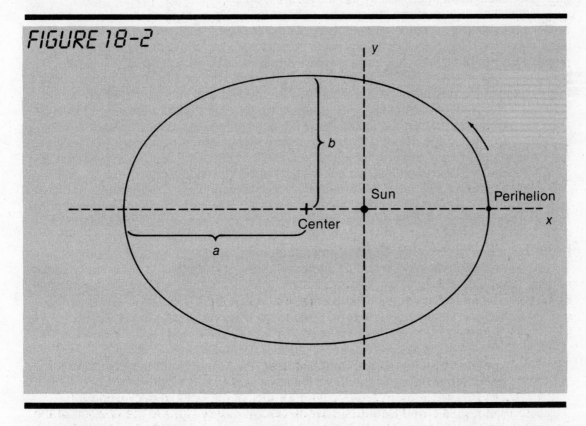

FIGURE 18-2

We'll draw in a standard x-y coordinate system, putting the x axis along the major axis of the ellipse. The origin of the coordinate system will be at the sun. That means that the center of the ellipse is the point $(-ea, 0)$; so the equation of the ellipse becomes

$$\frac{(x + ea)^2}{a^2} + \frac{y^2}{b^2} = 1$$

We need to decide what units of measure to use. It will be awkward to measure the distances in miles or kilometers because then the numbers would be very big. Let's measure distance in units of million-kilometers. It will be most convenient to measure time in units of days. Also, we'll need to know the position of the planet on the first day that we run the program. For example, if we start running the program on January 1, 1984, we'll need to know the position of the planet we're interested in on that date.

We'll use v_x to stand for the speed at which the planet is moving in the x direction, expressed as million kilometers per day. Then, in half an hour, the change in the x position will be

$$x = x + v_x \left(\frac{1}{48}\right)$$

But v_x also changes during that half hour, according to the equation

$$v_x = v_x + xcomp \left(\frac{1}{48}\right)$$

In this case, xcomp is the acceleration in the x direction, which is given by

$$xcomp = \frac{-Gx}{r^3}$$

where r is the distance from the planet to the sun, and $G = 991.047$, which is the gravitational constant multiplied by the mass of the sun.

We still need to perform the second general task. We must convert the planet's orbital motion into its position as seen from Earth. We need to break this job into four parts. First, we must calculate the sun-centered coordinates of the planet, relative to the plane of Earth's orbit, with the x axis pointed in a standard direction. We'll call these coordinates X1, Y1, and Z1. To perform this calculation, we need to know three numbers that determine the orientation of the planet's orbit: the angle of inclination, which tells how much the planet's orbit is tilted with respect to the orbit of Earth; the longitude of the ascending node, which tells the longitude of the point where the planet crosses the plane of Earth's orbit when the planet is going up; and the longitude of perihelion, which tells the longitude of the point where the planet is closest to the sun. (See Figures 18-3 and 18-4.) These calculations are carried out in the procedure called hlcent.

Second, we have to repeat exactly the same planetary motion program to find the position of Earth. We'll call the coordinates of Earth X5, Y5, and Z5. Third, once we know the sun-centered coordinates of Earth and the other planet, we need to calculate the Earth-centered coordinates of the planet. We'll call these coordinates X3, Y3, and Z3. Fourth, we need to convert the Earth-centered rectangular coordinates into right ascension and declination. (We should add one more task—we'll need to convert the day number we've been using in the calculations into a regular month and day of the month. Fortunately, we've already written a procedure to do this.)

Now that our strategy is all set, we need to go ahead and write the program.

```
PROGRAM planet (INPUT, OUTPUT);
    {This program calculates the motion of a selected
    planet and determines its position (right ascension
    and declination) as seen from earth.
    All distances are measured in units of million-kilometers.
    All times are measured in units of days.
    The program updates the position of the planet and the
    earth every half hour, and it displays the results
    once each day. The program starts on January 1, 1984.}
```

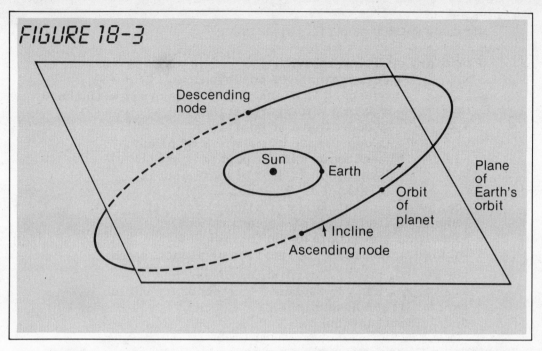

FIGURE 18-3

CONST
```
    earper = 1.78979;          {longitude of perihelion for earth}
    a0 = 149.5;                {semimajor axis of earth's orbit}
    b0 = 149.479;              {semiminor axis of earth's orbit}
    ecc0 = 0.01673;            {eccentricity of earth's orbit}
    etilt = 0.4092797;         {tilt of earth's axis in radians}
    g = 991.047;               {gravitational constant times mass of sun}
    pi = 3.14159;
    interval = 0.0208333;      {half-hour interval}
    numhours = 48;             {number of intervals in one day}
```

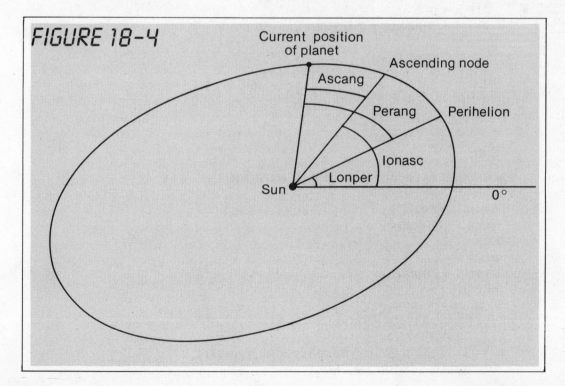

FIGURE 18-4

```
TYPE
    string = PACKED ARRAY[1..3] OF CHAR;
VAR
   {Planetary orbit variables:}
      x,          {x coordinate of position.
                   measured in plane of planet's orbit with the
                   x axis pointing at perihelion.}
      y,          {y coordinate of position}
      v,          {x coordinate of velocity of planet}
      a,          {semimajor axis of planet's orbit}
      b,          {semiminor axis of planet's orbit}
      r,          {distance from planet to sun}
      ecc,        {eccentricity of planet's orbit}
      lonasc,     {longitude of ascending node}
      lonper,     {longitude of perihelion}
      incline,    {angle of inclination of planet's orbit}

      x0, y0, r0, v0,     {coordinates of earth}
      x1, y1, z1, x3, y3, z3, test,    {temporary variables}
      ra,      {right ascension}
      dec:    {declination}
       REAL;
      mlist : ARRAY[1..12] OF STRING;
      m : ARRAY[1..13] OF INTEGER;
      m2 : ARRAY[1..13] OF INTEGER;
      month: string;
      date, daymax, day, flag, hour, decsign,
         year, count, numdays : INTEGER;

FUNCTION atn(y, x: REAL) : REAL;
   CONST pi = 3.14159;   {This function calculates the arctangent}
   VAR z : REAL;         {of y/x and places the result in the}
   BEGIN                 {correct quadrant.}
     IF x = 0
            THEN IF y > 0 THEN atn : = pi/2
                          ELSE atn : = 3*pi/2
            ELSE BEGIN
                    z : = ARCTAN(y/x);
                    IF x < 0 THEN z : = z + pi;
                    IF z < 0 THEN z : = z + 2 * pi;
                    atn : = z
                 END
   END;

PROCEDURE calendar(yeardate: INTEGER);
VAR
   stop : BOOLEAN;
   mnum : INTEGER;
BEGIN
   mnum : = 0;
   stop : = FALSE;
   REPEAT
     mnum : = mnum + 1;
      If yeardate < (m2[mnum+1]+1)
         THEN BEGIN
                 day : = yeardate − m2[mnum];
                 stop : = TRUE
```

```
              END
   UNTIL stop;
   month := mlist[mnum]
END;

PROCEDURE newyear;
VAR mn : INTEGER;
BEGIN
   year := year + 1;
   WRITELN(year:15);
   date := 0;
   FOR mn := 1 TO 13 DO m2[mn] := m[mn];
   numdays := 365;
   IF year MOD 4 = 0
        THEN BEGIN     {leap year}
                numdays := 366;
                FOR mn := 3 TO 13 DO m2[mn] := m2[mn] + 1
             END
END;

PROCEDURE vset;
        {initial values for Venus}
BEGIN
   WRITELN('Position of Venus: ');
   x := 72.461;
   v := -2.239;
   a := 108.1;
   ecc := 0.00679;
   lonasc := 1.3356;
   lonper := 2.2858;
   incline := 0.059236
END;

PROCEDURE mset;
        {Initial values for Mars}
BEGIN
   WRITELN('Position of Mars');
   x := -241.244;
   v := 0.506;
   a := 227.8;
   ecc := 0.09337;
   lonasc := 0.86268;
   lonper := 5.86067;
   incline := 0.03229
END;

PROCEDURE jset;
     {Initial values for Jupiter}
BEGIN
   WRITELN('Position of Jupiter. ');
   x := -277.558;
   v := 1.051;
   a := 778;
   ecc := 0.04844;
   lonasc := 1.7508;
   lonper := 0.2648;
   incline := 0.022776
END;
```

```
PROCEDURE sset;
     {Initial values for Saturn}
BEGIN
    WRITELN('Position of Saturn. ');
    x : = -888.952;
    v : = -0.665;
    a : = 1426;
    ecc : = 0.05568;
    lonasc : = 1.98105;
    lonper : = 1.6612;
    incline : = 0.043459
END;

PROCEDURE initial;
    {This procedure determines the initial
    setting of the orbital elements for the planets
    you choose.}
VAR
  p : CHAR;
BEGIN
        {Positions for Earth on January 1, 1984:}
    x0 : = 137.4141284;
    v0 : = 1.435896;
    test : = 1 - SQR((x0+ecc0*a0)/a0);
    IF test < 0 THEN test : = 0;
    y0 : = b0 * SQRT(test);
    IF v0 > 0 THEN y0 : = -y0;
    WRITELN('Enter the first letter of the planet you');
    WRITELN('would like to see: ');
    WRITELN('Venus, Mars, Jupiter, or Saturn. ');
    READLN(p);
    CASE p OF
        'V' : vset;
        'M' : mset;
        'J' : jset;
        'S' : sset
    END;
    b : = a * SQRT(1 - SQR(ecc));
    test : = 1 - SQR((x + ecc*a)/a);
    IF test < 0 THEN test : = 0;
    y : = b * SQRT(test);
    IF v > 0 THEN y : = -y;

        {These are the initial values that are needed
            for the calendar procedure:}

    m[1]:=0;  m[2]:=31;  m[3]:=59;  m[4]:=90;  m[5]:=120;
    m[6]:=151;  m[7]:=181;  m[8]:=212;  m[9]:=243;  m[10]:=273;
    m[11]:=304;  m[12]:=334;  m[13]:=365;

    mlist[1]:='Jan'; mlist[2]:='Feb'; mlist[3]:='Mar';
    mlist[4]:='Apr'; mlist[5]:='May'; mlist[6]:='Jun';
    mlist[7]:='Jly'; mlist[8]:='Aug'; mlist[9]:='Sep';
    mlist[10]:='Oct'; mlist[11]:='Nov'; mlist[12]:='Dec';
    year : = 1983   {note that the program starts on Jan 1, 1984}

    END;
```

```pascal
PROCEDURE plpos;
    {This procedure calculates the position
    of the planet within its own orbit.
    Global variables used are: r, x, y, and v.}
VAR
   xcomp, test : REAL;
BEGIN
   r : = SQRT (x*x + y*y) ;   {distance from planet to sun}
   xcomp : = -g*x/ (r*r*r) ;   {x component of acceleration}
   x : = x + v * interval;
   v : = v + xcomp * interval;
   test : = 1 - SQR ((x + ecc * a) /a) ;   {temporary variable}
     IF test < 0 THEN test : = 0;
     y : = b * SQRT (test) ;
     IF v > 0 THEN y : = -y
END;

PROCEDURE epos;
   {This procedure calculates the position of the Earth.}
VAR
    xcomp, test : REAL;
BEGIN
        r0 : = SQRT (x0*x0 + y0*y0) ;   {distance from Earth to sun}
        xcomp : = -g * x0/ (r0*r0*r0) ;
        x0 : = x0 + v0 * interval;
        v0 : = v0 + xcomp * interval;
        test : = 1 - SQR ((x0+ ecc0*a0) /a0) ;
          IF test < 0 THEN test : = 0;   {temporary variable}
          y0 : = b0 *SQRT (test) ;
          IF v0 > 0 THEN y0 : = - y0
END;

PROCEDURE hlcent;
      {This procedure calculates the heliocentric
      (sun-centered) coordinates of the planet.}
VAR
   perang, ascang, x2, y2, z2 : REAL;
BEGIN
   perang : = ATN (y, x) ;
      {angle from planet to perihelion}
   ascang : = perang - lonasc + lonper;
      {angle from planet to ascending node}
   x2 : = r * COS (ascang) ;
   z2 : = r * SIN (ascang) * SIN (incline) ;
   y2 : = SQRT (r*r*SIN (ascang) *SIN (ascang) - z2 * z2) ;
     IF SIN (ascang) < 0 THEN y2 : = - y2;
         {x2, y2, z2 are coordinates of the planet in plane of
         Earth's orbit with x axis pointing to ascending node.}
   x1 : = x2 * COS (lonasc) - y2 * SIN (lonasc) ;
   y1 : = x2 * SIN (lonasc) + y2 * COS (lonasc) ;
   z1 : = z2
          {x1, y1, z1 are coordinates of the planet with the
          x axis pointing to 0 degrees heliocentric longitude.}
END;

PROCEDURE ecent;
   {This procedure calculates Earth-centered coordinates.}
```

```pascal
VAR
  x5, y5, z5 : REAL;
BEGIN
  x5 := x0 * COS(earper) − y0 * SIN(earper);
  y5 := y0 * COS(earper) + x0 * SIN(earper);
  z5 := 0;
       {x5, y5 z5 are coordinates of the Earth with
        the x axis pointing to 0 degrees heliocentric
        longitude.}
  x3 := x1 − x5;
  y3 := y1 − y5;
  z3 := z1 − z5
       {x3, y3, and z3 are rectangular coordinates
        of the planet as seen from Earth.}
END;

PROCEDURE radec;
   {This procedure calculates right ascension and
      declination.}
VAR
  x4, y4, z4 : REAL;
BEGIN
  x4 := x3;
  y4 := y3 * COS(etilt) − z3 * SIN(etilt);
  z4 := y3 * SIN(etilt) + z3 * COS(etilt);
  ra := ATN(y4,x4);
  dec := ATN(z4, (SQRT(x4*x4 + y4*y4)));
  ra := ra * 12/pi;   {convert to hours}
  dec := dec * 180/pi;   {convert to degrees}
  IF dec > 180 THEN dec := dec − 360
END;

PROCEDURE printout;
        {This routine prints the output.}
VAR
  rahours, decdeg: INTEGER;
  ramin, decmin: REAL;
BEGIN
  calendar(date);   {Calculate the day and month.}
  rahours := TRUNC(ra);
  ramin := (ra − rahours)*60;
  IF dec < 0 THEN decsign := −1 ELSE decsign := 1;
  dec := ABS(dec);
  decdeg := TRUNC(dec);
  decmin := (dec − decdeg)*60;
  decdeg := decsign * decdeg;
  WRITELN(month, day:3, rahours:6, ramin:6:1, decdeg:8, decmin:6:1)
END;

BEGIN   {********** Main program block **********}
REPEAT
  initial;
  WRITELN('Type the number of days you wish the program to
      run.');
  READLN(daymax);
  newyear;
  WRITELN('  Date     RA      Dec');
```

```
      WRITELN('     Hrs  Min  Deg  Min');
    FOR count : = 1 TO daymax DO
      BEGIN
        date : = date + 1;
        FOR hour : = 1 TO numhours DO
          BEGIN
            plpos;   {position of planet}
            epos     {position of Earth}
          END;
        hlcent;  {sun-centered coordinates}
        ecent;   {Earth-centered coordinates}
        radec;   {calculate right ascension and declination}
        printout; {output routine}

        IF date = numdays THEN newyear
      END;
      WRITELN('Type 1 to look at another planet.');
      WRITELN('Type 0 to stop program.');
      READLN(flag);
    UNTIL flag = 0
END.
```

Here are some samples of the output from this program:

```
Enter the first letter of the planet you
would like to see:
Venus, Mars, Jupiter, or Saturn.
S
Position of Saturn.
Type the number of days you wish the program to run.
40


          1984
  Date      RA        Dec
         Hrs  Min   Deg  Min
Jan  1   14  56.3   −14  30.4
Jan  2   14  56.9   −14  32.8
Jan  3   14  57.5   −14  35.4
Jan  4   14  58.2   −14  38.0
Jan  5   14  58.9   −14  40.8
Jan  6   14  59.7   −14  43.8
Jan  7   15   0.8   −14  47.6
Jan  8   15   2.1   −14  52.6
Jan  9   15   2.4   −14  53.7
Jan 10   15   2.6   −14  54.8
Jan 11   15   2.9   −14  55.8
Jan 12   15   3.1   −14  56.9
Jan 13   15   3.3   −14  57.9
Jan 14   15   3.5   −14  58.9
Jan 15   15   3.7   −14  59.8
Jan 16   15   3.9   −15   0.7
Jan 17   15   4.1   −15   1.7
Jan 18   15   4.3   −15   2.5
Jan 19   15   4.5   −15   3.4
Jan 20   15   4.7   −15   4.3
Jan 21   15   4.9   −15   5.1
Jan 22   15   5.1   −15   5.9
```

```
Jan 23    15    5.2    -15    6.6
Jan 24    15    5.4    -15    7.4
Jan 25    15    5.6    -15    8.1
Jan 26    15    5.7    -15    8.8
Jan 27    15    5.9    -15    9.5
Jan 28    15    6.0    -15   10.2
Jan 29    15    6.2    -15   10.8
Jan 30    15    6.3    -15   11.4
Jan 31    15    6.5    -15   12.0
Feb  1    15    6.6    -15   12.6
Feb  2    15    6.7    -15   13.2
Feb  3    15    6.8    -15   13.7
Feb  4    15    7.0    -15   14.2
Feb  5    15    7.1    -15   14.7
Feb  6    15    7.2    -15   15.2
Feb  7    15    7.3    -15   15.7
Feb  8    15    7.4    -15   16.1
Feb  9    15    7.5    -15   16.5
```
Type 1 to look at another planet.
Type 0 to stop program.
1
Enter the first letter of the planet you
would like to see:
Venus, Mars, Jupiter, or Saturn.
J
Position of Jupiter.
Type the number of days you wish the program to run.
40

```
                    1984
      Date        RA        Dec
                Hrs  Min   Deg  Min
      Jan  1    17  35.8   -23   2.2
      Jan  2    17  37.3   -23   3.1
      Jan  3    17  38.8   -23   4.0
      Jan  4    17  40.5   -23   4.9
      Jan  5    17  42.3   -23   5.8
      Jan  6    17  44.4   -23   6.7
      Jan  7    17  47.2   -23   7.7
      Jan  8    17  51.0   -23   8.8
      Jan  9    17  51.4   -23   8.9
      Jan 10    17  51.8   -23   9.1
      Jan 11    17  52.1   -23   9.3
      Jan 12    17  52.5   -23   9.5
      Jan 13    17  52.8   -23   9.6
      Jan 14    17  53.2   -23   9.8
      Jan 15    17  53.5   -23  10.0
      Jan 16    17  53.9   -23  10.1
      Jan 17    17  54.2   -23  10.3
      Jan 18    17  54.5   -23  10.4
      Jan 19    17  54.9   -23  10.6
      Jan 20    17  55.2   -23  10.7
      Jan 21    17  55.5   -23  10.8
      Jan 22    17  55.9   -23  11.0
      Jan 23    17  56.2   -23  11.1
      Jan 24    17  56.5   -23  11.2
```

```
          Jan 25    17 56.8   -23 11.3
          Jan 26    17 57.1   -23 11.5
          Jan 27    17 57.4   -23 11.6
          Jan 28    17 57.7   -23 11.7
          Jan 29    17 58.1   -23 11.8
          Jan 30    17 58.4   -23 11.9
          Jan 31    17 58.7   -23 12.0
          Feb  1    17 59.0   -23 12.1
          Feb  2    17 59.3   -23 12.2
          Feb  3    17 59.5   -23 12.3
          Feb  4    17 59.8   -23 12.4
          Feb  5    18  0.1   -23 12.5
          Feb  6    18  0.4   -23 12.6
          Feb  7    18  0.7   -23 12.7
          Feb  8    18  1.0   -23 12.7
          Feb  9    18  1.3   -23 12.8
```
Type 1 to look at another planet.
Type 0 to stop program.
1
Enter the first letter of the planet you
would like to see:
Venus, Mars, Jupiter, or Saturn.
V
Position of Venus:
Type the number of days you wish the program to run.
10

	1984	
Date	RA	Dec
	Hrs Min	Deg Min
Jan 1	15 10.6	-15 51.9
Jan 2	15 17.3	-16 19.0
Jan 3	15 24.3	-16 46.3
Jan 4	15 31.8	-17 14.1
Jan 5	15 39.9	-17 42.7
Jan 6	15 49.2	-18 13.3
Jan 7	16 1.4	-18 49.1
Jan 8	16 18.3	-19 32.3
Jan 9	16 21.4	-19 43.3
Jan 10	16 24.4	-19 53.8

Type 1 to look at another planet.
Type 0 to stop program.
1
Enter the first letter of the planet you
would like to see:
Venus, Mars, Jupiter, or Saturn.
M
Position of Mars
Type the number of days you wish the program to run.
10

	1984	
Date	RA	Dec
	Hrs Min	Deg Min
Jan 1	13 21.4	-7 4.0

```
Jan  2    13 24.3    -7 20.5
Jan  3    13 27.2    -7 37.2
Jan  4    13 30.3    -7 54.4
Jan  5    13 33.5    -8 12.3
Jan  6    13 37.0    -8 31.3
Jan  7    13 41.2    -8 53.0
Jan  8    13 46.6    -9 19.8
Jan  9    13 49.0    -9 33.9
Jan 10    13 51.2    -9 47.7
```
Type 1 to look at another planet.
Type 0 to stop program.
0

These results are not perfectly accurate, since there are other factors that complicate planetary motion that we have not considered.

By now you have seen some examples of the many tasks that can be done by computers, and you have seen how to give the instructions to a computer to get it to do what you want it to do. Your skill with programming will grow even more with further practice. If you have a home computer, you will most likely think of many more jobs that you would like your computer to do for you. Or you might be interested in one of the many jobs that involve working with computers, in which case your knowledge of Pascal will help you understand computers.

Once you have a computer to spare you from having to do boring work, you are free to concentrate on much more creative and interesting tasks. This is only the beginning of what you might be able to accomplish.

Chapter 18 Exercises

1. Suppose *P* is a one-dimensional array in which $P[I]$ is the number of people in the country of age *I*. Suppose that, for every 1,000 people from ages 20 to 35, there are 66 people born each year. Suppose that, from ages 0 to 50, 90 percent of the people will survive to the next age; and that for people over age 51, 60 percent will survive to the next age. Write a program that calculates what the age distribution of the population will look like each year for the next 20 years.

2. Follow the same procedure as for Exercise 1, using the age distribution of the U.S. population in 1980, as well as actual values for the birthrate and death rate by age. Forecast what the age distribution of the population will look like every year for the next 20 years. For each year, calculate the ratio of working-age people (ages 20 to 64) to retirement age people (ages 65 and above).

3. Follow the same procedure as for Exercise 2, but compare the effects of the following contrasting assumptions:
    Assumption 1: The birthrate at all ages falls to 80 percent of its current value, and the death rate at all ages falls to 80 percent of its current value.
    Assumption 2: The birthrate at each age rises to 120 percent of its current value, and the death rate at each age also rises to 120 percent of its current value.

4. Write a program that demonstrates Kepler's law of planetary motion, which states that the ratio of the cube of a planet's mean distance from the sun divided by the square of its orbital period is the same for all nine planets in the solar system.

5. Write a program that reads in the values for the coefficients a, b, c, d, e, and r, and then performs the division problem

$$\frac{ax^4 + bx^3 + cx^2 + dx + e}{x - r}$$

by using synthetic division. (Refer to a book on algebra to see how synthetic division works.)

6. Write a program that reads in the size of an object and its distance and then computes its apparent angular size. Here are some sample objects:

Object	Size	Distance
Mt. Rainier, seen from Seattle	2.7 miles	60 miles
Width of Central Park, seen from the Empire State Building	3000 feet	8000 feet
Earth, seen from a space shuttle	8000 miles	100 miles
Moon	3500 kilometers	384,000 km
Sun	864,000 miles	93 million m
Saturn	75,000 miles	800 million m
Star Antares	5.5×10^8 miles	2.3×10^{15} miles
Andromeda galaxy	130,000 light years	2.2 mil. light yrs

7. Suppose an economy is governed by these three equations:

$$Y_t = C_t + I_t$$
$$C_t = 50 + 0.5Y_t$$
$$I = 0.5 \times (Y_{t-1} - Y_{t-2})$$

where Y_t is the gross national product (GNP) in year t, Y_{t-1} is the gross national product last year, Y_{t-2} is the GNP 2 years ago, C_t is consumption spending in year t, and I_t is investment spending. If $Y = 105$ in 1983 and $Y = 95$ in 1984, what will Y be for each year for the next 20 years? (In economics this type of model is called a multiplier accelerator model.) How will the results change if the third equation becomes as follows?

$$I = 0.65 \times (Y_{t-1} - Y_{t-2})$$

8. Modify the planet program included in the chapter to also tell in what zodiac constellation the planet will appear.

9. When parallel light rays strike a parabolic mirror, they will be reflected back. Write a program that reads in the distance of a particular light ray from the axis of the parabola and then calculates where that light ray will cross the axis after it has been reflected.

10. Write a program similar to the one for Exercise 9, but have the light rays strike a spherical mirror.

11. Ohm's law says that $I = V/R$, where V is the voltage in an electronic circuit, D is the resistance (in ohms), and I is the current (in amperes). Write a program that reads in values for V and R and then calculates I.

12. Write a program that calculates the total impedance in an ac electrical circuit that has frequency *f*, a capacitor of capacitance *C*, and an inductor with inductance *L*. (Refer to a book on electronics.)

13. Write a program that prints a triangle such that each number in the triangle is equal to the sum of the two numbers above it. (This arrangement is known as Pascal's triangle.) The top part of the triangle looks like this:

```
      1
    1 1
   1 2 1
  1 3 3 1
 1 4 6 4 1
```

14. Some gases obey the van der Waals equation of state, which tells the temperature of 1 mole of the gas if the pressure is *P* and the volume is *V*:

$$\left(P + \frac{a}{V^2}\right)(V - b) = RT$$

R is the gas constant, which has the value 8.31; *a* and *b* are two constants that depend on the type of gas. Write a program that reads in values for *P*, *V*, *a*, and *b* and then calculates the temperature.

15. Write a program that reads in the mass of two objects (in kilograms) and their distance apart (in meters) and then calculates the force of gravity between them from the following formula:

$$F = \frac{Gm_1m_2}{r^2}$$

where $G = 6.67 \times 10^{-11}$ m^3/kg-sec.

16. Write a program that reads in the longitude and latitude of two points on the surface of Earth and then prints the longitude and latitude of five points along the shortest route between them. (The shortest distance is known as the great circle distance.)

17. Write a program that calculates the correlation coefficient between the measurement of two variables. (Refer to a book on statistics.)

18. Write a program that reads in the mass of an object in grams and then calculates the equivalent energy from the formula $E = mc^2$. Here *c* is the speed of light, which is 3×10^{10} cm/sec. The result for energy will be measured in a unit called the erg.

19. The theory of relativity says that, if an object is traveling past you at a high speed, it will appear shorter to you than it would if you observed it when it was at rest. If the length of a rod at rest is *L* and it is moving with velocity *v*, then its length as it will look to you is given by $\dfrac{L}{\sqrt{1 - r^2/c^2}}$ Write a program to calculate its length.

20. Write a program that calculates how much the frequency (i.e., the color) of light will shift because of the Doppler effect when the light source is moving away from you at velocity *v*. (Refer to a physics book.)

Appendixes

Answers to Selected Exercises

Here are suggested solutions for some of the exercises. In some cases only part of the program is included. You will need to fill in the declaration section and other missing parts. Remember that a program that is to be used regularly should also include explanatory messages and checks for bad input data.

Chapter 1

3. Most programs will need to have INPUT and OUTPUT on the first line. As we will see in Chapter 15, the first line must also include the names of external files your program will use.

4. (a) 4.73926 E+03
    (b) 4.50000 E−04
    (c) 1.60000 E+08
    (d) 1.04900 E−01
    (e) 3.00000 E+05

Chapter 2

1. $a = -4$, $b = 61$, $c = 34$, $d = -22$

2. Test this on your own system. If the last two goodbyes are not displayed then it means that your system will not print the output from a WRITE command unless it is followed by a WRITELN statement.

3. (a) 17.
    (b)   16.9
    (c)   16.89
    (d)   16.890
    (e) 16.89
    (f)   16.9

4. The computer never needs to have comments included in a program. However, a program must have comments if it is to be read by humans.

Chapter 3

1. Use these statements:

    ```
    feet : = numinches DIV 12;
    inches : = numinches MOD 12;
    ```

6. Use these statements:

    ```
    d : = 10 ** b;
    result : = ( (n/d) − TRUNC (n/d) ) *d;
    ```

7. Use this statement:

    ```
    result : = (x + ABS (x) ) /2;
    ```

8. Use this statement:

    ```
    result : = e + x* (d + x* (c + x* (b + x*a) ) );
    ```

15. (11/8) / (7/3)

16. 1/ (1−a)

17. 1/ (1 + SQR (a))

18. 1/ (1/x + 1/y)

19. SQRT(SQR(x−h) + SQR(y−k))

20. (−b + SQRT (SQR (b) − 4*a*c)) / (2*a)

21. r * SIN (A) * COS (B)

Chapter 4

3. {Assume team 1 has win1 wins and loss1 losses.
    Team 2 has win2 wins and loss2 losses. Team 1
    has games1 games left and team 2 has games2 games left.}

    ```
    s1 : = win1 − loss1;
    s2 : = win2 − loss2;
    gamesback : = (s1 − s2) /2;
    ```

```
        avgames := (games1 + games2)/2;
        c := avgames - gamesback + 1;
        IF c < 1
          THEN WRITELN('Team 1 has clinched first place!')
          ELSE WRITELN('Clinching number is ',c);
```

4. {quadratic equation solution using quadratic formula}
```
    IF a = 0
        THEN IF b = 0
                    THEN IF c = 0 THEN WRITELN('Any value of x will do. ')
                                  ELSE WRITELN('No solutions. ')
                    ELSE WRITELN('Solution is: ',-c/b) {linear
                    equation}
        ELSE BEGIN
                disc := SQR(b) - 4 * a * c;   {discriminant}
                IF disc = 0
                    THEN WRITELN('Solution is: ',-b/(2*a))
                    ELSE IF disc > 0
                    THEN BEGIN
                            WRITELN('Solution 1: ',
                                    (-b+SQRT(disc))/(2*a));
                            WRITELN('Solution 2: ',
                                    (-b-SQRT(disc))/(2*a))
                        END
                    ELSE BEGIN
                            WRITELN('2 Complex solutions: ');
                            WRITELN('Real part: ',
                                    -b/(2*a));
                            WRITELN('Imaginary part: ',
                            ' + or -', (SQRT(-disc))/(2*a))
                        END
    END;
```

Chapter 5

1.
```
    PROGRAM average (INPUT, OUTPUT);
    VAR
        count : INTEGER; avg, num, sum : REAL;
    BEGIN
        sum := 0;
        count := 0;
        WRITELN('Enter a positive integer to continue. ');
        READLN(num);
        WHILE num > 0 DO
            BEGIN
                count := count + 1;
                sum := sum + num;
                WRITELN('Enter a positive integer to continue. ');
                READLN(num)
            END;
        avg := sum / count;
        WRITELN('Average is ', avg:1)
    END.
```

```
2.    PROGRAM average (INPUT, OUTPUT);
      VAR
         count: INTEGER; avg, num, sum : REAL;
      BEGIN
         sum : = 0;

         count : = 0;
      REPEAT
            WRITELN ('Enter a positive integer to continue. ');
            READLN (num) ;
            IF num > 0
               THEN BEGIN
                         count : = count + 1;
                         sum : = sum + num
                     END;
            WRITELN ('Enter a positive integer to continue. );
            READLN (num)
      UNTIL num < 0;
      avg : = sum / count;
      WRITELN ('Average is ', avg: 1)
      END.
```

3. Two main differences between a WHILE loop and a REPEAT loop:
    (a) The condition of a WHILE loop is checked before the loop is entered and it
        is possible that the loop will never be performed. The condition of a
        REPEAT loop, however, is checked after the loop has been performed so
        the loop will be performed at least once.
    (b) A WHILE loop is performed as long as the condition tested is true. A
        REPEAT loop is performed as long as the condition tested is false.

4. No, the second program uses a REPEAT loop and will therefore be performed
    at least once even if the user initially enters a negative number. Also the sums
    will not be the same since the second program will actually add the negative
    number used to end the loop to the sum of the numbers before checking for
    the ending condition of the REPEAT loop.

```
10.  PROGRAM prmfct (INPUT,OUTPUT);
         {This program prints a list of the prime factors
         of all of the whole numbers from 2 to 50.}
     VAR
         divisor, adder, n, number : INTEGER;
     BEGIN
        FOR number := 2 TO 50 DO
           BEGIN
              n := number;
              WRITELN('-------');
              WRITELN('Prime Factors of ',n);
              divisor := 2;
              adder := 1;
              WHILE n > 1 DO

                  BEGIN
                    IF (n MOD divisor) = 0
                        THEN BEGIN
                                n : = n DIV divisor;
                                WRITE (divisor, '  ')
                             END
```

```
                    ELSE BEGIN
                        divisor : = divisor + adder;
                        adder : = 2
                        END;
                END;
            END;
    END.


11.  PROGRAM trz (INPUT, OUTPUT);
        {This program calculates the number of trailing zeros in an
        integer.}
     VAR
       n, number : INTEGER;
     BEGIN
         READLN (n);
         number : = 0;
         WHILE ((n MOD 10) = 0) DO
           BEGIN
              number : = number + 1;
              n : = n DIV 10
           END;
         WRITELN ('Number of zeros: ', number)
     END.


12.  PROGRAM bin (INPUT, OUTPUT);
        {This program reads in a number less than
        64 and then prints the digits of the
        binary representation of that number.}
     VAR compare, number, n: INTEGER;
     BEGIN
       REPEAT
          compare : = 32;
          READLN (number);
          n : = number;
          REPEAT
           IF n < compare
              THEN WRITE (0 : 2)
              ELSE BEGIN
                       WRITE (1 : 2);
                       n : = n - compare
              END;
           compare : = compare DIV 2;
          UNTIL compare < 1;
          WRITELN;
       UNTIL number = 0 {The program stops when you type 0}
     END.


13.  PROGRAM solve (INPUT, OUTPUT);
        {This program solves the third-degree
        equation ax**3 + bx**2 + cx + d = 0}
     VAR
       a, b, c, d, x, y, y2 : REAL;
     BEGIN
       WRITELN ('Enter a, b, c, d: ');
       READLN (a, b, c, d);
```

```
WRITELN('Enter initial guess solution: ');
READLN(x);
y := d + x*(c + x*(b + x*a));
WHILE ABS(y) > 0.01 DO
  BEGIN
        y2 := 3*a*SQR(x) + 2*b*x + c;
        x := x - y/y2;
        y := d + x*(c + x*(b + x*a))
     END;
   WRITELN('Solution: ', x)
END.
```

Chapter 6

```
8.    FOR n := 1 TO 20 DO
        BEGIN
          WRITELN(n, ' games played');
          FOR wins := 0 TO n DO
            BEGIN
               percent := wins/n;
               WRITELN(wins: 6, percent: 7: 3)
            END
        END;


17.   PROGRAM sine (INPUT, OUTPUT);
          {This program reads in a number
          and calculates an approximation for
          the sine of that number.}
     VAR
        sign, result, total, x: REAL;
        count, i, j: INTEGER;
     BEGIN
        REPEAT
          READLN(x);
          sign := 1; count := 1; result := 0;
          FOR i := 1 TO 10 DO
            BEGIN
              total := 1;
              FOR j := 1 TO count DO
                     total := total *x/j;
              result := result + sign * total;
              sign := - sign;
              count := count + 2
            END;
          WRITELN('Sin is: ', result: 7: 5);
        UNTIL x = 0 {The program stops when you type 0}
     END.
```

Chapter 7

1.   The value of *correct* is never initialized. Within the WHILE loop the value of *correct* is not altered, and so the loop will never end.

2. Yes, it is valid to check the condition *legal* = TRUE although it is redundant. It would be just as valid to write the condition as WHILE *legal*.

3. False

4. True

5. True

6. False

7. False

Chapter 8

1. ```
FUNCTION meters (inches: REAL) : REAL;
   BEGIN
      meters : = inches/39.38
   END;
```

8. One volt RMS equals 1/2.8 volts peak to peak.

10. ```
FUNCTION annrate (monrate: REAL) : REAL;
   BEGIN
      annrate : = ((1 + monrate) **12) - 1
   END;
```

13. ```
PROGRAM sroot (INPUT, OUTPUT) ;
      {This program uses the function sqroot to calculate
       the square root of a number using Newton's method.}
VAR x: REAL;
FUNCTION sqroot (x: REAL) : REAL;
   VAR test, estimate : REAL;
   BEGIN
      estimate : = x/2;
      test : = SQR (estimate) ;
      WHILE ABS (test-x) > 0.001 DO
         BEGIN
            estimate : = (estimate + x/estimate) /2;
            test : = SQR (estimate)
         END;
      sqroot : = estimate
   END;
BEGIN {Main program block}
   REPEAT
      READLN (x) ;
      WRITELN (TRUNC (x) : 6, sqroot (x) : 10:4) ;
   UNTIL x = 0 {The program stops when you type in 0}
END.
```

15. ```
PROGRAM bc (INPUT, OUTPUT) ;
      {This program reads in n and j and
       calculates the binomial coefficient n!/[j! (n-j)!] }
VAR n, j : REAL;
FUNCTION bin (n, j : REAL) REAL;
VAR result: REAL;
    count, i : INTEGER;
```

```
         BEGIN
           result : = 1;
           IF j > (n - j) THEN count : = TRUNC (n - j)
                          ELSE count : = TRUNC (j);
           FOR i : = 1 TO count DO
                result : = result * (n - i + 1) /i;
             bin : = result
         END;
     BEGIN {Main program block}
        REPEAT
           WRITELN ('Enter n, j');
           READLN (n, j);
           WRITELN (bin (n, j) : 10 : 0);
        UNTIL n = 0 {The program stops when you enter 0}
     END.
```

Chapter 9

3.
```
   {Program segment to test if an array a
       containing n numbers is in order}
   notfinished : = TRUE;
   inorder : = TRUE;
   previous : = a [1];
   i : = 1;
   WHILE (inorder AND notfinished) DO
     BEGIN
        i : = i + 1;
        current : = a [i];
        inorder : = (current >= previous);
        notfinished : = (i <= n);
        previous : = current
     END;
   IF inorder
      THEN WRITELN ('In order')
      ELSE WRITELN ('Not in order');
```

5.
```
   {Program segment to determine the longest
       consecutive stretch of nonzero numbers
       in the 162-element array h.}
   streak : = 0;
   long : = 0;
   FOR game : = 1 TO 162 DO
     BEGIN
        IF h [game] = 0 THEN streak : = 0
                       ELSE streak : = streak + 1;
        IF streak > long THEN long : = streak
     END;
     WRITELN ('Longest hitting streak: ', long);
```

7.
```
   {m is a list containing n numbers. This
   program segment will count the number of
   times each number occurs in m.
   numlist is a 50-element array of real numbers.
   count is a 50-element array of integers
   that has been set to zero.
```

We are assuming that the array m does not
contain more than 50 distinct numbers.
After this segment is executed, the array
element count[j] will tell the number of times
that numlist[j] occurs in the array m.}
```
FOR i := 1 TO n DO
   BEGIN
      number := m[i];
      j := 1;
      found := FALSE;
      newnum := FALSE;
      REPEAT
         IF count[j] = 0
           THEN BEGIN
                   count[j] := 1;
                   numlist[j] := number;
                   newnum := TRUE
                END;
           ELSE IF numlist[j] = number
                   THEN BEGIN
                           count[j] := count[j] + 1;
                           found := TRUE
                        END;
         j := j + 1;
      UNTIL (newnum OR found)
   END;
```

17.   {This program segment multiplies two 4 by 4
matrices. The result is stored in the 4 by 4
matrix called result.}
```
FOR row := 1 TO 4 DO
   BEGIN
      FOR column := 1 TO 4 DO
         BEGIN
            total := 0;
            FOR k := 1 TO 4 DO
               total := total + a[row, k] * b[k, column];
            result[row, column] := total
         END
   END;
```

Chapter 10

1. An ordinal type is ordered and *countable*. As was pointed out in the chapter, a REAL type is not countable.

2. Black

3. White

4. Red

5. 6

6. This represents the CHAR value chr(6) and not the color value green.

7. The value circle cannot represent both a constant value of a type and be a variable identifier at the same time.

8. *gpa* is illegal since a subrange cannot be of a REAL type. *alphabet* is illegal since the beginning value of the subrange is greater than the ending value.

9. No, since the values of the subrange must be defined before the program is compiled.

10. The values of a user-defined type cannot be input to a program so the READLN (day) statement is illegal.

Chapter 14

1. A, B, C, D, E, F, G, I, O, U

2. B, C, D, F, G

3. [ ], the empty set.

4. A, E

5. V, W, X, Y, Z

6. A, C, E, F, I, O, U

7. False

8. True

9. False

10. True

11. [ ], [A], [C], [F], [A, C], [A, F], [C, F], [A, C, F]

12. The set *legalnum* is not initialized before it is used in the main body of the program.

14.
```
TYPE
    string = PACKED ARRAY [1..25] OF CHAR;
    bookinfo =
        RECORD
            isbn: INTEGER;
            title, author, pub: string;
            price: REAL
        END;
VAR
    bookrec: bookinfo;
```

16. The record type definition does not contain the necessary END statement to indicate the end of the record *name*.

Chapter 15

1. With sequential access files to get to a specific element all the preceding elements must first be accessed. With a random, or direct, access file you can access a specific element without first accessing each previous element. A Pascal file is a sequential access file.

2. The predefined Pascal file parameters are INPUT and OUTPUT.

3. READLN (somefile, value) is the same as

```
WHILE NOT EOLN(somefile) DO
```

```
        GET(somefile);
      GET(somefile);
```

WRITELN(somefile, value) is the same as

```
    somefile^ : = value;
    PUT(somefile);
```

4. (a) students^[7]
   (b) studentmstr^.firstname

5.
```
    VAR
      somefile: TEXT;
      count: INTEGER;
    BEGIN
      count : = 0;
      RESET(somefile);
      WHILE NOT EOF(somefile) DO
        BEGIN
          IF EOLN(somefile)
            THEN count : = count + 1;
          READLN(somefile)
        END;
```

7. You only need to include those nonstandard files which are used that are external to the program. If the file is a temporary file (one which is used only within the program), it is not included in the program header.

8. The *grades* file is not initialized by a REWRITE statement before it is written to.

9. A WHILE loop is recommended because there may be a case in which the file you are trying to read is an empty file. If you use a REPEAT loop, the statement which attempts to read the empty file will be executed at least once.

How Do I Run Pascal on My Computer?

When you first buy a computer, you will most likely find that the computer will not understand Pascal. You will need to buy a separate software package that will allow your computer to execute Pascal programs. There are several different versions of Pascal available. Fortunately, the basic features of Pascal are standardized, so any version that you obtain will be similar to the version we have described in this book. In this section we will mention some of the most popular versions and describe some of their idiosyncrasies.

Before you buy a version of Pascal, you must make sure that it will work on your computer. You must check that your computer will be able to understand the system's disks and that your computer has enough memory to make the system work. The first thing you will have to learn is how to make programs run. This procedure will be different for different versions. You will learn one annoying feature of most Pascal systems: it is a lot of work just to tell the computer to run the program. If you are used to BASIC, where you just type in the program and then type RUN, you will find it very cumbersome to run Pascal programs. However, you will find one advantage: because the Pascal programs are compiled into machine language, they will run much faster.

You should find that the programs included in this book will run just as they are written, and you will also find that your version probably includes some added special features that we have not described in the text. You will need to consult your manual to learn more of the details of your system. Here are some of the features that vary with different implementations:

- The size of the maximum allowable integer

- The largest allowable real number

- The number of significant digits in real numbers

- The number of significant characters in a variable name (Some versions will consider two variables to be different only if they differ in their first eight characters; in those versions the two names varname11 and varname12 will be indistinguishable.)

- The values of ORD('a'), ORD('A'), and ORD('0')

- Whether you use { } or (* *) for comments

- Whether you use [ ] or (..) for array subscripts

- Whether you can use lowercase letters in variable names and, if so, if they are distinguished from uppercase letters

- If your version includes an exponentiation operator (Most versions don't.)

Some of the popular Pascal versions available for microcomputers are described briefly here.

UCSD p-System

The UCSD p-system is a Pascal compiler combined with a file management system. The UCSD system is available for the IBM PC and other computers. It was developed at the University of California at San Diego.

FILE MANAGEMENT SYSTEM

To start the system put the p-system disk in your drive. You will see the system's introductory command line:

```
Command: E(dit, R(un, F(ile, ...
```

This list gives you a choice of what you want to do. The first thing you will need to do is type your program, which you do in edit mode. Type E for edit. The p-system keeps track of the file you are currently working with (called the *workfile*). If you already have a workfile, then you may start editing it. Otherwise, you have two choices: you may start from scratch, or you may call for a file currently stored on the disk to be moved into the workfile location. When you are ready to edit, you will see the basic edit command line:

```
Edit A(djust C(opy D(elete F(ind I(nsert ...
```

To start typing your program, type I for insert. Then type away. Your manual will describe the edit commands that allow you to move the cursor around the screen and make changes to your program. When you are finished with the program, type "control C." Control C means to hold down the control key (which is on the left-hand side of the keyboard) and then press the C key. You will see the edit command line again. Type Q for quit, then type U in response to the next set of choices to update the workfile. Now your program is saved in the workfile. To run the program you must make sure that the disk with the Pascal compiler is also loaded in the computer. When you see the initial command line, type R for run, and before your very eyes, the program will run! Actually, it will go to the compiler first. The compiler will print some messages on the screen to reassure you that it is still working. The compiler produces a special coded version of the program (called P-code). Once the compilation is completed, the program will run. The advantage of the system will become clear if you want to run the program again. If you type R again, the computer will see that the P-code has already been produced so it will run the program immediately.

There are two more operations you will need to learn. Since you will not want to type your program again each time, you will need to learn how to transfer a file from the workfile to disk storage and also how to retrieve a file from storage to the workfile. When you see the initial command line, type F for filer. Here are the filer options:

1. Type S for save. The computer will ask you for the name you wish to use. Then it will store the workfile under that name.

2. Type N for new. This will destroy the workfile.

3. Type G for get. The computer will ask you for a file name. Then it will copy the file you name to the workfile.

When you are finished with the filer, type Q to quit the filer and return to the beginning command line.

ARITHMETIC

Pascal provides a standard identifier name, called MAXINT, that identifies the largest allowable integer. The value will depend on the computer you are using. A common value for MAXINT is 32,767. What if you must keep track of an integer with a larger value? UCSD Pascal allows a special type of number called a *long integer.* When you declare a long integer you specify the maximum number of digits that the number might have (up to a limit of 35 decimal digits). The declaration for a long integer looks like this:

VAR

longintegername : INTEGER[12]

The declaration is the same as for a regular integer except that you enclose the maximum number of digits (which is 12 in this example) in square brackets following the word INTEGER.

STRINGS

We found that it was essential to define our own variables of type string since the one-character CHAR variables provided in standard Pascal cannot be used to store names and words. The UCSD system includes strings as a predefined type, so you may declare variables to be of type STRING without first defining string with the TYPE command. A string declaration looks like this:

VAR

stringname : STRING[20]

In this case the string has a maximum length of 20 characters. If you do not explicitly include the string length, then the compiler will assume a maximum length of 80 characters. No string can be longer than 255 characters.

Some standard functions are included to work with strings. In each case, *string1* and *string2* may be either variable names of type string or literal string expressions enclosed in quotes, such as 'This is a literal string enclosed in quotes'.

- LENGTH(*string*) calculates the length of the string.

- CONCAT(*string1,string2*) glues the two strings together to form a longer string. CONCAT stands for concatenation, and you may concat together as many strings as you like. For example, if string1 is 'George' and string2 is 'Washington' then

- CONCAT(*string1,",string2*) is 'George Washington' (What would happen if you left out the blank string ' '?).

- COPY(*string1,n1,n2*) creates a new string by tearing apart the original string. In particular, it selects a total of *n2* characters from the original string, starting with the character at position *n1* in the original string.

- DELETE(*string1,n1,n2*) deletes *n2* characters from *string1,* starting at character *n1*.

- INSERT(*string2,string1,n*) inserts *string2* into *string1* starting at character *n*.

- POS(*string1,string2,n*); looks through *string1,* starting at character *n,* and sees if *string2* is contained in *string1*; if it is, it gives the number of the character that tells where in *string1* that *string2* starts.

FILES

Suppose you have a data file on your disk named INFO.DAT. If you would like to read data from this file into your Pascal program, then you must declare a Pascal variable of type FILE and tell your computer that you want it to associate this file variable with the disk file INFO.DAT. Let's suppose F1 is the Pascal file variable name, declared like this:

```
VAR F1: TEXT; {We are assuming F1 is meant to be a text file.}
```

Before you start reading from the file, use this command:

```
RESET(F1, 'INFO.DAT')
```

This commands opens the file F1 so you can read data from it, just as we have done in Chapter 15. The statement also tells the computer to look for the data to be read in the file INFO.DAT. Note that F1 is not in quotation marks because it is a valid Pascal variable. However, INFO.DAT must be in quotation marks because the Pascal compiler does not recognize the name INFO.DAT; however it will tolerate the string expression 'INFO.DAT'.

When you are finished with the file you must close it with a CLOSE command:

```
CLOSE(F1);
```

If you will be writing data from a Pascal file named F1 to a disk file named INFO.DAT then you open the file with the REWRITE command:

```
REWRITE(F1, 'INFO.DAT');
```

If you want to keep the data you wrote to the file, then you must close the file when you are finished with a command like this:

```
CLOSE(F1, LOCK);
```

GRAPHICS

UCSD Pascal allows you to do graphics—that is, draw pictures on the screen. We describe a little bit about UCSD graphics in the following section on Apple Pascal.

Apple Pascal

The Apple Pascal system is the system that you will use if you have one of the models of Apple II computers. The Apple Pascal system is based on the UCSD system described above—so you should read that section first. When you first start the system, you will see the command line prompt. To type in programs you must type E to enter the editor mode, to use the file manager to store or retrieve files you type F, and to run your programs type R. This section will look at some of the special features of Apple Pascal.

The first thing you may find is that your screen may only contain 40 columns, in which case you will not see the entire display on your screen at once. The other 40 columns which make up the right-hand half of the display will be hidden somewhere inside the computer. To see the right-hand half of the display, type control A. To see the left-hand half again, type control A again. Older models of Apple computers do not allow you to type lowercase letters. In that case your entire program will be in capital letters. If you do not have square brackets on your keyboard, then you type control K for a left bracket and shift M for a right bracket.

Apple Pascal includes features that allow you to make sounds and read in input from game paddles. If your program uses these special routines, you must include the statement USES APPLESTUFF; in the declare section. To make a musical note sound when the program is being run, use the statement NOTE(*pitch,duration*); NOTE is a built-in function that sounds a note that will be determined by the values of the two parameters given it. In this example the two parameters are variables named *pitch* and *duration*. You may also connect the computer to game paddles: PADDLE(0) and PADDLE(1). While the computer is executing your program, it can read in values that will depend on the settings of the paddles.

You can draw pictures by giving commands that cause an imaginary turtle to move around the screen. To use the graphics, you must include the statement USES TURTLEGRAPHICS; in the declare section. The statement INITTURTLE; in the action part of the program tells the turtle to be ready for motion. Then the statement MOVETO(X,Y) causes the turtle to move to the point on the screen that is a distance X from the left edge and a distance Y down from the top. As the turtle moves, it draws a line. If you have a color screen you may include the statement PENCOLOR(ORANGE); to tell the turtle to draw in orange. Or you may use other colors such as white, blue, green, or violet. The statement PENCOLOR(NONE); means that the turtle will move around the screen without leaving any lines. You may use this statement to move the turtle to a new location to begin a new line.

One more note about the USES command: if your program will use mathematical functions such as SQRT, SIN, COS, EXP, ATAN, or LN, you must include the command USES TRANSCEND; at the beginning of the program.

IBM Pascal

The IBM Pascal system is a version of Pascal designed by Microsoft especially for the IBM PC. The IBM Pascal system will produce machine language programs that execute quickly. The complete system is so large that it occupies three disks.

Before you can run your program you must type the program into the computer using a text editor. The IBM PC comes with an editor called EDLIN that allows you to type programs and make changes in them. You will need to become familiar with this editor (or else learn to use a word processing editor to enter your programs). File names in the IBM PC consist of a name followed by a period followed by a file extension of up to three letters, for example,

TAXCALC.PAS

Your Pascal programs should be given names with the file extension PAS.

To execute your program, you need to insert the first Pascal disk and then execute the command PAS1. PAS1 is the first stage of the Pascal compiler. When PAS1 is finished, it has translated your program into a rough-draft machine code version. Then you must insert the second disk and execute the command PAS2. PAS2 looks over the machine code generated by PAS1 and fixes it up so that it will run more efficiently. Then you must insert the third disk (called PASCAL.LIB) and execute the command LINK which merges the machine code version from PAS2 with the standard routines that your program needs to perform arithmetic and handle input and output. Finally, the program is ready to go! The result from the final stage is a file with the same name as your original program file, but now with the file extension EXE. For example, if your program file was called TAXCALC.PAS, then the final file will be called TAXCALC.EXE. The EXE file is a machine code file that the PC can execute just as it is, so all you need to do to run the program is type its name. For example, we would type the command TAXCALC and then see our program execute right before our eyes.

STRINGS

IBM Pascal includes two types of strings: the type STRING, which is of fixed length, and the type LSTRING, which can have varying length. A STRING variable is declared by specifying the length of the string, and an LSTRING variable is declared by fixing the maximum length of the string, for example,

```
VAR
   name : STRING(20);   {name is a STRING variable of fixed
                            length 20}
   sentence : LSTRING(60); {sentence is an LSTRING variable of
                            maximum length 60}
```

The built-in functions for LSTRING variables are:

- CONCAT(*lstring1,lstring2*) connects *lstring1* and *lstring2* together.

- DELETE(*lstring,n1,n2*) deletes *n2* characters from *lstring,* starting at character *n1.*

- INSERT(*lstring1,lstring2,n*) inserts *lstring2* into *lstring1* starting at character *n.*

- POSITN(*lstring1,lstring2,n*); looks through *lstring1,* starting at character *n* and sees if *lstring2* is contained in *lstring1;* if it is, it gives the number of the character that tells where in *lstring1* that *lstring2* starts.

FILES

Suppose you have data stored in a disk file named INFO.DAT, and you would like to read this data as a Pascal file named F1. You must use the ASSIGN command to tell the computer to associate the Pascal file variable F1 with the disk file INFO.DAT. The ASSIGN command looks like this:

```
ASSIGN(F1, 'INFO.DAT');
```

Then, before you start reading from the file you must include the command RESET (F1).

In order to write data to a file, you must first use an ASSIGN command to assign the Pascal file name to the external file name, and then use a REWRITE command to open the file.

PRINTER

You may also find it useful to direct all your program's output to your printer. Here is a way to do that. When your Pascal program starts, the computer automatically opens the files INPUT (corresponding to the keyboard) and OUTPUT (corresponding to the screen). Now, let's close the file OUTPUT, and then reopen it—only this time we will assign it to the printer. To direct all your output to the printer, include these statements at the beginning of your program:

```
CLOSE (OUTPUT);
  ASSIGN (OUTPUT, 'LPT1:');
  REWRITE (OUTPUT);
```

LPT1: is a special file name that corresponds to the printer.

BREAK AND CYCLE STATEMENTS

Suppose your program is in the middle of a loop and you would like it to get out of the loop quickly in some cases. IBM Pascal allows you to include the command BREAK in the middle of a loop. The BREAK command causes an immediate exit. For example, consider these statements (continue and mistake are boolean variables)

```
WHILE continue DO
  BEGIN
      . . .
  IF mistake THEN BREAK;
      . . .
  END;
```

If the boolean variable mistake is TRUE when the computer reaches the BREAK command, then the computer will skip over the statements in the loop that follow the BREAK command and start executing the statements that follow the loop.

The command CYCLE tells the computer to jump back to the beginning of a loop, for example,

```
FOR count : = 1 TO total DO
  BEGIN
      . . .
  IF count : = 7 THEN CYCLE;
      . . .
  END;
```

The computer will execute the entire loop when count has the values 1, 2, 3, 4, 5, and 6. When count equals 7, the computer will execute the loop until it reaches the CYCLE command. Then it will skip the rest of the loop and jump back to the beginning, proceeding to execute the loop again with count having the value 8.

OTHERWISE COMMAND

The OTHERWISE command is used with the CASE command. It specifies what action you want the computer to take if the CASE variable does not have any of the indicated values. Here is an example:

```
CASE place OF
    1: WRITELN ('Gold Medal');
    2: WRITELN ('Silver Medal');
    3: WRITELN ('Bronze Medal');
    OTHERWISE WRITELN ('No Medal')
  END;
```

You may also include an OTHERWISE clause that does not specify any action. In that case the computer will not do anything if the CASE variable does not have one of the indicated values.

MT-PLUS

The MT-PLUS system is a powerful Pascal system developed by Digital Research. Versions of the MT-PLUS system are available for several different computers, including the IBM PC and Kaypro computers. The programs included in this book were run under the MT-PLUS system. The general procedure for running programs is described in Chapter 1. You must first type the program using a text editor of some kind. Your program should be saved as a file with file extension .SRC (SRC stands for source). If your program source file is called TAXCALC.SRC, then the command to execute the Pascal compiler is

```
MTPLUS TAXCALC
```

The compiler produces an intermediate file called TAXCALC.ERL. Before you can run the program, you must perform a second stage. You must use a program, called the linker, that connects your program with the standard information it needs. The exact form for the linker command will depend on what routines you will need. Here is one possibility:

```
LINKMT TAXCALC, FPREALS, PASLIB/S
```

If the program uses mathematical functions such as SQRT or SIN or EXP, you must include the word TRANCEND in the LINKMT command. For example, if the name of the program is PLANET, the link command might look like this:

```
LINKMT PLANET, TRANCEND, FPREALS, PASLIB/S
```

The manual describes other options available with the linkmt command. In each case the LINKMT command creates a file with file extension COM that can be executed by the computer. To execute the program just type its name. For example, type TAXCALC to cause the file TAXCALC.COM to be executed.

MT-PLUS includes string operations similar to those described above, and it also includes some special debugging tools.

Summary of Pascal

This summary of Pascal is for reference purposes. You may refer to it while you are writing your Pascal programs. For more detailed information you should consult the main text and the manual for your version.

In this summary, words in capital letters must be typed exactly as shown; words in *italics* may be replaced by any appropriate item of your own choosing. In particular:

- *x* is used to represent a real expression or variable name.

- *i, j* are used to represent integer expressions or variable names.

- *k* is used to represent an item of any ordinal type (integer, boolean, char, or user-defined).

- *m, n* can be expressions of any type.

- *c* is used to represent any character.

Items in braces { } are comments that are there for the benefit of human readers. They are ignored by the computer. Three dots . . . mean that more than one item may be supplied of that form.

The general structure of a Pascal program looks like this:

```
PROGRAM programname (INPUT, OUTPUT);
    {Constant declarations (optional):}
```

```
CONST
    name = value , . . . ;   {see chapter 3}
      {Type declarations  (optional): }
TYPE
    name = (item1, . . . );   {see chapter 10}
    {Variable declarations:}
VAR
    name1, name2 , . . . : typea;
    name3, name4 , . . . : typeb;  . . .
    {Function and procedure declarations -- see
     below and see chapter 8}
    BEGIN    {start of main program block}
     statement1 ;
     statement2 ;

       . . .
     last statement
  END.
```

Each name used in the program must be declared in the declaration section. The four standard data types are INTEGER, REAL (see Chapter 3), BOOLEAN (see Chapter 7), and CHAR (see Chapter 10). You may also define your own types (see Chapter 10).

A semicolon is placed at the end of each statement.

A compound statement is formed by inserting the word BEGIN, followed by some statements, and is ended by the word END. Note that you do not put a semicolon after the BEGIN or before the END in a compound statement.

ARITHMETIC OPERATIONS

The symbols for arithmetic operations and built-in functions are:

+	addition
−	subtraction
*	multiplication
/	real number division
i DIV j	integer division
i MOD j	remainder when two integers are divided
SQR(x)	square of x
SQRT(x)	square root of x
TRUNC(x)	calculate the integer part of x
ROUND(x)	calculates the integer closest to x
ABS(x)	calculates the absolute value of x
SIN(x)	sine of x, x expressed in radians
COS(x)	cosine of x, x expressed in radians
EXP(x)	exponential function e
LN(x)	natural logarithm of x
ODD(j)	has the boolean value TRUE if j is odd
ARCTAN(x)	arctan of x, expressed in radians

BOOLEAN VARIABLES

Boolean variables have only two possible values: TRUE or FALSE. The logical operators AND, OR, and NOT may be used with boolean variables. Suppose A and B are boolean variables. Then

A AND B is TRUE only if both A and B are TRUE

A OR B is TRUE if either A or B is TRUE

NOT A is TRUE if A is FALSE and NOT A is FALSE if A is TRUE

SPECIAL FUNCTIONS

These functions may be applied to the ordinal types CHAR, INTEGER, BOOLEAN, and user-defined types:

PRED(k)   the predecessor of k

SUCC(k)   the successor of k

ORD(k)   the ordinal position of k within its type

[For character variables, the value of the ORD function will depend on your computer. If your computer uses the ASCII coding sequence you will find ORD('A') is 65, ORD('a') is 97, and ORD('0') is 48.]

CHR(i)   the character whose ordinal number is i:

IF i = ORD('c'), then c = CHR (i)

CONTROL STRUCTURES

The Pascal structures that you will use to control the order of execution of your statements are IF, CASE, REPEAT, WHILE, and FOR. The general form of the IF command is

IF *condition*

THEN *statement1*

ELSE *statement2;*

If the *condition* is true, then *statement1* is executed; otherwise *statement2* is executed. Note that you do not put a semicolon before the word ELSE. *statement1* and *statement2* may be compound statements. You may leave out ELSE *statement2* if you do not want to do anything if the condition is false. The *condition* may be a boolean variable or it may be one of these logical expressions:

$m = n$ Does m equal n?

$m > n$ Is m greater than n?

$m < n$ Is m less than n?

$m >= n$ Is m greater than or equal to n?

$m <= n$ Is m less than or equal to n?

$m <> n$ Is m not equal to n?

The general form of the CASE command is

CASE *variable* OF

    value1 : *statement1;*

    value2 : *statement2;*

    . . .

    last value : *last statement*

END;

The *variable* may be of any type other than REAL. If it is equal to *value1*, then *statement1* will be executed, and so on.

The general form of the REPEAT command is

REPEAT

    statements

UNTIL *condition;*

First, the computer will execute the *statements.* Then it will check to see if the *condition* is true. If not, then the computer will return to the beginning of the loop. If it is, then it will continue on to the next statements following the loop.

The general form of the WHILE command is

WHILE *condition* DO

BEGIN

    statements

END;

When the computer comes to the WHILE command, it will first check to see if the *condition* is true. If it is, then the computer will execute the statements in the middle of the loop. After passing through the loop, the computer will check the *condition* again. The computer will keep executing the *statements* until the condition becomes false.

The general form of a FOR loop is

FOR *counter* := *start* TO *stop* DO

    BEGIN

        statements

    END;

counter is a variable of an ordinal type. The computer will first execute the loop with *counter* having the value *start.* Then the computer will execute the loop again with *counter* having the next value; then the loop will be repeated again using the value after that; and so on until finally the loop will be executed for the last time when *counter* has the value *stop.*

PROCEDURES

A procedure is a mini-Pascal program that is called by the main program. A procedure declaration for a procedure with no parameters looks like this:

PROCEDURE *procedurename;*
    {constant declarations, type declarations, variable
    declarations, nested procedure declarations (optional)}

```
BEGIN   {start of main block for procedure}
   statements
END;
```

To execute the procedure, merely include the name of the procedure somewhere in the main program block. Objects declared within a procedure are *local* to that procedure and their names will not be recognized elsewhere (unless they are also declared elsewhere in which case the same name can be used to represent something totally different at another point in the program).

ARRAYS

The general form of the declaration for a one-dimensional array is

```
VAR arrayname : ARRAY[lowsub..highsub] OF type
```

An element of the array can be identified by specifying a subscript value.
The general form of the declaration for a two-dimensional array is

```
VAR arrayname : ARRAY[lowsub1..highsub1,
                      lowsub2..highsub2] OF type
```

SETS

The general form of a set declaration is

```
TYPE setname = SET OF base type
```

RECORDS

The general form of a record declaration is

```
TYPE
  recordname =
      RECORD
          field identifier : type;
          field identifier, field identifier : type
                     . . .
      END;
```

FILES

The general form of a file declaration is

```
TYPE
    filetype = FILE OF element type identifier;
  VAR
      filename : filetype;
```

or you may write

```
  VAR
      filename : FILE OF element type identifier
```

List of Reserved Words

AND	NIL
ARRAY	NOT
BEGIN	OF
CASE	OR
CONST	PACKED
DIV	PROCEDURE
DO	PROGRAM
DOWNTO	RECORD
ELSE	REPEAT
END	SET
FILE	THEN
FOR	TO
FUNCTION	TYPE
GOTO	UNTIL
IF	VAR
IN	WHILE
LABEL	WITH
MOD	

INDEX

Notes

Notes